*The Campus History Series*

# LINCOLN UNIVERSITY
## 1920–1970

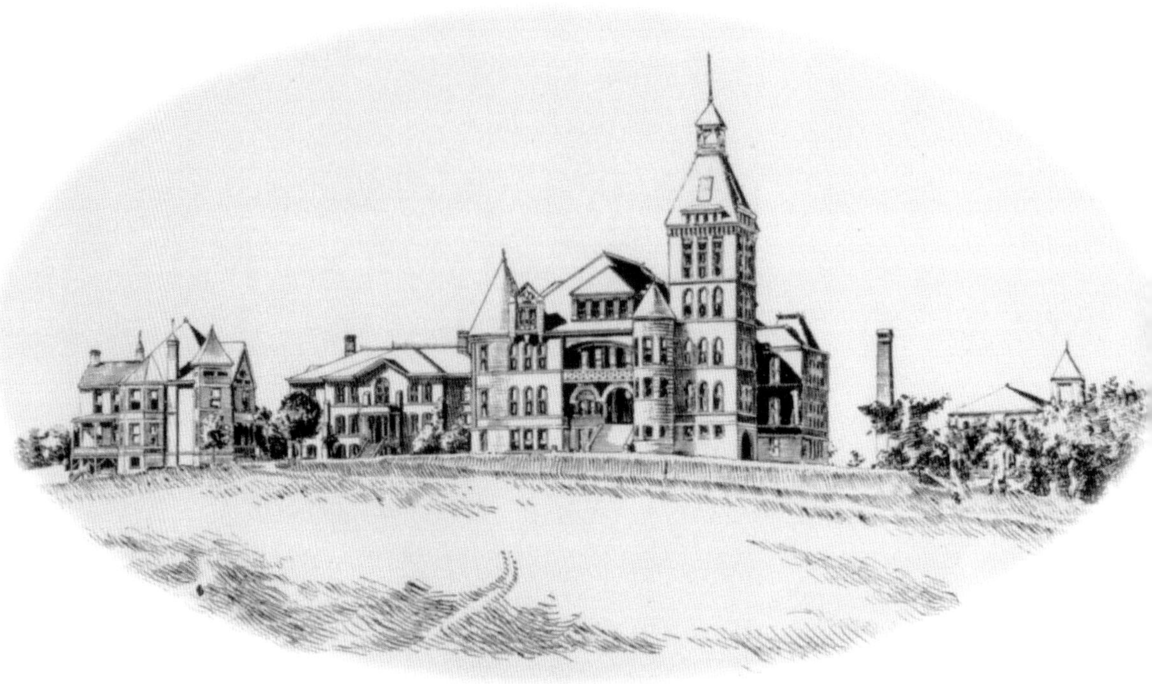

The campus as it appeared about 1900 was captured in this pen sketch from an old catalog. The president's home appears on the left with Barnes-Krekel Hall sitting in the background beside Memorial Hall, which is the building with the bell tower. Also in the picture is the chimney to the heating plant and Chinn Hall, which was an industrial arts building. The black soldiers and their white officers of the 62nd and 65th United States Colored Infantries founded Lincoln University in 1866. The gates leading up the driveway to the campus buildings proudly displays the original name of the institution, which was Lincoln Institute. The school began offering college-level classes in 1887 and became Lincoln University in 1921 with the passage of a bill sponsored by the first black Missouri state legislator, Walthall M. Moore, who represented St. Louis in the general assembly.

*On the cover*: This photograph shows the Lincoln University History Club and its sponsor Dr. Lorenzo J. Greene, a renowned historian. The history club was formally organized in 1934 with the purpose of not only discussing history but exploring any topic of current social, religious, or political interest. The membership was limited to history majors and minors and other students who showed a singular interest in history. The club was particularly active during Negro History Week. (Courtesy of the Lincoln University Archives.)

*The Campus History Series*

# LINCOLN UNIVERSITY
## 1920–1970

ARNOLD G. PARKS

ARCADIA
PUBLISHING

ISBN 978-0-7385-5132-6

Published by Arcadia Publishing
Charleston SC, Chicago IL, Portsmouth NH, San Francisco CA

Printed in the United States of America

Library of Congress Catalog Card Number: 2007920807

For all general information contact Arcadia Publishing at:
Telephone 843-853-2070
Fax 843-853-0044
E-mail sales@arcadiapublishing.com
For customer service and orders:
Toll-Free 1-888-313-2665

Visit us on the Internet at www.arcadiapublishing.com

*The gates to the driveway leading to the campus buildings at the top of the hill proudly display the original name of the school, Lincoln Institute.*

# Contents

# ACKNOWLEDGMENTS

My deepest appreciation and gratitude is extended to Elizabeth Briscoe Wilson, university librarian/director of the Lincoln University Inman E. Page Library, for allowing me access to historical documents related to Lincoln University in the university archives. Without access to these materials, this book would not have been possible. Equally supportive was her assistant, university archivist Carmen Beck, who willingly dug through files and folders to identify images that well represented the history of Lincoln University during the time period 1920–1970. These two individuals have earned my immeasurable gratitude. The images appearing in this book are from the Lincoln University Archives.

I also wish to thank my editor at Arcadia Publishing, Anna Wilson, for her patience in working with me, expert guidance (when requested), and prodding (when needed). Thanks also to Maggie Cantrell of the Lincoln University Center for Teaching and Learning for her assistance with the technical aspects of readying the manuscript for the publisher.

Most importantly, the writings of a couple of friends who are both excellent historians unknowingly provided a beacon of light for this book. Both individuals, Dr. Gary Kremer and Dr. Antonio F. Holland, have produced several books on either Lincoln University or Jefferson City history. Reading their works inspired me to attempt to "synthesize" in pictorial and brief narrative form a more limited historical presentation of the solid scholarship that these two scholars produced devoted to the university. Humbly I submit that as a sociologist rather than a historian, I may not have done justice to the topic. Also, from a distance, I have admired the work of an individual who graduated from high school with me, Dr. John A. Wright Sr., who has published several books for Arcadia Publishing on topics particularly related to our hometown of St. Louis. After reading his publications, I approached Arcadia with the idea for a book spotlighting Lincoln University. Finally, to my wife, Lennette, a retired Lincoln University nursing faculty member, thank you for your helpful suggestions, love, and encouragement, not just for this book but also in everything.

# INTRODUCTION

Prior to the Civil War it was illegal in Missouri to educate African Americans, whether slave or free, for fear that literacy among the slave population would lead to their rebellion. However, at the close of the Civil War, soldiers and officers of the 62nd United States Colored Infantry stationed at Fort McIntosh, Texas, but composed primarily of Missourians, decided to establish an educational institution in the state. This was particularly enlightening because many of those soldiers who were ex-slaves had learned to read and write at classes around campfires on the battlefield. Despite their low pay, the infantrymen contributed generously. One private who earned only $13 per month gave $100. Astonishingly, two African American regiments collected more than $6,000 for the project, with members of the 62nd Colored Infantry contributing $5,000 supplemented by almost $1,400 given by the 65th Colored Infantry. It was a difficult mission. Raising additional funds proved tough, and an attempt to locate the school in St. Louis failed, but the gallant soldiers would not be denied. On January 14, 1866, Lincoln Institute was formally established under an organizational committee. By June of the same year, the committee incorporated and became a board of trustees. The group focused on locating in Jefferson City, with considerable help from white officers and supporters who were inspired by their cause. Especially notable among them was Lt. Richard Baxter Foster. The doors of Lincoln Institute opened in September 1866. The following stipulations were set for the school: the institution shall be designed for the special benefit of freed African Americans; it shall be located in the state of Missouri; its fundamental idea shall be to combine study and labor.

In 1869, Lincoln Institute moved to the present campus location and in 1870 began to receive aid from the State of Missouri for teacher training. Therefore, the institution became the state normal school for African Americans. Its primary mission was to educate black teachers who would teach black students throughout the state. College-level work was added to the curriculum in 1877. Lincoln Institute formally became a state institution in 1879 with the deeding of its property to the state. Under the second Morrill Act of 1890, Lincoln Institute became a land-grant institution, and the following year industrial and agricultural courses were added to the curriculum. In 1921, the Missouri legislature changed the name from Lincoln Institute to Lincoln University. The North Central Association of Colleges and Secondary Schools accredited the four-year college of arts and sciences in 1934. Graduate instruction was begun in the summer session of 1940 with majors in education and history and minors in English, history, and sociology. In 1954, the United States Supreme Court handed down its ruling in *Brown v. Board of Education of Topeka*, and Lincoln University responded by opening its doors to all applicants meeting its entrance criteria. Today Lincoln University serves a diverse clientele, both residential and nonresidential, and is racially integrated with the student body being approximately 55 percent white and 45 percent African American.

Although Lincoln University today is 141 years old, it would appear that to highlight only 50 years of this rich history the other 90-plus years of valuable university history is not significant. This is by no means the case. The author selected the 1920–1970 time frame because this is a period that might be considered the golden era of the university's development. For example, in 1921 when the transformation from an institute to a university occurred, an intellectual explosion took place, and the advent of racial integration after 1954 significantly changed the complexion of the student body and the school's focus. Therefore, the rationale for concentration on this 50-year time span is justified.

# *One*

# Campus Buildings

Lincoln Institute was started in a dilapidated, abandoned two-room shack built in 1842 as a public school. It was located on "Hobo Hill," which had the distinction of being one of the tallest hills in Jefferson City. Classes were held in this building from 1866 until 1871 when financial donations and assistance of persons such as John Milton Turner and Lt. Richard Baxter Foster helped Lincoln Institute move to the site where the university is located. An initial building at the institute's new location was a structure called the "main building," which was a three-story, 60-by-70-foot building with a basement. The building served multiple purposes, including space for student life activities, a library, and a gymnasium. On September 4, 1895, the first building on the Lincoln University campus, named Memorial Hall, was dedicated and paid recognition to the soldiers of the 62nd and the 65th Colored Infantries who gave money to start Lincoln Institute. The latter structure was a sturdy stone building of late-Tudor architecture and was actually an addition to the main building constructed in 1871. Also, in 1891, the state legislature appropriated money to Lincoln Institute for construction of an industrial arts building named Chinn Hall, although it was soon destroyed by fire. The insurance proceeds from this loss, along with the money appropriated by the state legislature, helped to build the Memorial Hall structure.

During the 1930s and 1940s, Lincoln University was aggressively adding buildings. Notable among the new additions was the current main administration building called College Hall (now Young Hall) completed in 1931; Allen Hall (1936), which was a dormitory for men; Damel Hall (1937), which was an industrial arts building; Bennett Hall (1938), which was a dormitory for junior and senior women; and Anthony Hall (1940), a residence for freshman and sophomore women. Plans were also developed in the early 1940s for a stand-alone library, but this building (Inman E. Page Library) was not completed until 1948 because of World War II.

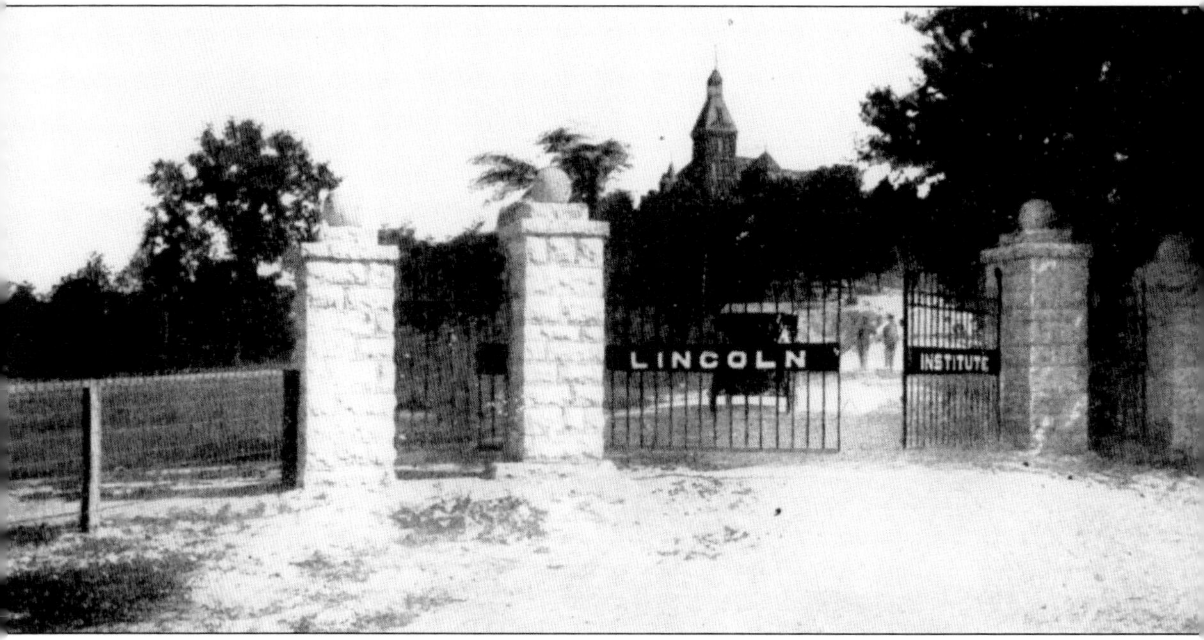


This image shows a prominent view of the entrance gates that lead to the top of the hill where the main campus buildings of Lincoln Institute were located.

Pvt. Logan A. Bennett was one of the last survivors of the 62nd United States Colored Infantry, which contributed money for Lincoln University's founding. A lifelong resident of Jefferson City, Bennett remained an ardent supporter of Lincoln University throughout his life. The Bennett residence hall, now a cooperative research living learning center, is named for him.

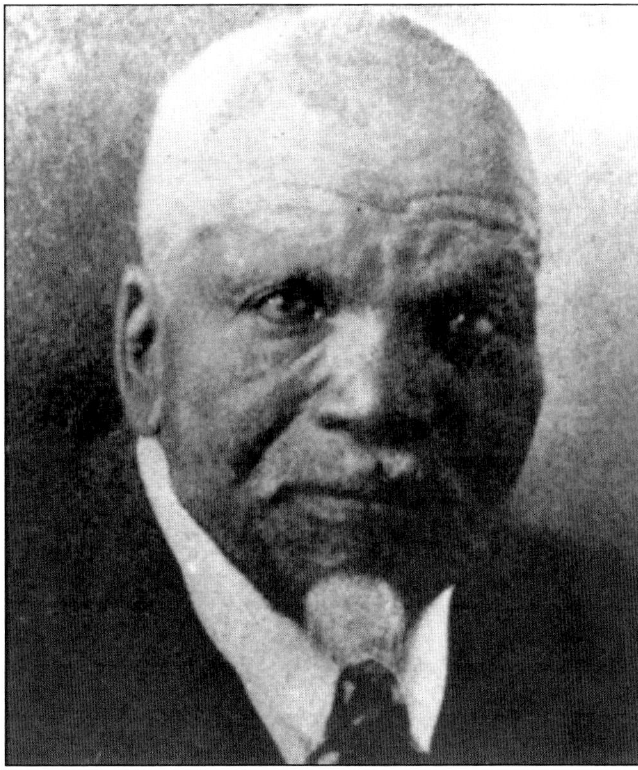

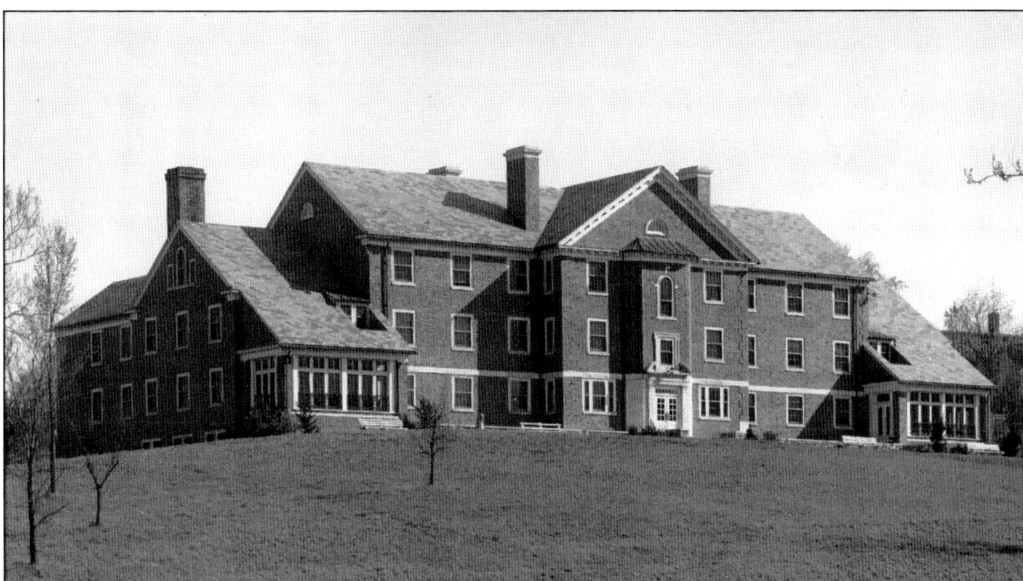

Bennett Hall, shown here, was erected in 1938. This three-story brick building was designed to house 100 women and included such features as three dressing rooms, recreational halls, laundry rooms, sorority rooms, study rooms, and two large sunporches on each side of the first floor. Today the building serves as an 1890 land-grant living and learning center whereby students both live in the facility and have opportunities for learning to take place in the students' living environment.

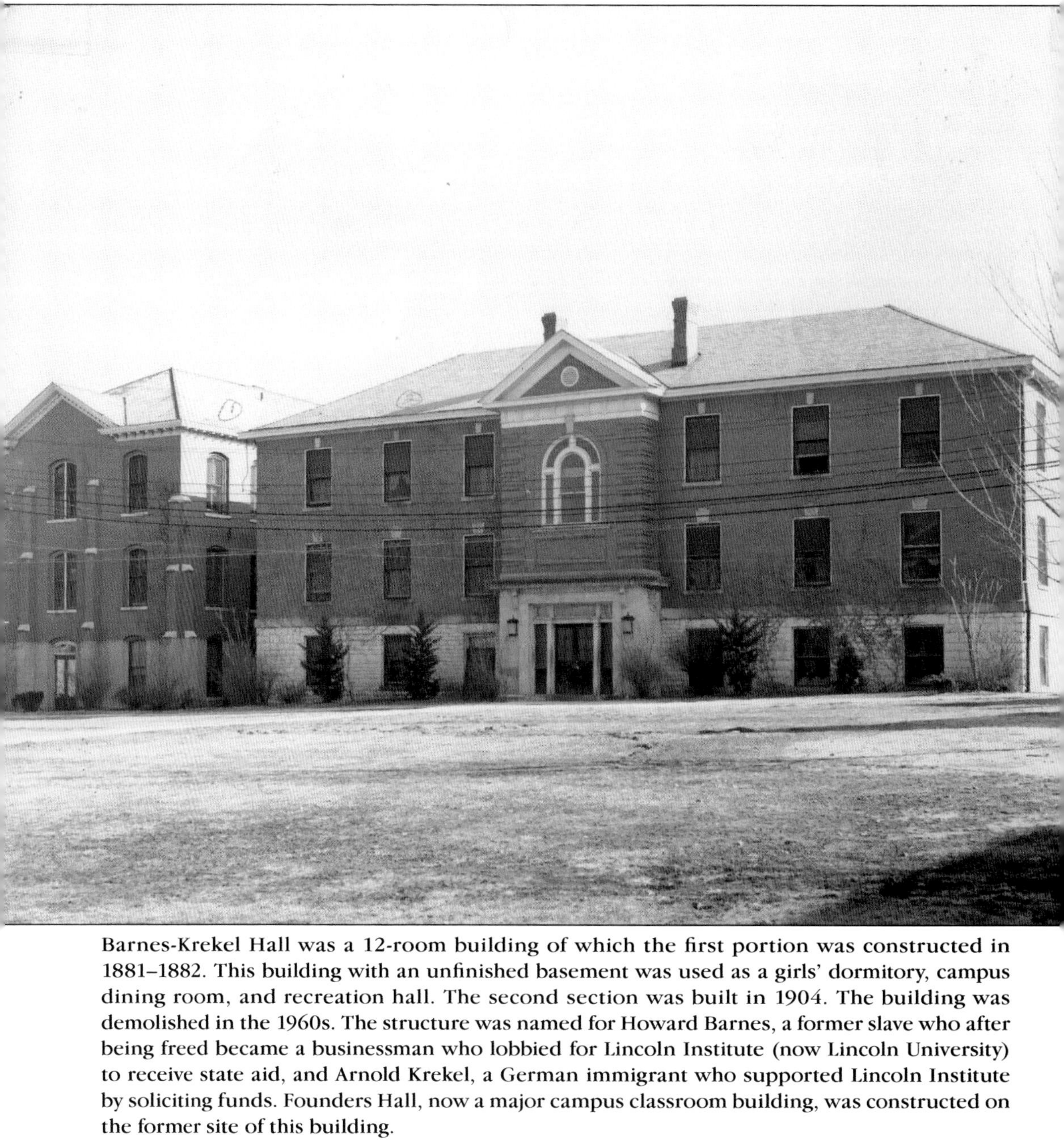

Barnes-Krekel Hall was a 12-room building of which the first portion was constructed in 1881–1882. This building with an unfinished basement was used as a girls' dormitory, campus dining room, and recreation hall. The second section was built in 1904. The building was demolished in the 1960s. The structure was named for Howard Barnes, a former slave who after being freed became a businessman who lobbied for Lincoln Institute (now Lincoln University) to receive state aid, and Arnold Krekel, a German immigrant who supported Lincoln Institute by soliciting funds. Founders Hall, now a major campus classroom building, was constructed on the former site of this building.

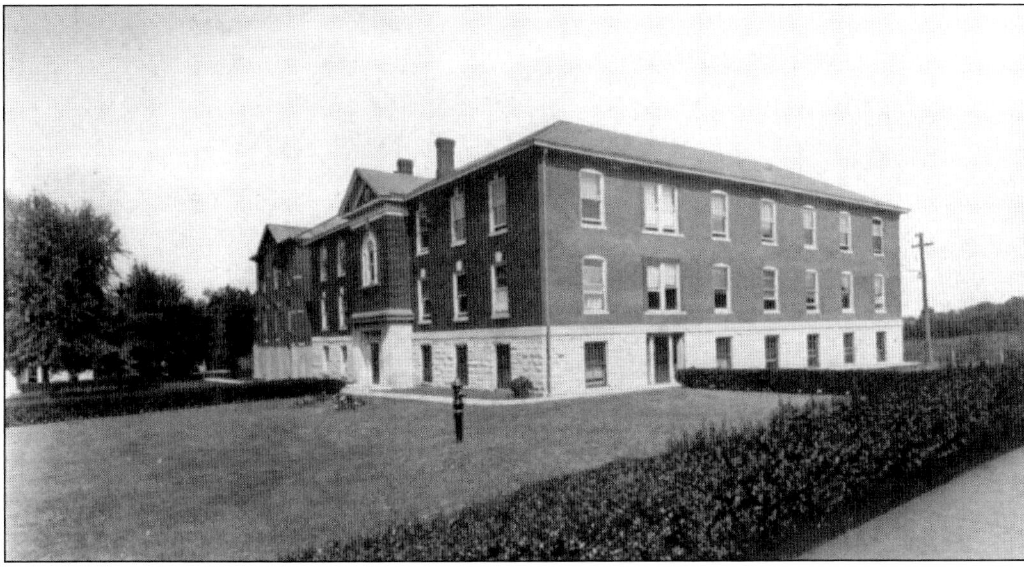

This is another view of Barnes-Krekel Hall.

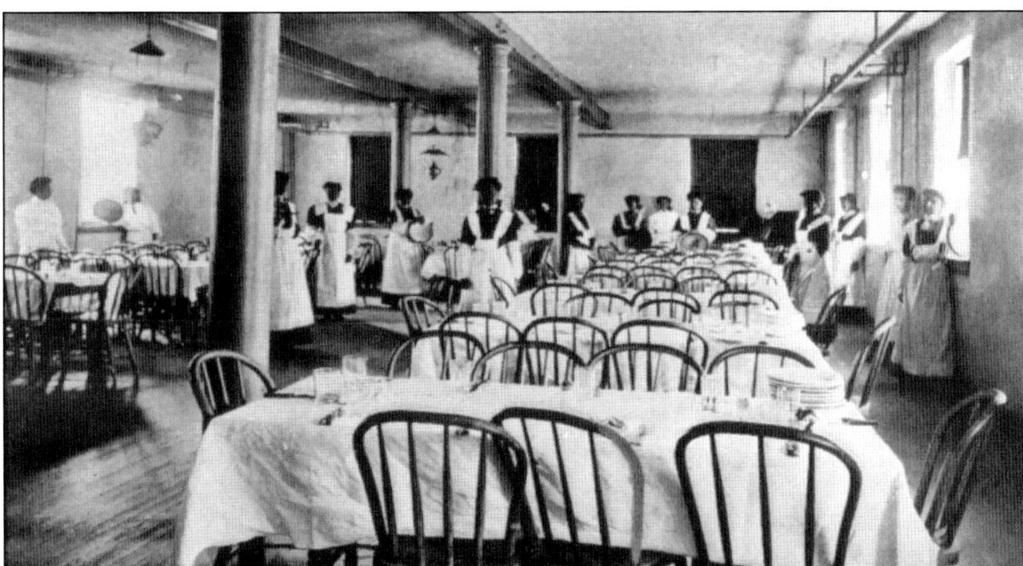

The Barnes-Krekel Hall dining hall, shown in this photograph, was the campus dining facility until Anderson M. Schweich Hall was constructed in 1930, at which time the basement dining room became a recreational hall.

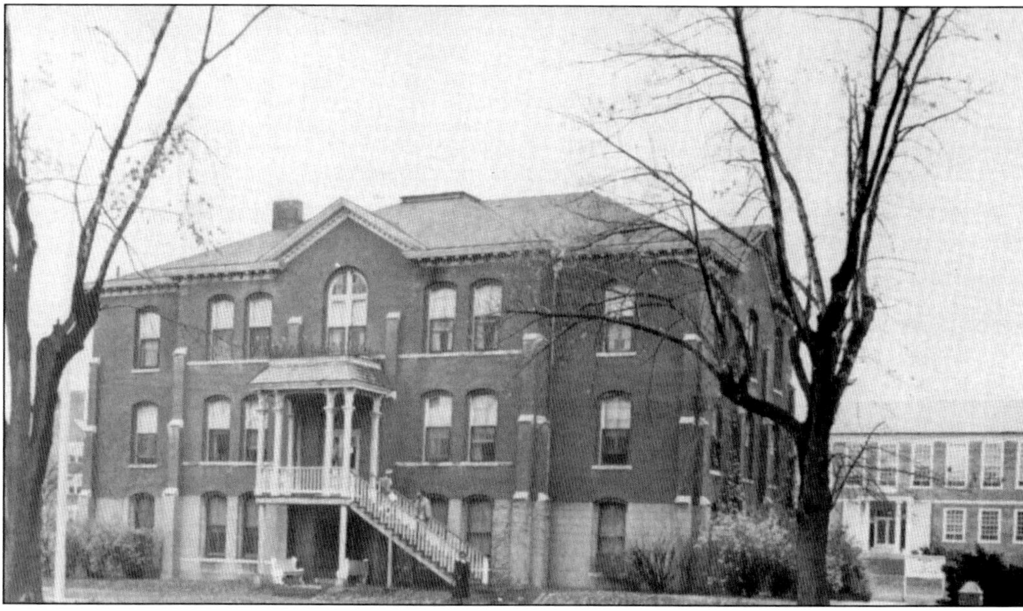

Barnes-Krekel Hall is pictured here in 1902.

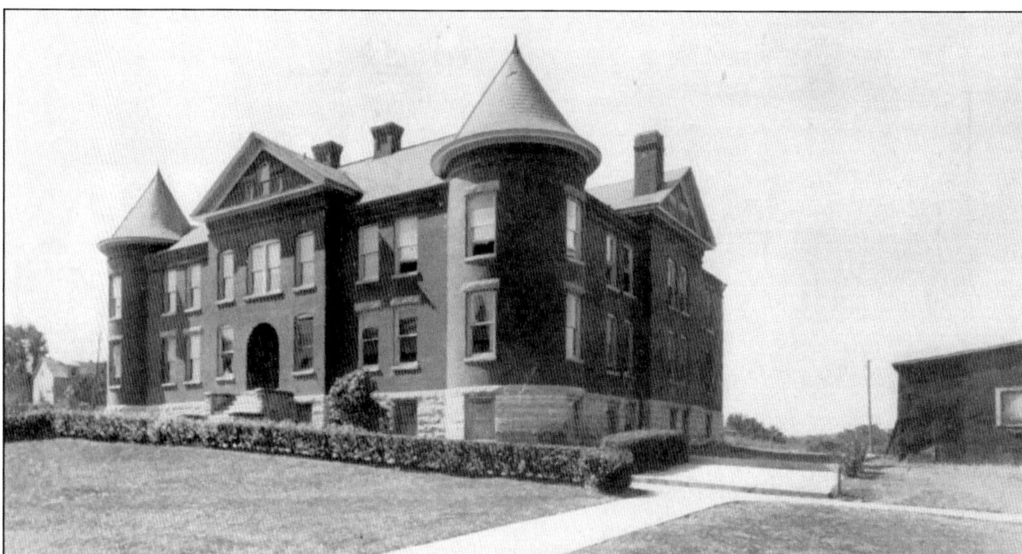

Yates Hall was named for Josephine Silone Yates, a native of Mattituck, New York, who took a teaching job at Lincoln Institute in 1881. Yates taught chemistry, elocution, and English literature. The structure was built in 1884 as a men's dormitory and served later as a women's residence hall, then reconverted to a men's dormitory after Anthony Hall was built in 1940 to house women. The building was demolished in 1948 for the construction on that site of the first Inman E. Page Library. The latter building now is named Stamper Hall after a former dean.

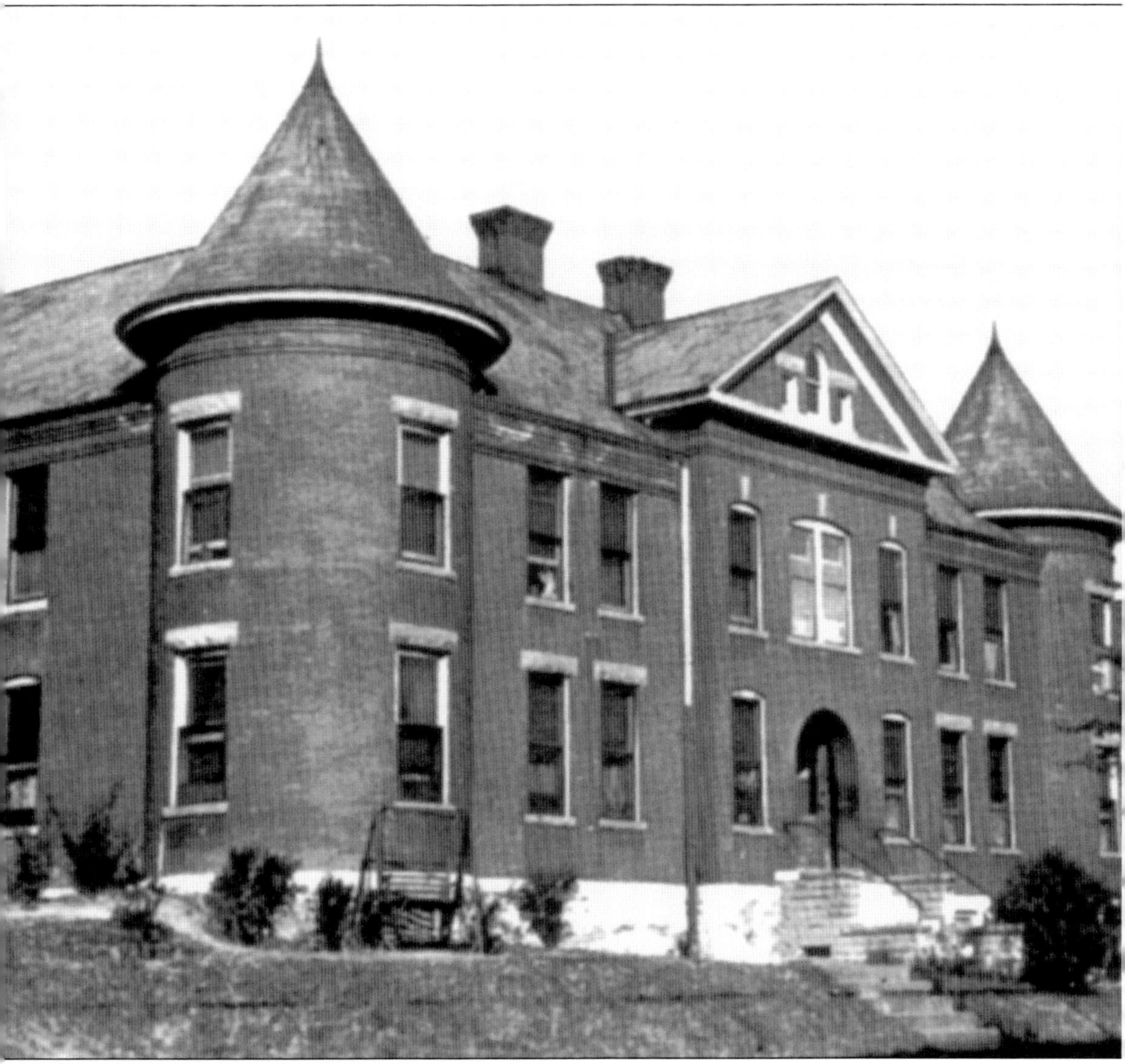

Pictured here is another view of Yates Hall.

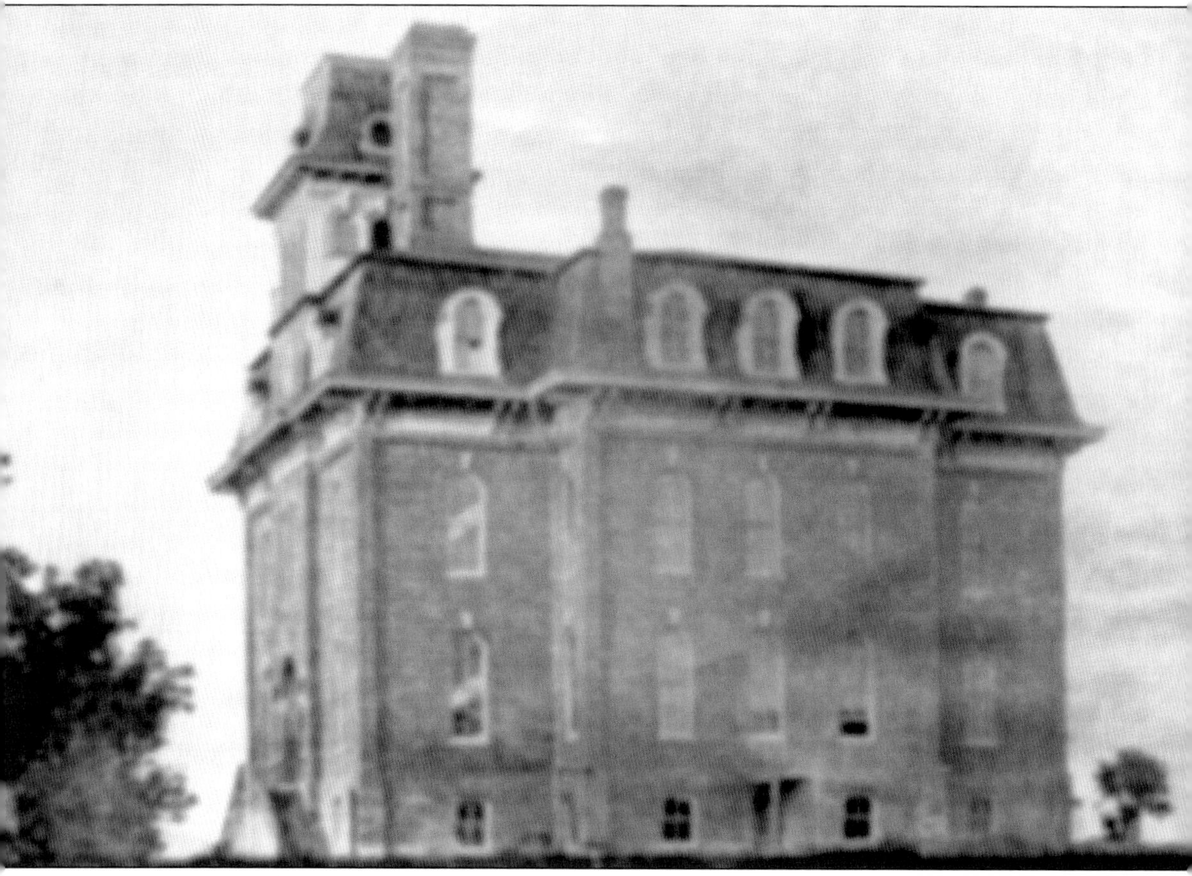

Alexander R. Chinn Hall, built in 1891–1892, was the first industrial arts building built prior to the construction of J. W. Damel Hall. This building was named for Alexander R. Chinn, a native of Glasgow, Missouri. He was a prominent educator who taught in the Glasgow school system more than 50 years. Chinn was referred to as a race scholar, a leader, and an influential citizen of the Glasgow community. He served on the board of regents of Lincoln Institute and did much for the school's development. Chinn Hall was torn down to make room for the current Anderson M. Schweich Hall.

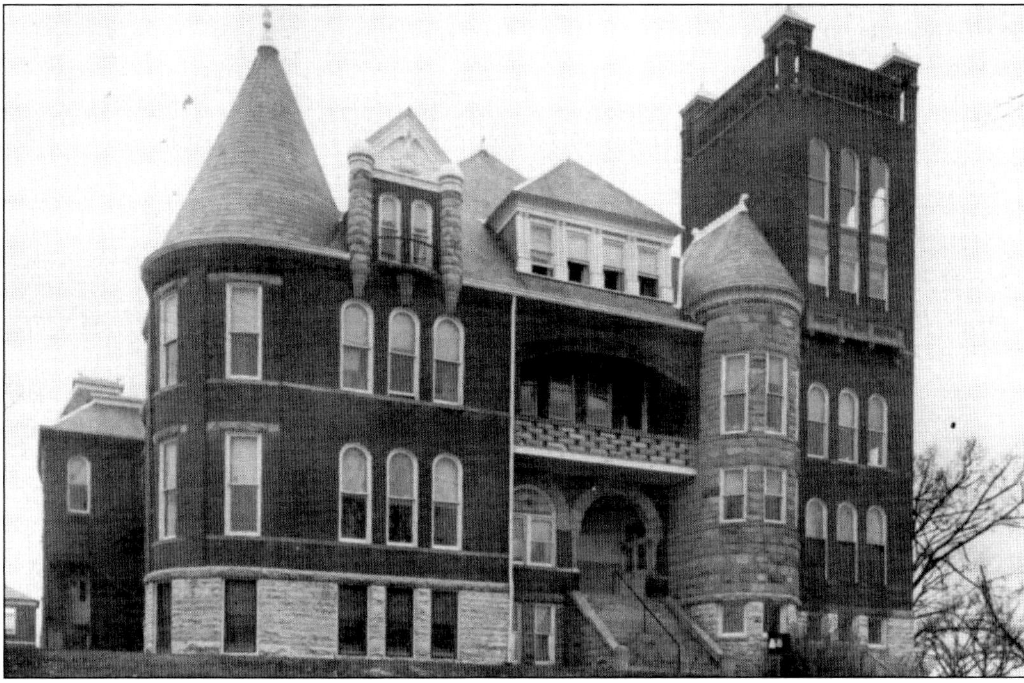

This photograph is of the second of three buildings on the Lincoln University campus called Memorial Hall. The first Memorial Hall was completed on the hilltop campus in 1871 as a memorial to the Civil War soldiers who not only gave money for the founding of Lincoln Institute but also contributed money toward that building. A fire damaged this building on August 2, 1893.

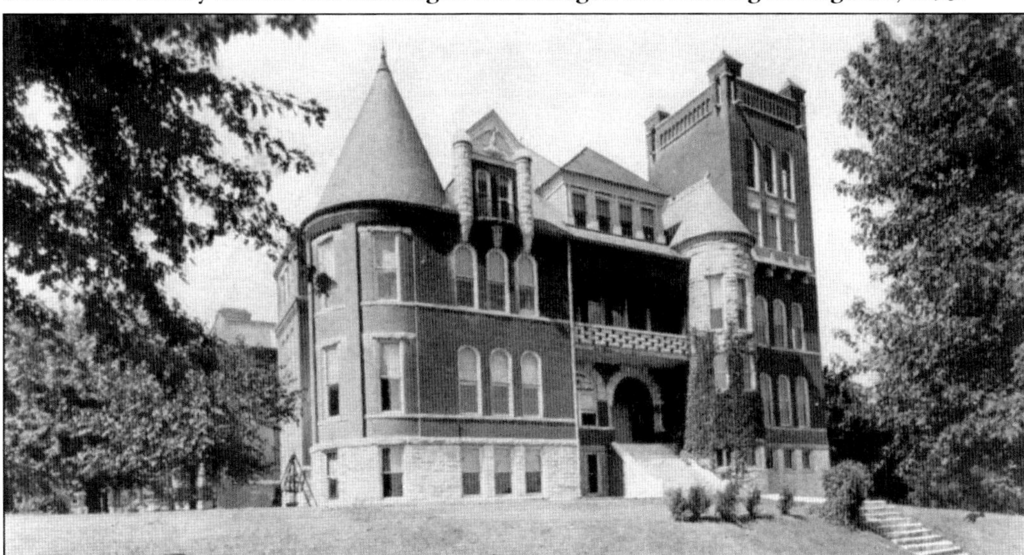

In 1895, the second Memorial Hall (shown here), also known as the "main building" prior to 1895, was struck by lightning on August 2, 1893. In 1895, the building was renamed Memorial Hall, but only the "new half" was ever shown in publicity photographs. By the 1930s, aerial photographs showed the "two Memorial Halls" (the 1871 side and the 1895 side). Both were torn down in 1972. During its heyday, Memorial Hall was a major campus classroom and office building. The current Memorial Hall was completed in 1992 and is an alumni center.

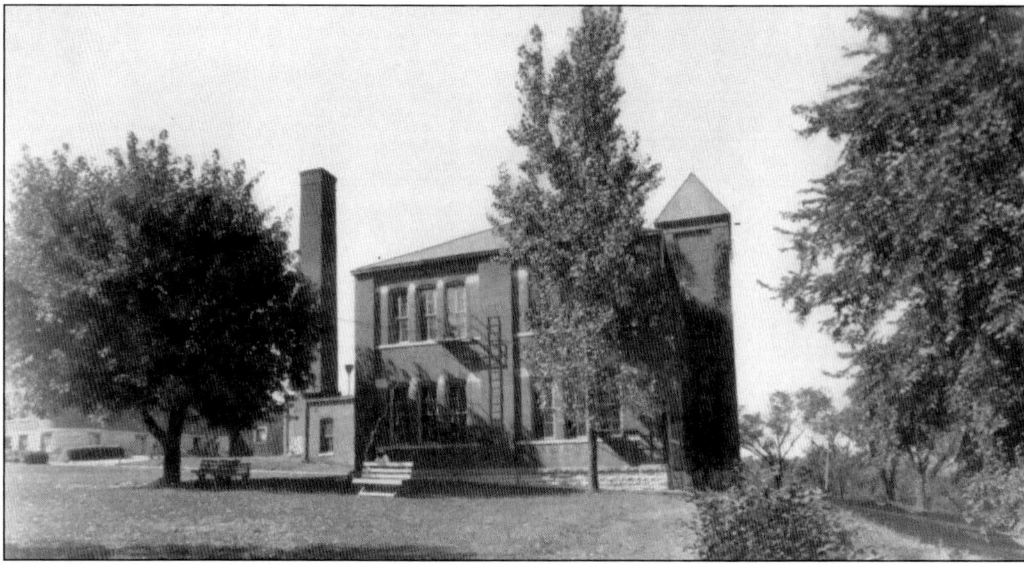

Memorial Hall is seen in this photograph.

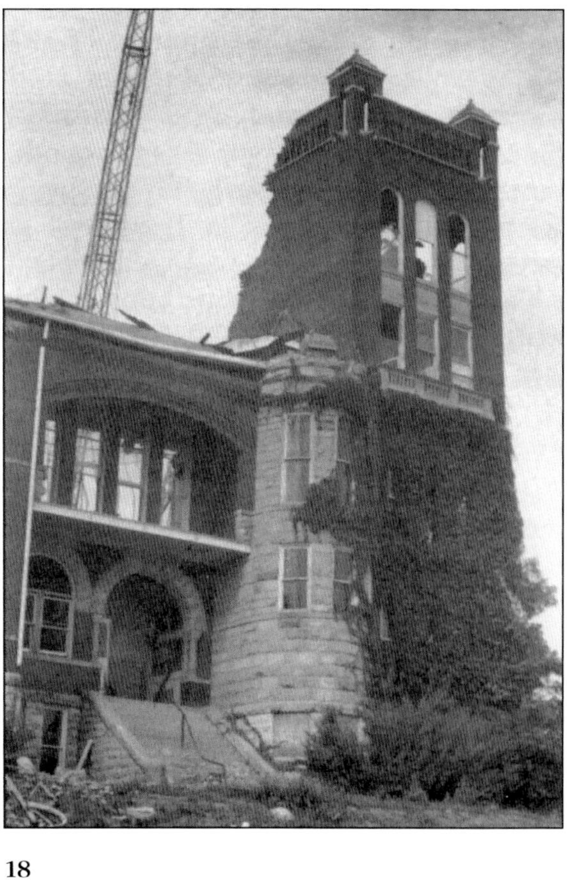

The demolition of the second Memorial Hall, in 1972, is pictured here.

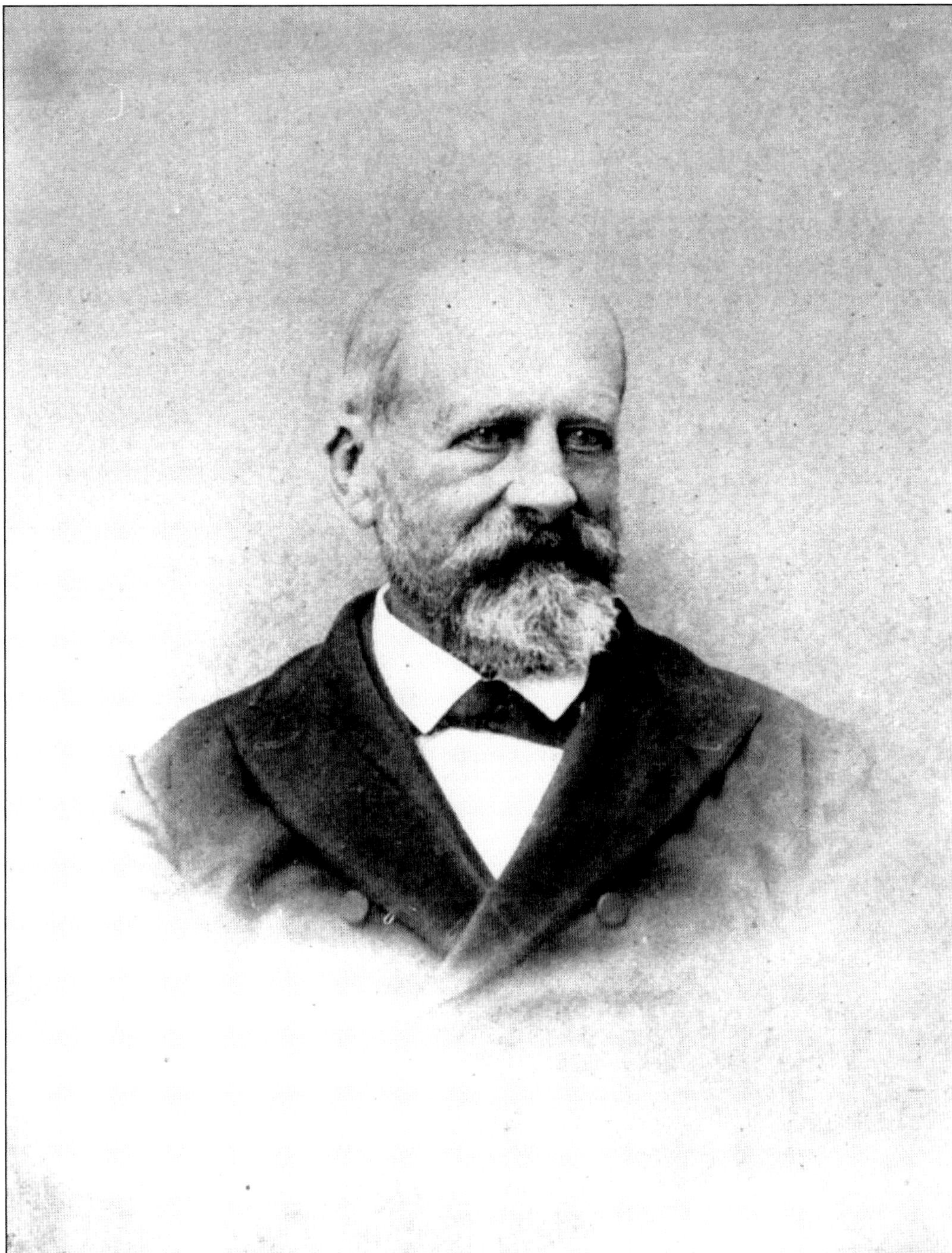

Richard Baxter Foster was a Connecticut-born Civil War lieutenant who, because of his interest in furthering the education of African American soldiers in the 62nd and 65th United States Colored Infantries, organized the first board of Lincoln Institute in St. Louis on January 14, 1866. The school formally opened in September 1866. Foster served as the first and third principal of Lincoln Institute. Foster Hall, a former residence hall named for him, is now an office building for the 1890 land-grant cooperative extension/cooperative research program.

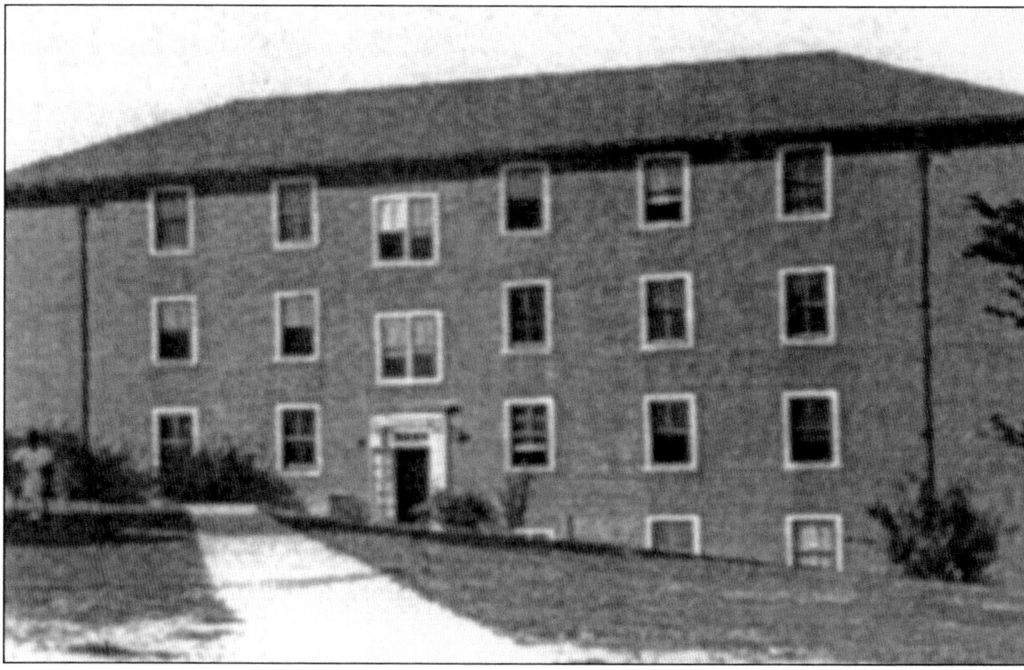

Foster Hall, shown here, was constructed in 1923 as a dormitory for male students. The building, when used as a residence hall, contained a recreation room, a reception room, a barbershop, and an office for the dean. In 1994, the building underwent an extensive renovation using funds granted by the United States Department of Agriculture (USDA) and was converted to an office building and research laboratories for the Lincoln University 1890 land-grant program.

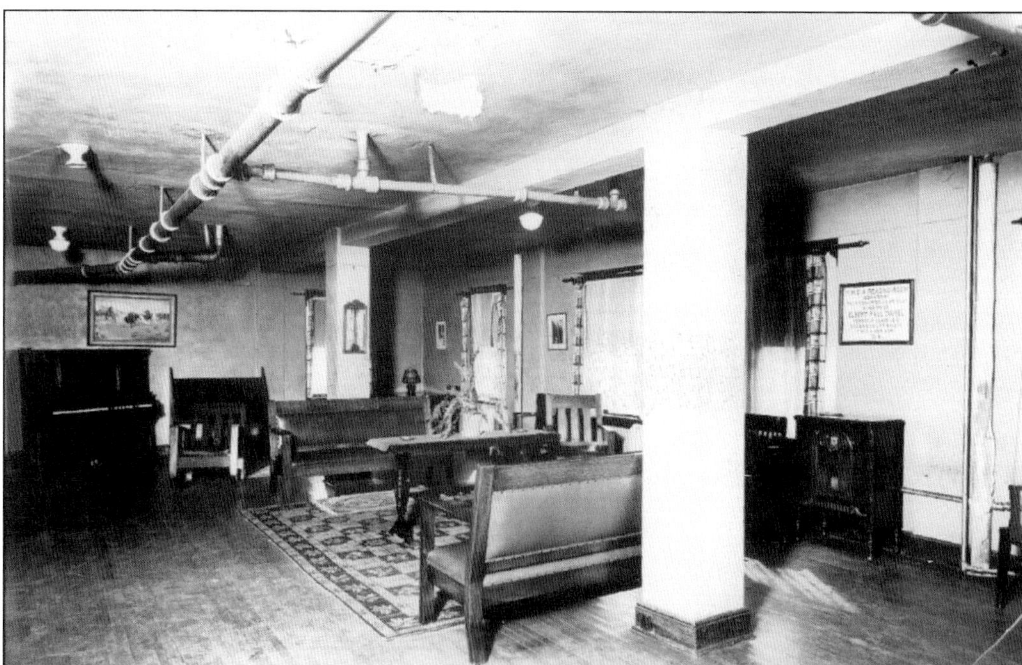

The student recreation lounge of Foster Hall between 1920 and 1930 is pictured here.

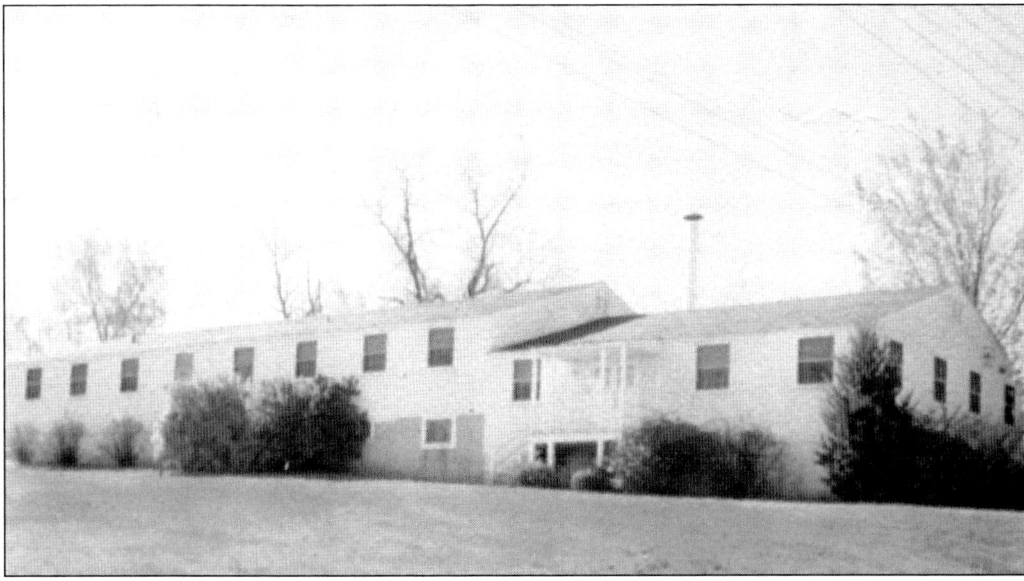

This asbestos-sided building served as the campus infirmary until the Thompkins Health Center was constructed in 1969.

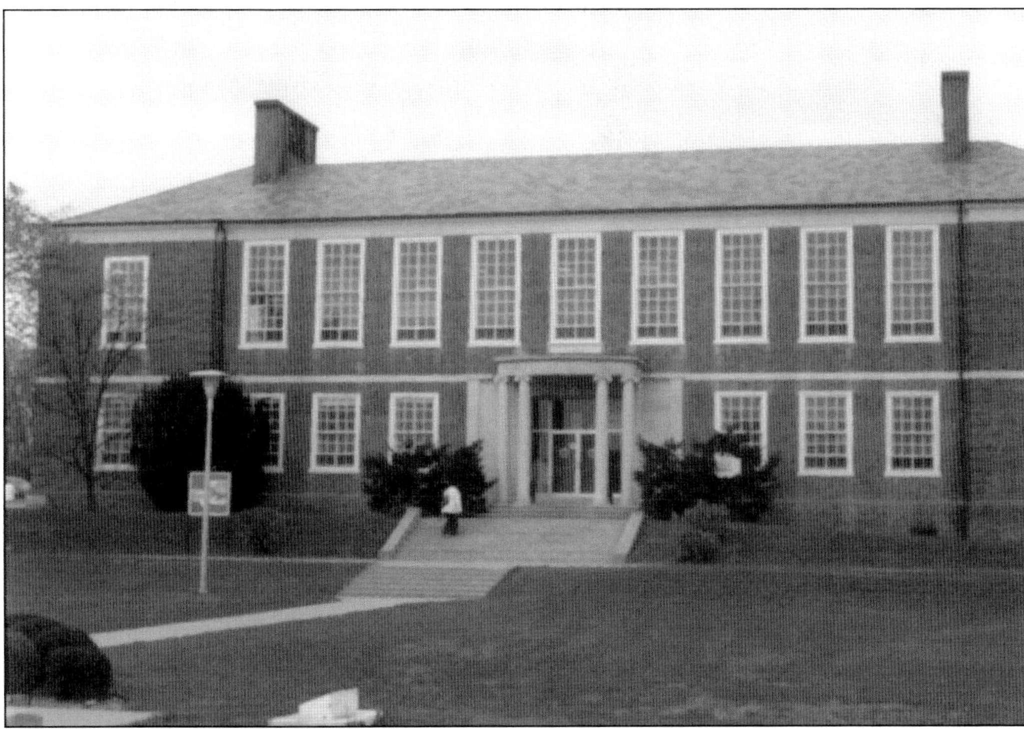

The first Inman E. Page Library was completed in 1950 on land where Yates Hall formerly set and could hold 120,000 volumes. There was seating capacity for approximately 450 persons in the building. It was the first campus structure devoted completely to library services because the university library had shared space in the Young Hall administration building.

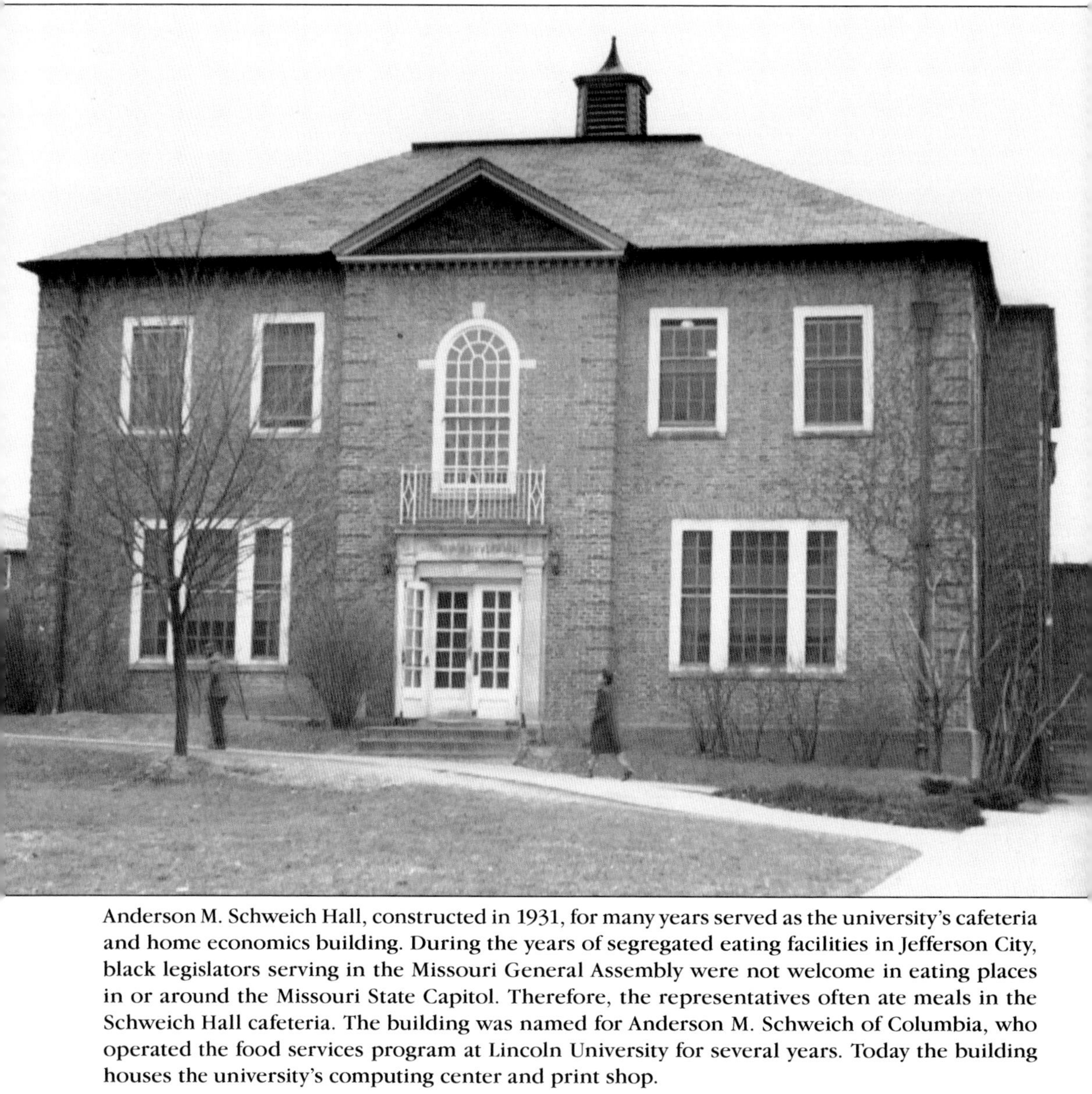

Anderson M. Schweich Hall, constructed in 1931, for many years served as the university's cafeteria and home economics building. During the years of segregated eating facilities in Jefferson City, black legislators serving in the Missouri General Assembly were not welcome in eating places in or around the Missouri State Capitol. Therefore, the representatives often ate meals in the Schweich Hall cafeteria. The building was named for Anderson M. Schweich of Columbia, who operated the food services program at Lincoln University for several years. Today the building houses the university's computing center and print shop.

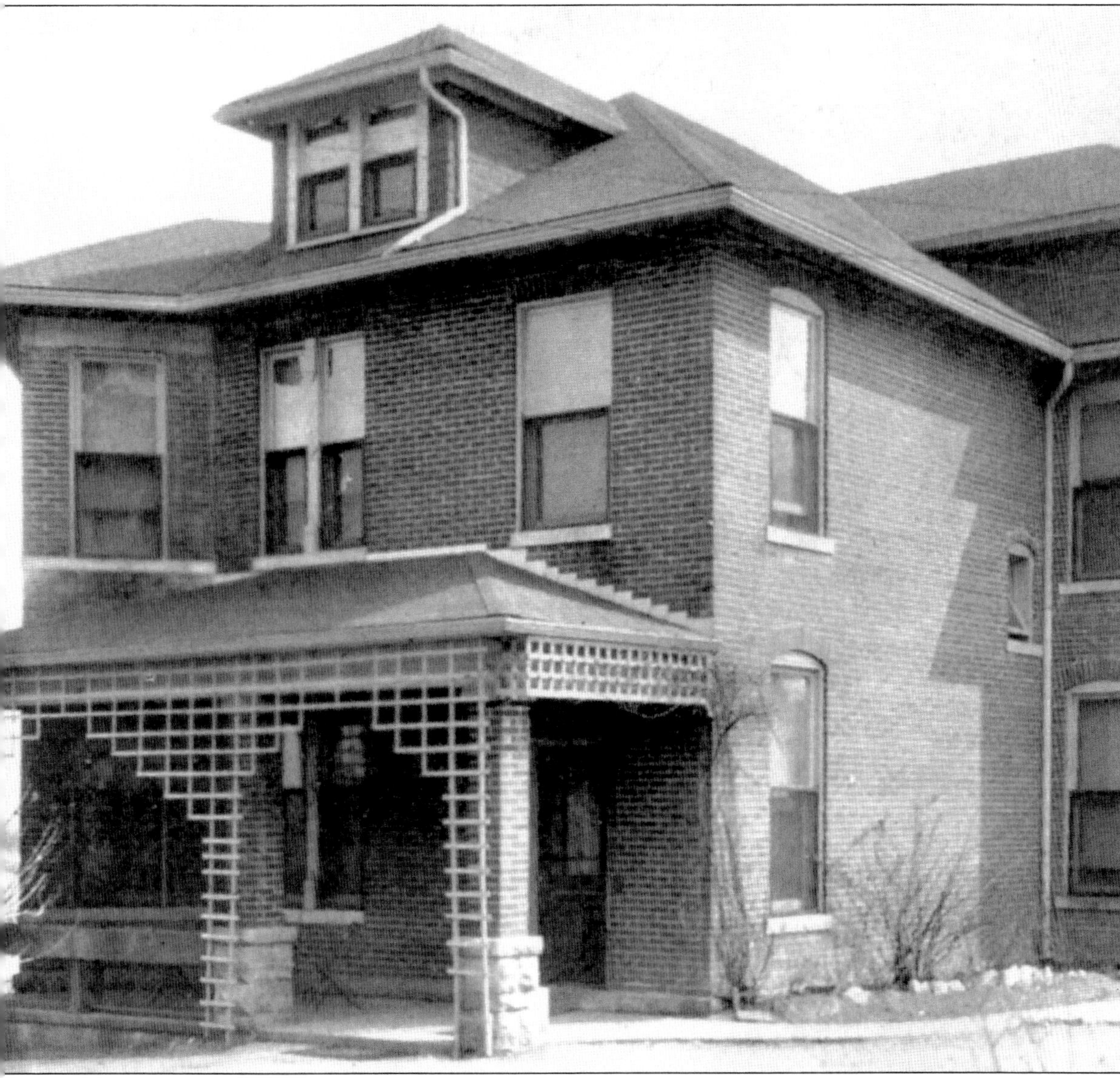

The first Lincoln University presidents' home was constructed in 1892 by students of the Department of Industrial Arts at a cost of $1,000. The two-and-one-half-story, 12-room brick building served during the administration of Pres. Charles Florence as a guesthouse for visiting dignitaries because hotels in Jefferson City would not accommodate African Americans. Among the guests who stayed at the presidents' house during that time were Dr. George Washington Carver, Mary McLeod Bethune, Dr. W. E. B. DuBois, and Dr. Carter G. Woodson. In 1965, the current presidents' residence, located at 601 Jackson Street, was purchased from the estate of Hugh Stephens, who built the house in 1913.

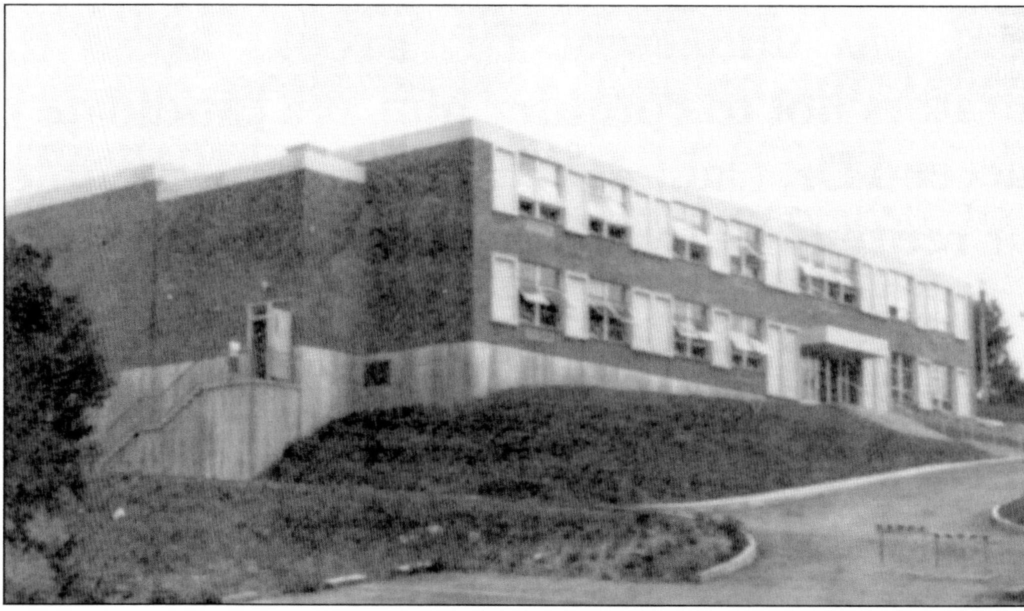

Eliff Hall was named for Dr. J. D. Eliff of the University of Missouri-Columbia who was a longtime member of the Lincoln University Board of Curators. The building initially was the Laboratory High School, which educated black students through the eighth grade until the school was closed in 1975. The building now houses the nursing program and university cable access television station.

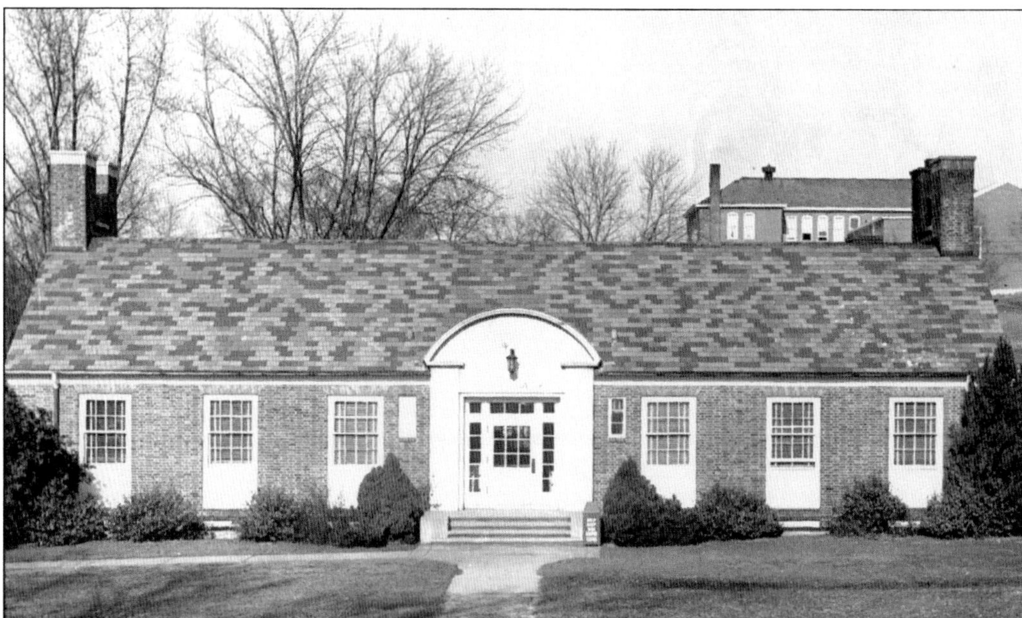

Mitchell Hall, originally called the Journalism Building, opened in the fall of 1942 for the School of Journalism. The building was named for Joseph E. Mitchell, the founder and publisher of the once influential African American newspaper the *Saint Louis Argus*. Included in the building were laboratories for news editing, reporting, photography, photoengraving, advertising, and typography, classrooms, and a library with more than a thousand volumes.

# *Two*

# LINCOLN UNIVERSITY PRESIDENTS

Between the years 1920 and 1970, Lincoln University had eight presidents. The tenure of presidents in the early years was generally short-lived, with most of the persons staying two to three years. In fact, one president only held office for one year. The major cause of the short tenures of early presidents was the political atmosphere and influence those leaders had to endure. As a state-supported institution, the Missouri governor, often from a distance, provided oversight over the university. Secondly, the governing board of curators appointed by the governor was usually partisan and likewise made governing difficult for the chosen leader. It was not until the late 1930s that political influence seemed less an issue a president had to consider in managing the institution. A ninth individual—Dr. James Frank, who assumed the presidency in 1972—is added to the list because of the special significance and meaning his presidency brought to Lincoln University. Frank is the first and only alumnus to serve as president (although Lincoln University alumnus Dr. Henry Givens from St. Louis served a brief stint in the mid-1980s as the university's chief executive officer during an interim period while the university searched for a new leader). The Lincoln University presidents from 1920 to 1970 were Clement Richardson, 1918–1922; Inman E. Page, 1880–1898, 1922–1923; Nathan B. Young, 1923–1927, 1929–1931; William B. Jason, acting president 1927, president 1928–1929, acting president 1937–1938; Charles Florence, 1931–1937; Sherman D. Scruggs, 1938–1956; Earl E. Dawson, acting president, 1952–1954, president, 1954–1969; Walter Daniel, 1969–1972; and Dr. James Frank, 1973–1982.

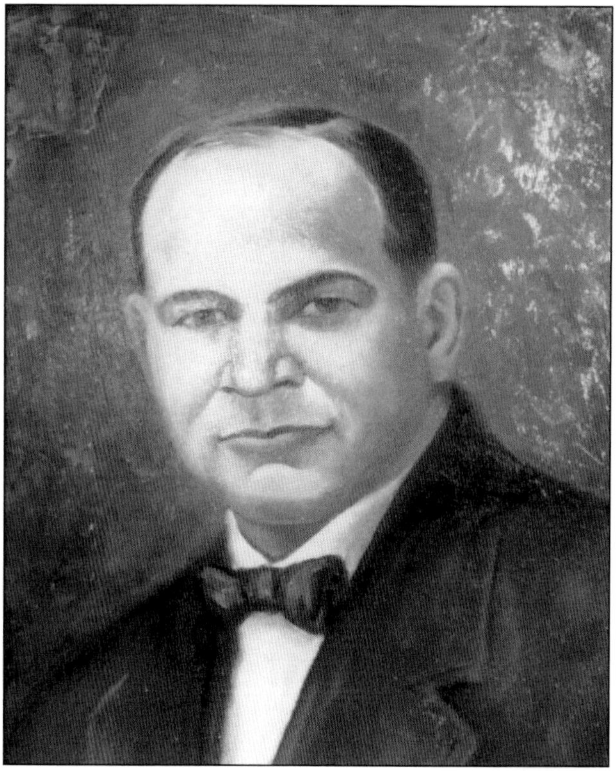

Dr. Clement Richardson, a former faculty member of Tuskegee Institute, was appointed to lead the school in 1918. One of the main goals of Richardson was to improve the industrial and agricultural programs, but a managing board of curators hampered him. Richardson traveled the state promoting Lincoln Institute by speaking to various groups. It was during his tenure that the name Lincoln Institute was changed to Lincoln University and the curriculum was strengthened with a view toward full accreditation.

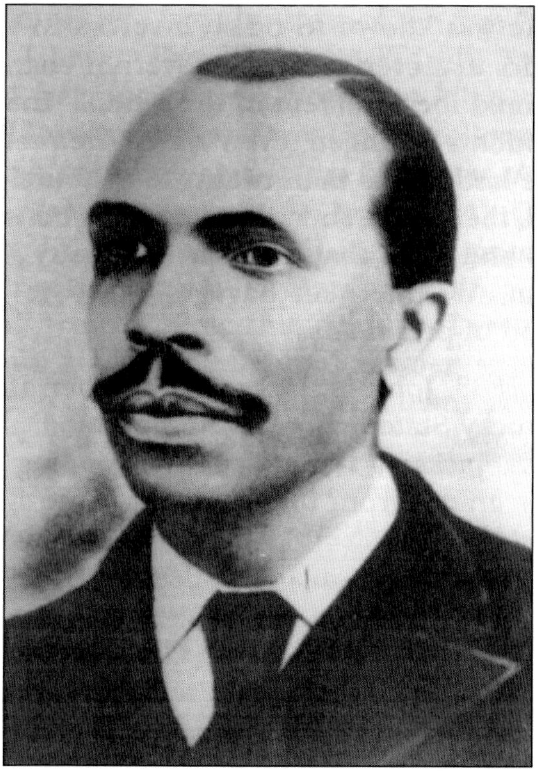

Inman E. Page, who was born into slavery, purchased his own freedom and then entered school in Washington, D.C., later graduating from Brown University where he was class orator. Page, who served two separate terms as university president, first from 1880 to 1898 and again from 1922 to 1923, brought a period of stability to the school. During his tenure in 1891, Lincoln Institute became a land-grant institution under the federal second Morrill Act of 1890. Page added the first significant college work to the curriculum and greatly enhanced the school's physical plant. In 1891, the state legislature gave money for the erection of Chinn Hall, which was an industrial arts building. Further, he was able to attract outstanding teachers and added college work in 1887.

Nathan B. Young served as the president of Lincoln University between 1923 and 1927 and again from 1929 to 1931. He is considered to be one of the most significant figures in the institution's history. Upon assuming the presidency, he soon realized that little had been done academically to change the school from an institute to a university. One of Young's initial tasks was to raise the quality of Lincoln University's faculty by attracting people with degrees from prestigious northern institutions such as Harvard, Cornell, the University of Chicago, Boston University, and Massachusetts Institute of Technology. Many of these faculty members spent their entire teaching careers at Lincoln University.

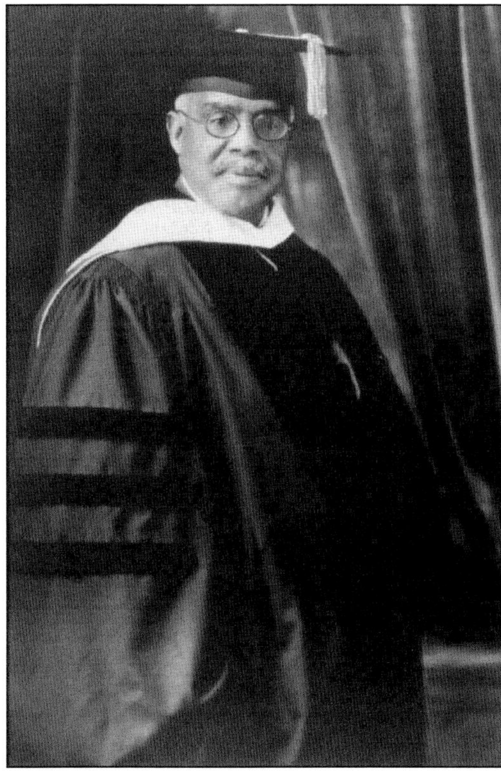

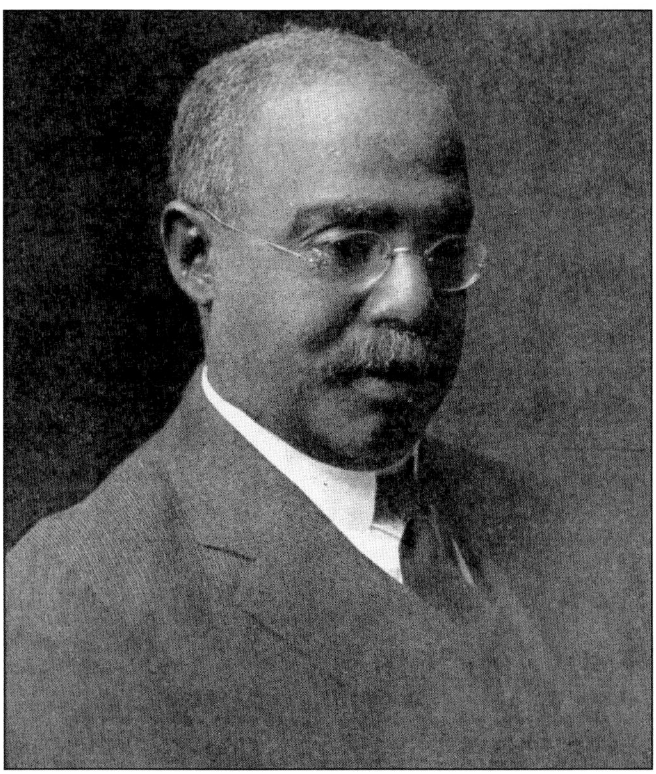

This is another view of Pres. Nathan B. Young.

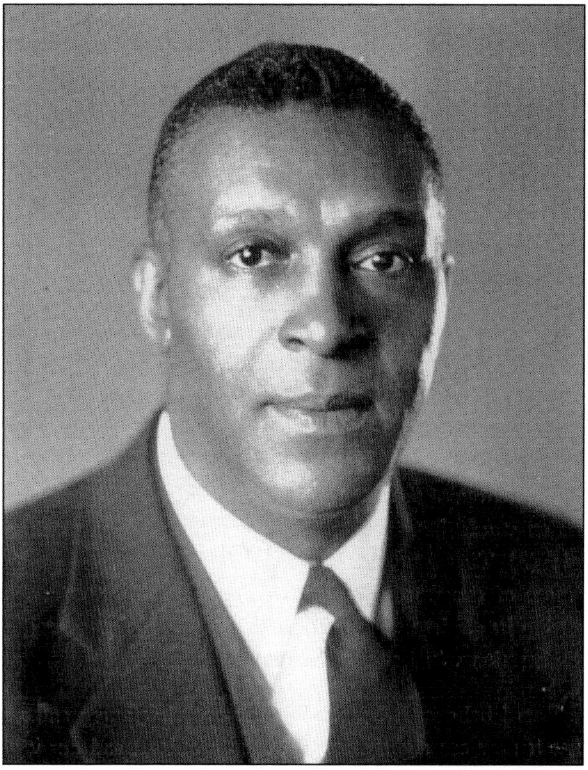

William B. Jason first came to Lincoln University in 1918 to teach mathematics and serve as a coach. Named acting president in 1927, he was made president in 1928. Under his leadership, the state legislature appropriated money for the erection of an educational building that was completed in September 1931. The building was named College Hall but later renamed Young Hall in honor of former president Nathan B. Young. Today this building houses the university's main administrative offices. Jason resigned in 1929 but later served as dean of students, dean of instruction, and finally as vice president and again as acting president in 1937–1938. By the time he became acting president in 1937, Jason had accumulated 19 years of continuous service to Lincoln University.

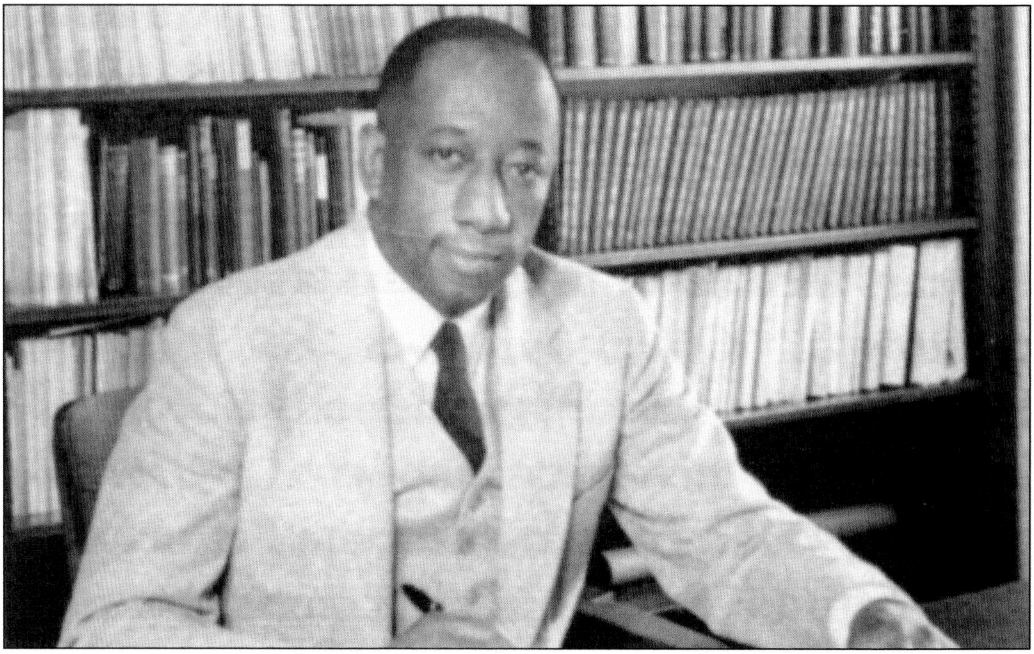

Charles W. Florence guided Lincoln University to full accreditation and membership in the North Central Association of Colleges and Secondary Schools. Also under his leadership a strong effort was made to upgrade faculty by providing sabbatical leaves for persons who wished to work toward advanced degrees.

Sherman D. Scruggs assumed the presidency of Lincoln University in 1938. During his tenure, Lincoln University was freed from political influences and the Schools of Journalism and Law were established.

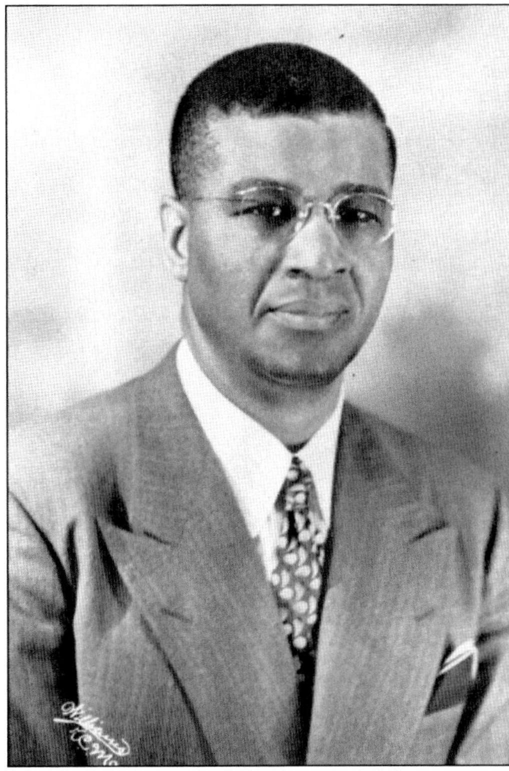

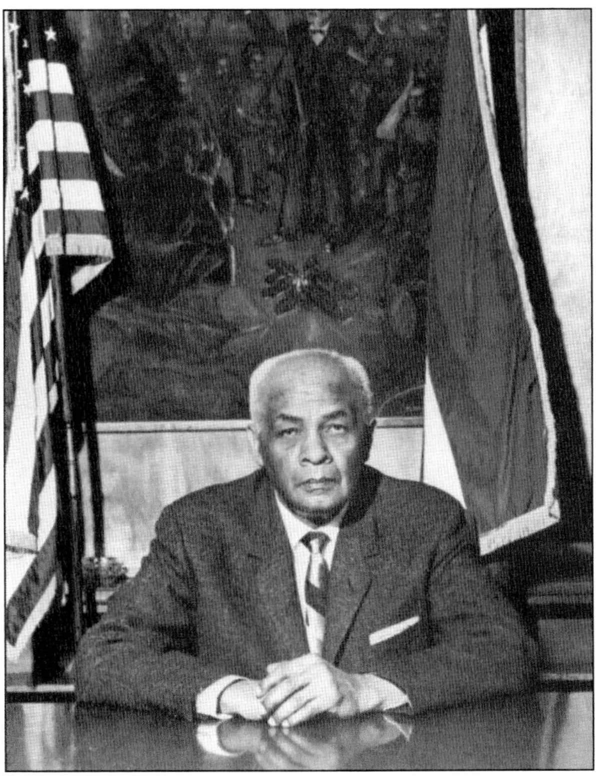

Lincoln University showed tremendous growth in student enrollment during the presidency of Dr. Earl E. Dawson. In 1954, the year of the historic *Brown v. Board of Education of Topeka* Supreme Court decision outlawing "separate but equal" school systems, the university enrolled approximately 700 students. However, with racial integration, by 1961 enrollment was almost 1,500 students with one-third of the students coming from Jefferson City and neighboring communities. The other two-thirds were mainly African Americans from 31 states and several foreign countries. During Dawson's administration, the Martin and Perry Hall dormitories were built.

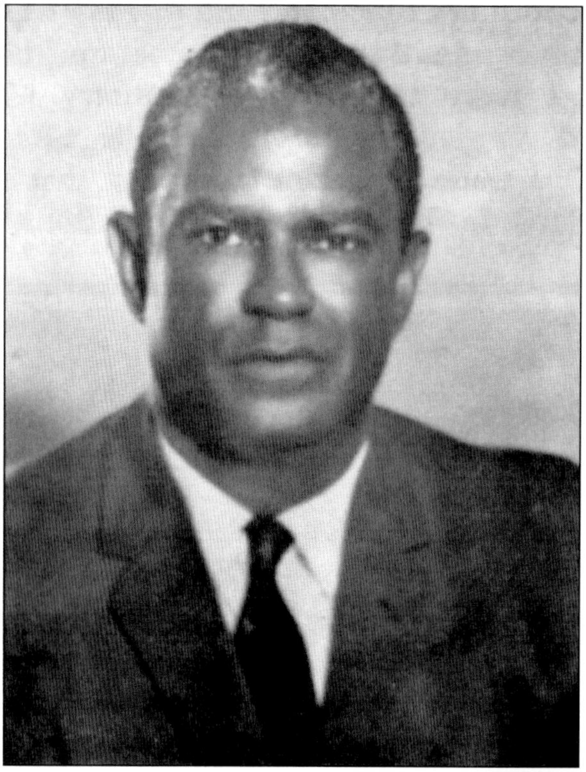

Dr. Walter Daniel had a short tenure of only three years as president before resigning to accept a vice chancellor position at the University of Missouri–Columbia. Daniel's major contributions at Lincoln University include uniting students, faculty, and administration and giving the university a national recognition. He coined the familiar rallying cry for the university at that time, which was "Might Proud of Lincoln."

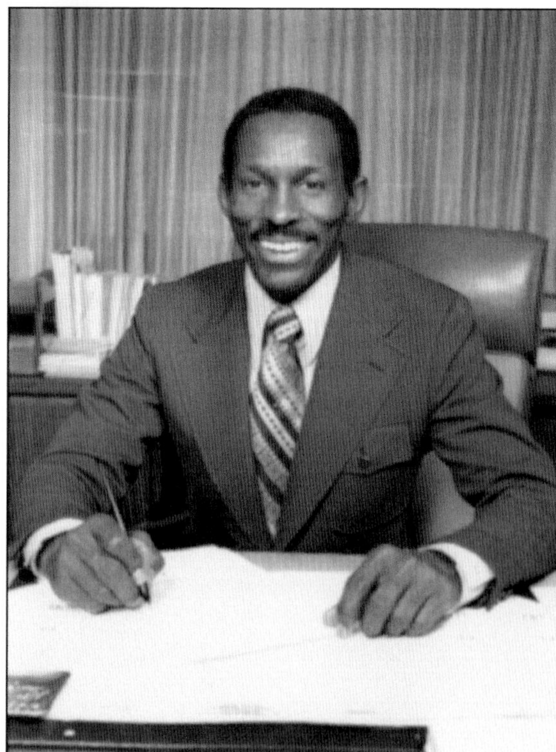

Dr. James Frank in 1973 became the first and only alumnus to serve as president of Lincoln University. A 1953 graduate of the university, Frank served early in his professional career as a Lincoln University physical education instructor and head basketball coach. Additionally in 1981, Frank was both the first African American and college president elected president of the National Collegiate Athletic Association (NCAA) in its then 87-year history. After leaving Lincoln University, Frank served as head of the Southwestern Athletic Conference from 1983 to 1998. (Please note that while this book only covers up to 1970, the author thought it was important that Frank be included among presidents, given his long tradition with Lincoln University).

# *Three*

# Organizations and Societies

Organizations and societies during the 1920–1950 time period tended to be organized around either intellectual or cultural enrichment activities. The formal debate club participated in national debating tournaments competing against prestigious Ivy League schools or well-known historically black colleges and universities. Also, a string ensemble frequently gave campus-based performances. Complementing the school's musical talent was a university orchestra. During the decades of the 1920s, 1930s, and 1940s, student social life at Lincoln University was very much organized around clubs and black men's and women's fraternal organizations. It is important to note that the clubs had more than a social purpose. For example, most, if not all, the academic disciplines have formal student membership support groups whose members were academic majors within the respective departments.

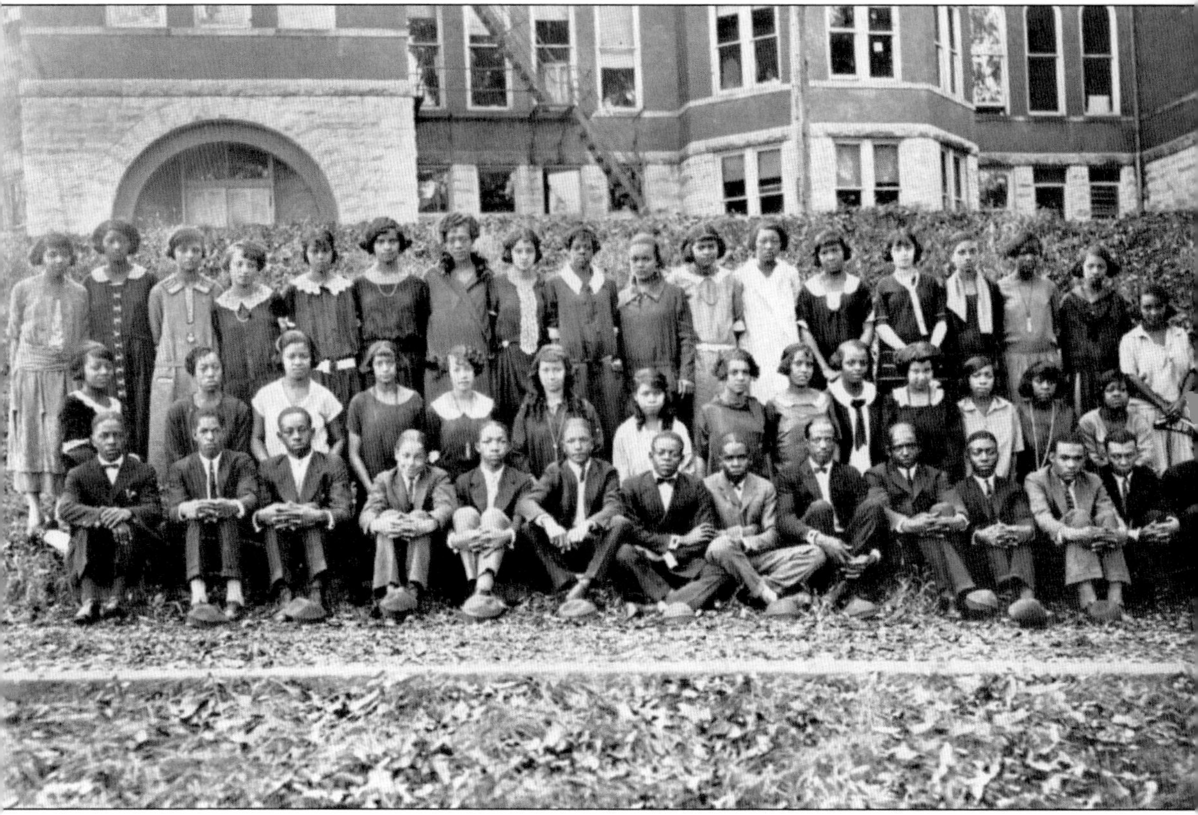

The 1925 freshman college class is pictured here.

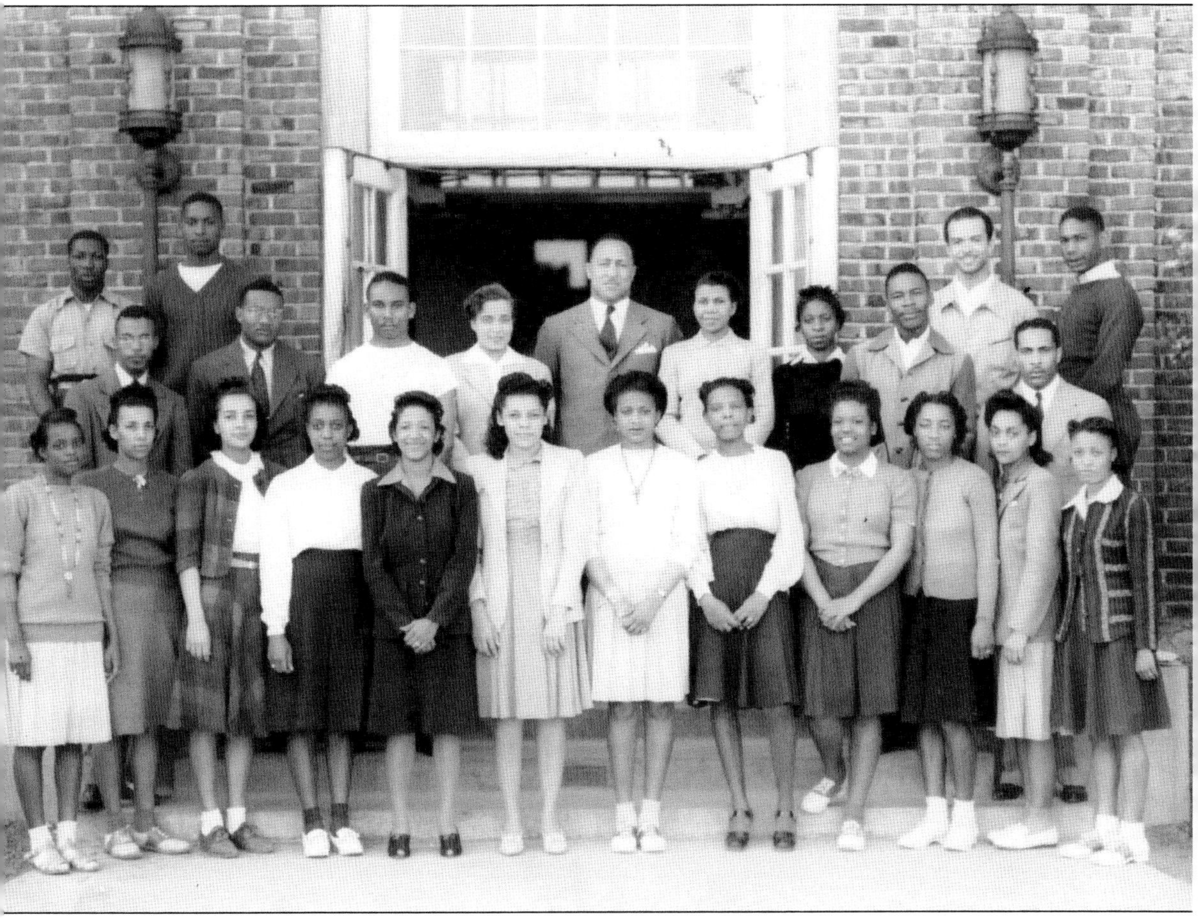

The staff and majors of the Department of Health and Physical Education are pictured here in 1942.

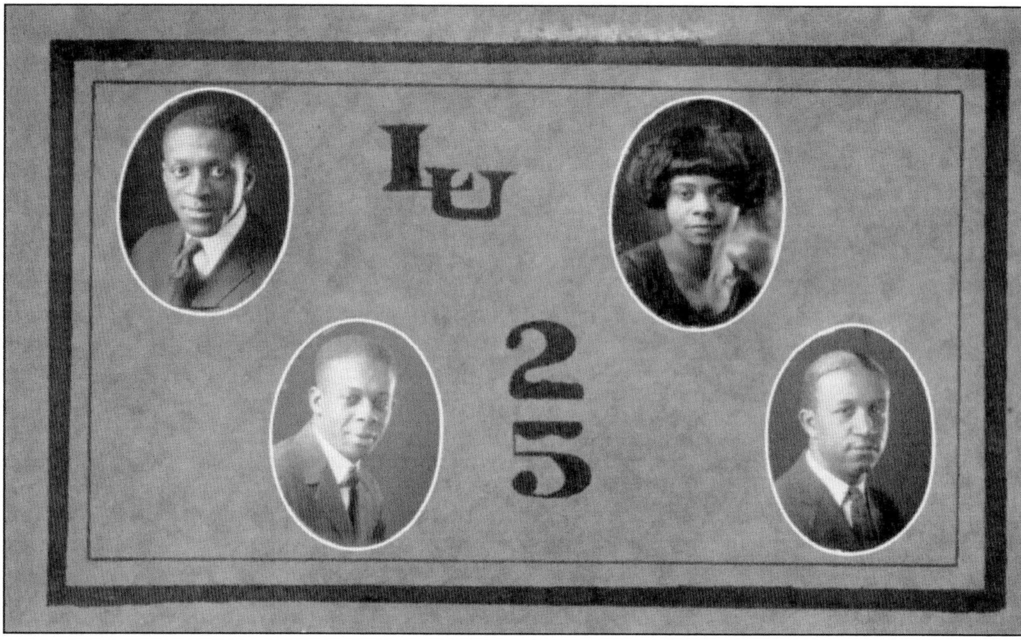


Senior class officers in 1925 include, from left to right, (top row) Marion Lunderman (Paducah, Kentucky), vice president, and Eulalia Hubbard (Sedalia), secretary; (bottom row) Joel Johnson (Williamsburg), treasurer, and Onward Abbington (Jefferson City), president.

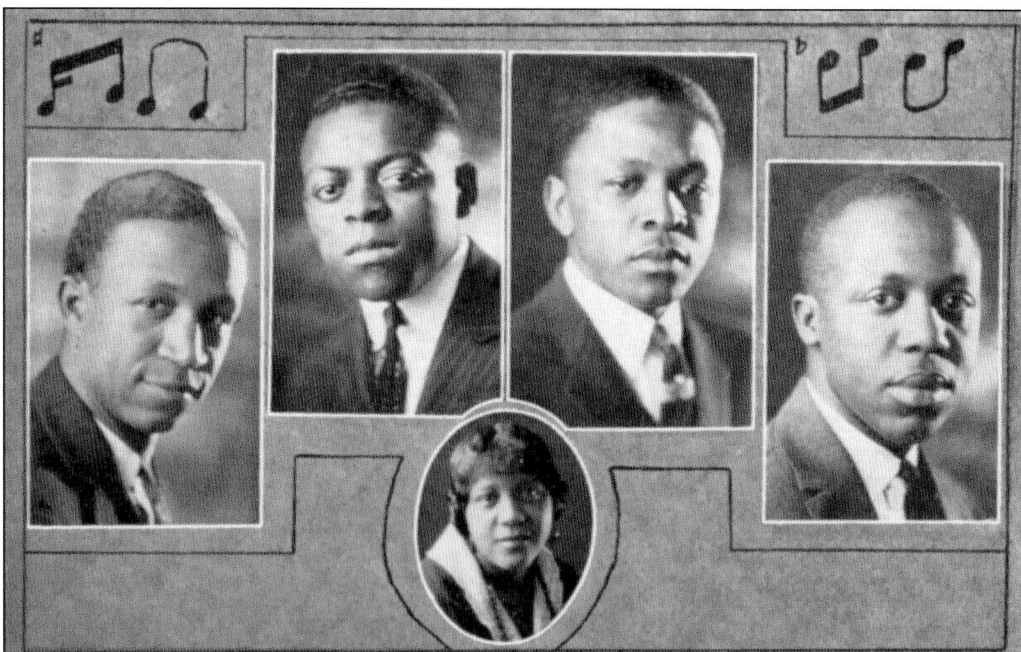

In the 1920s, Lincoln University had a university quartet that broadcast often on radio station WOS of Jefferson City and received cards, letters, and telegrams of appreciation from every state in the union plus Canada, Mexico, and Hawaii. In 1925, members of the quartet include, from left to right, Onward Abbington (baritone), Clement S. Smith (first tenor), James E. Clinton (second tenor), and Bragg T. Douglass (bass). The supervisor is a Miss Cottrell.

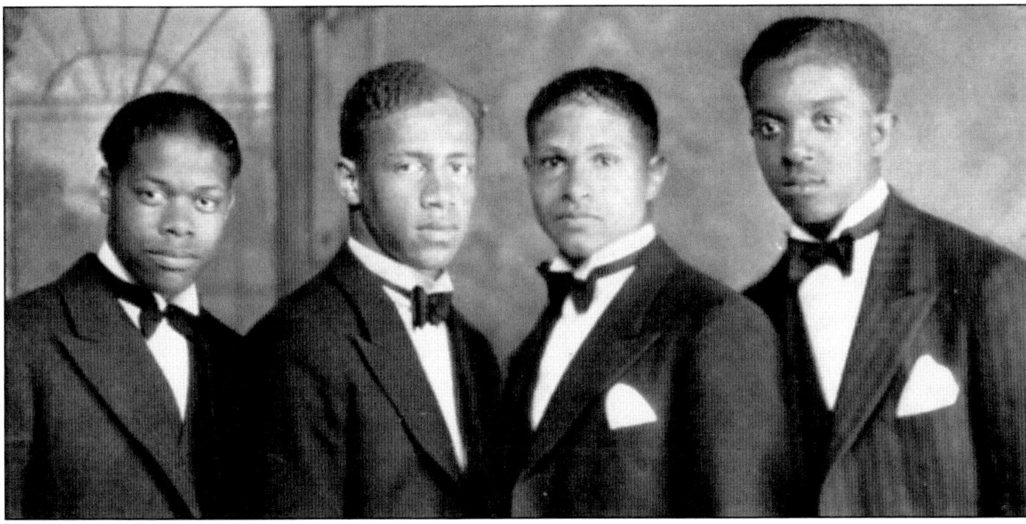

Members of the male quartet in 1929 include, from left to right, DeArmond C. Stewart (bass), Ennis Whaley (baritone), George Brown (second tenor), and Finis Simms (first tenor).

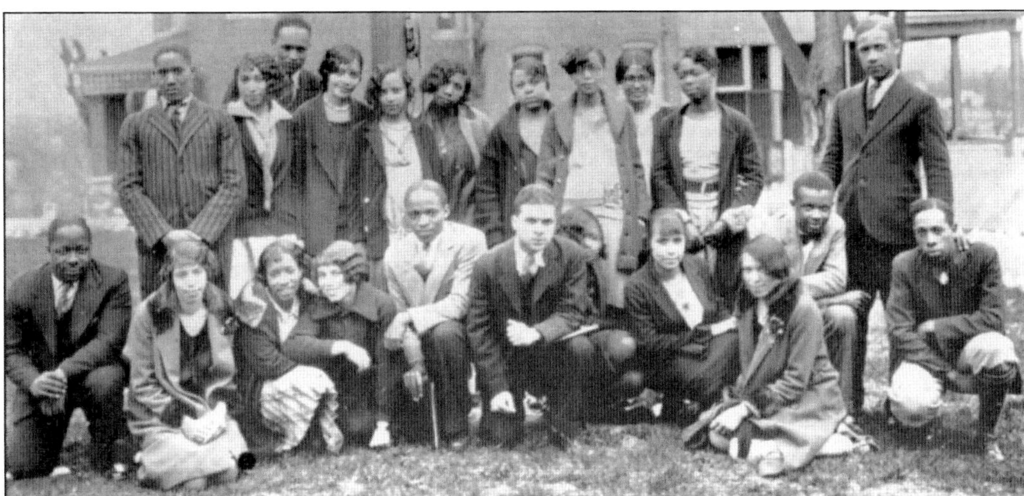

A few sophomore and freshmen students interested in discussing current events organized the Forum Debating Club in October 1928 to debate selected topics. The aim of the Forum Debating Club was to instill and develop self-confidence in sophomore and freshman students. Further, the organization afforded an avenue for training in debating, both formally and informally, because ordinarily students did not receive this instruction in their classes. Meetings were held biweekly at which time discussions were conducted by members of the club. Every other meeting was a social meeting in which formal discussions were held and refreshments served.

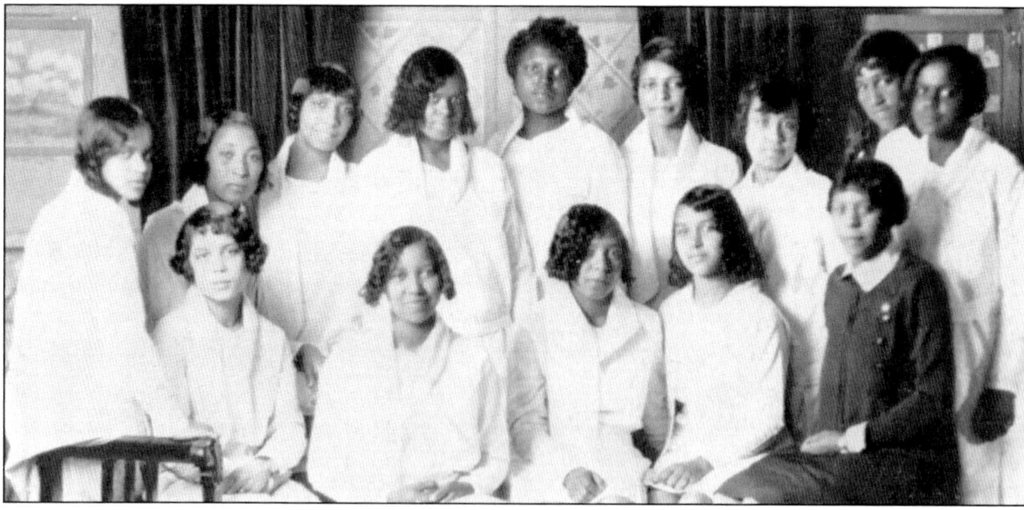

One of the active organizations at Lincoln University in 1929 was a girls' glee club. Members pictured here include E. Louise Thornton, Opal Woods, Marinda Ferguson, Margaret Cravens, Margarette Burton, Wilhelmina Harrison, Clementine Sexton, Mary E. Cobbs, Clyde Easter, Frances Randall, Josephine Payne, and Rose Mary Smith. The accompanist was Mary L. Ray, and Roena Muckelroy was the directress.

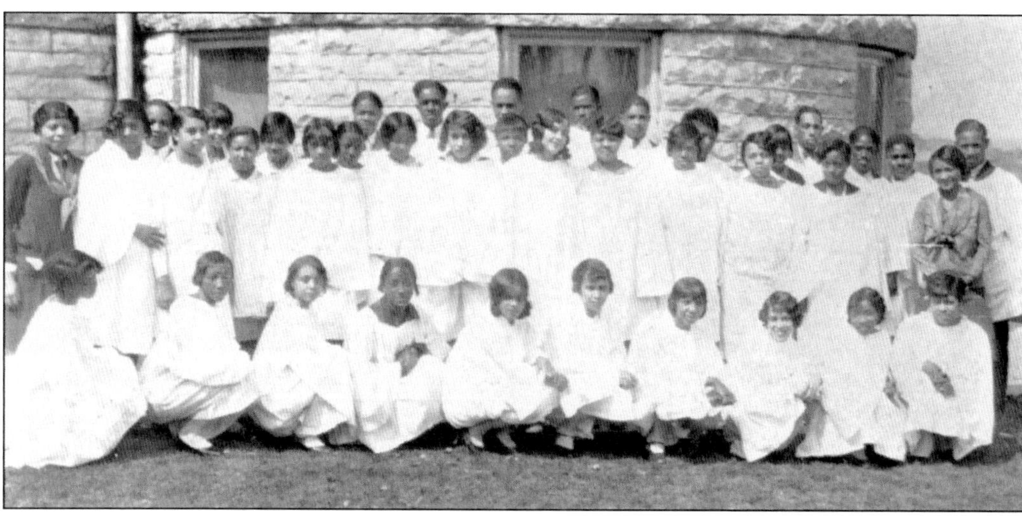

Pictured here is the 1929 Lincoln University Chorus.

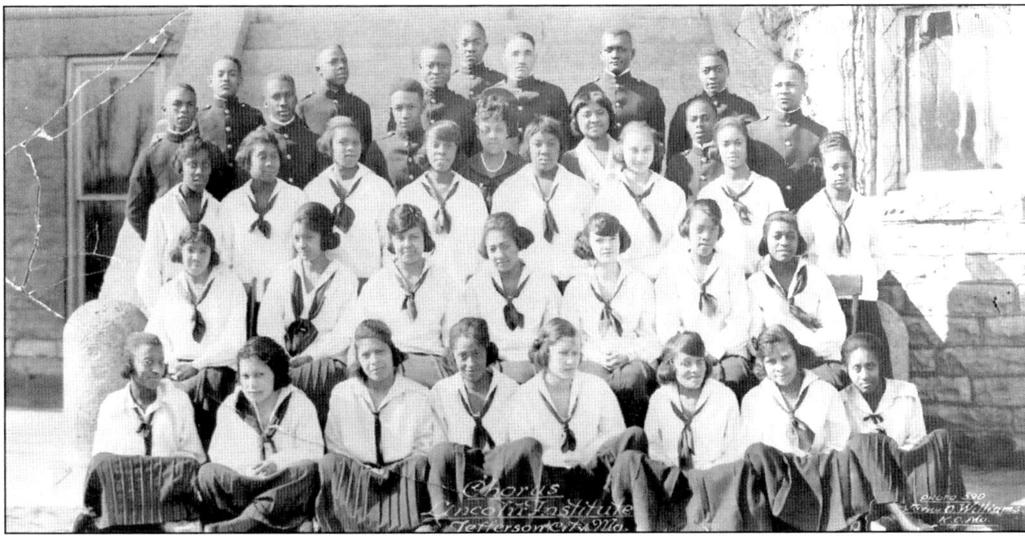


This is a choral group in the 1930s.

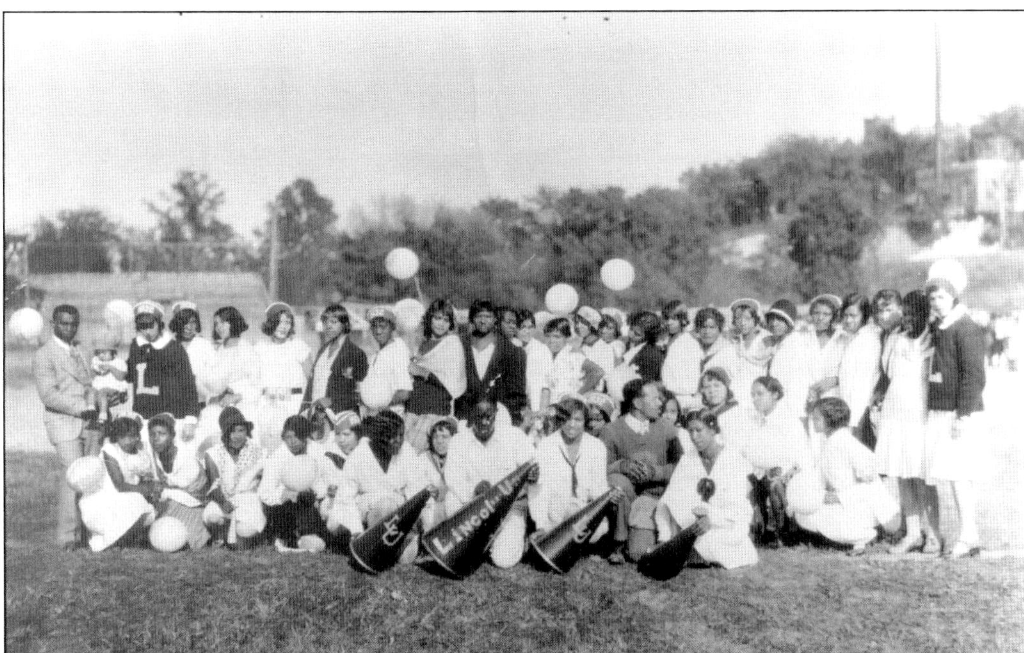

Lincoln University cheerleaders in the 1930s are pictured here.

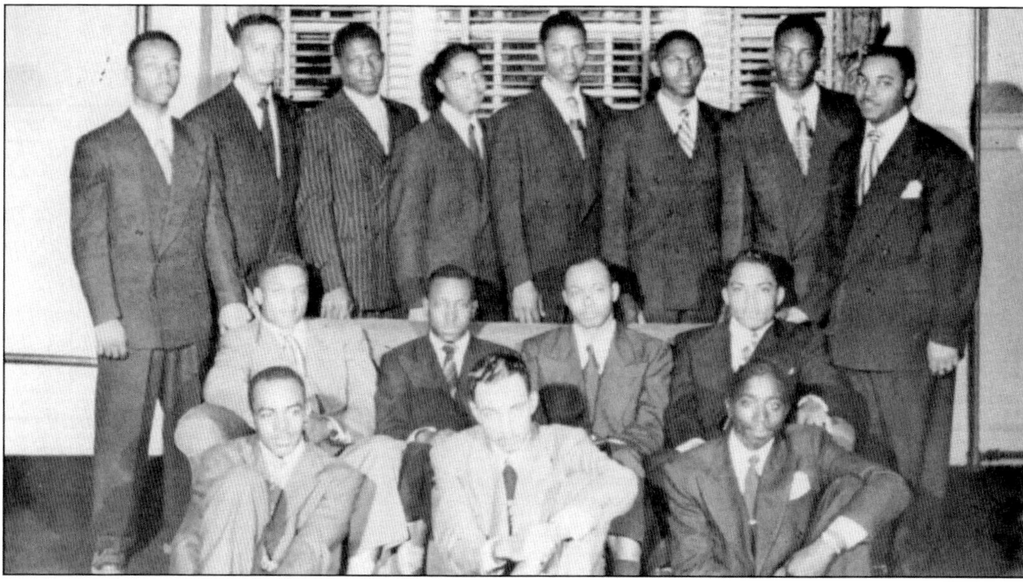

The Agonanhus Club was organized in September 1946 to stimulate thinking and promote scholarship in the field of agriculture and all related sciences, to promote leadership among students enrolled in the Department of Agriculture, and to promote wholesome recreational and social activities. In 1949, the members include Norman Barber, Bennie Britt, Charles Brooks, James Carroll, Roy Cooper, Edward D. Dobbins, Robert Dodson, George Farris, Marion Franklin, Elmer Harris, William Harris, Marshall James, Jodie McDonald, Benjamin Owusu, and Obie Richardson.

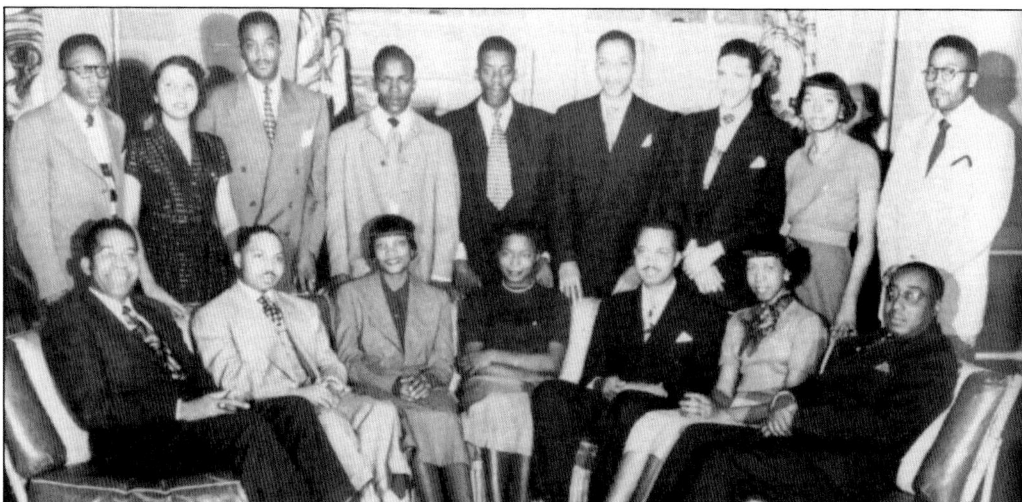

The Sociology Club was organized in 1939 shortly after the school offered the field as a major with a purpose of inspiring students to develop a greater interest in the study of people through community projects. Some projects that the club participated in included supervising juvenile recreation at the local community center and volunteer teaching at the Missouri Penitentiary. From left to right they are (first row) Dr. Oliver C. Cox (sociology professor), Lloyd Marshall (treasurer), Emma Ackerman (president), Pearlie Ingram (secretary), Samuel Q. Parks, Opal Daniels (assistant secretary), and Dr. R. Clyde Minor (sponsor); (second row) Virgil Wright, Clarice Boyd, Thomas Lawson (vice president), Thomas Jackson, Orrell Ellison, Ulysses Thompson, Walter Hopps, Marion Searcy, and Ambrose Brodus.

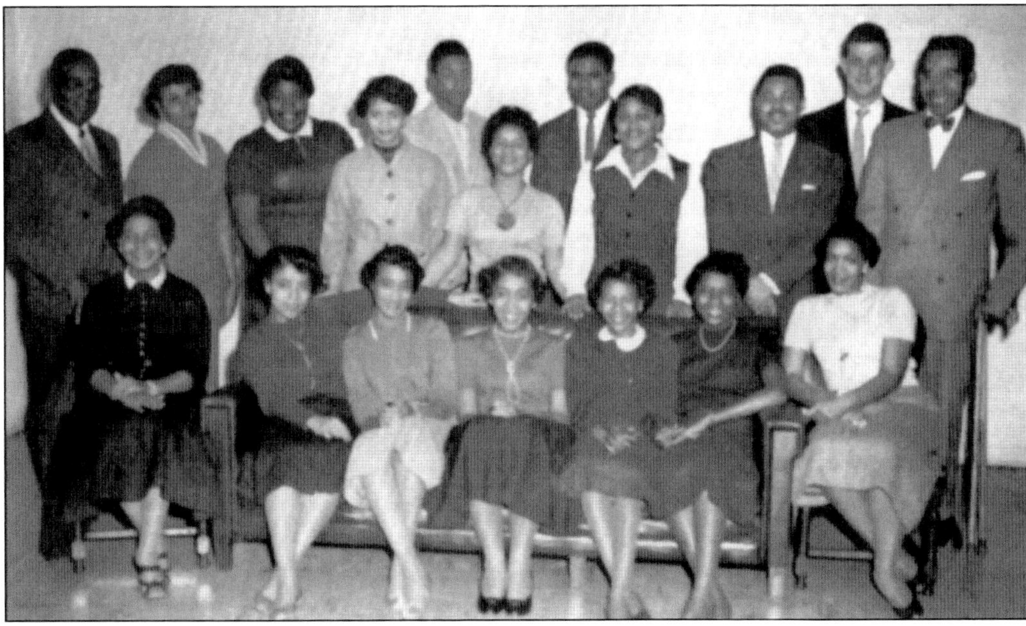

This is the Sociology Club in a later year.

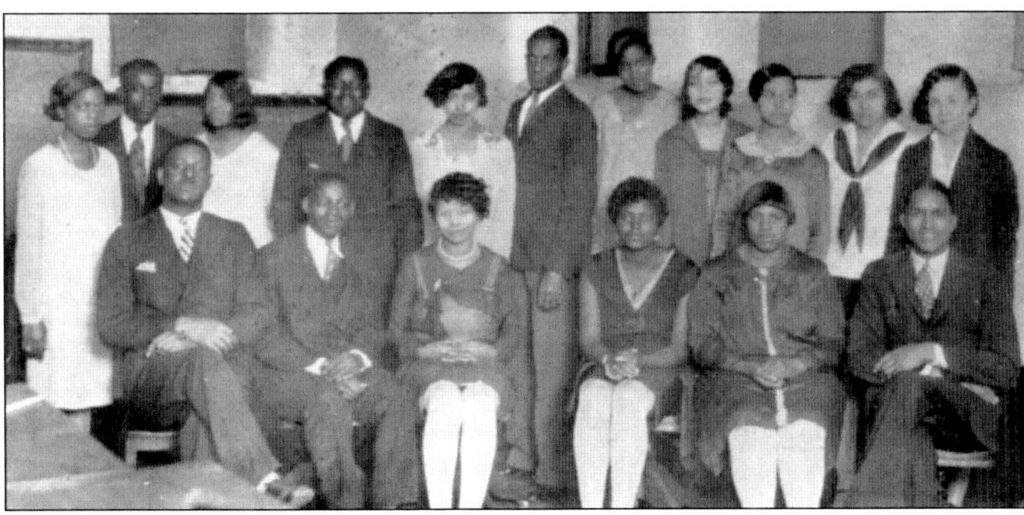

The Commercial Club in 1929 was an organization of students pursuing courses given by the Department of Commerce. Its activities were educational, inspirational, and social to help students acquire a practical knowledge of business as a profession.

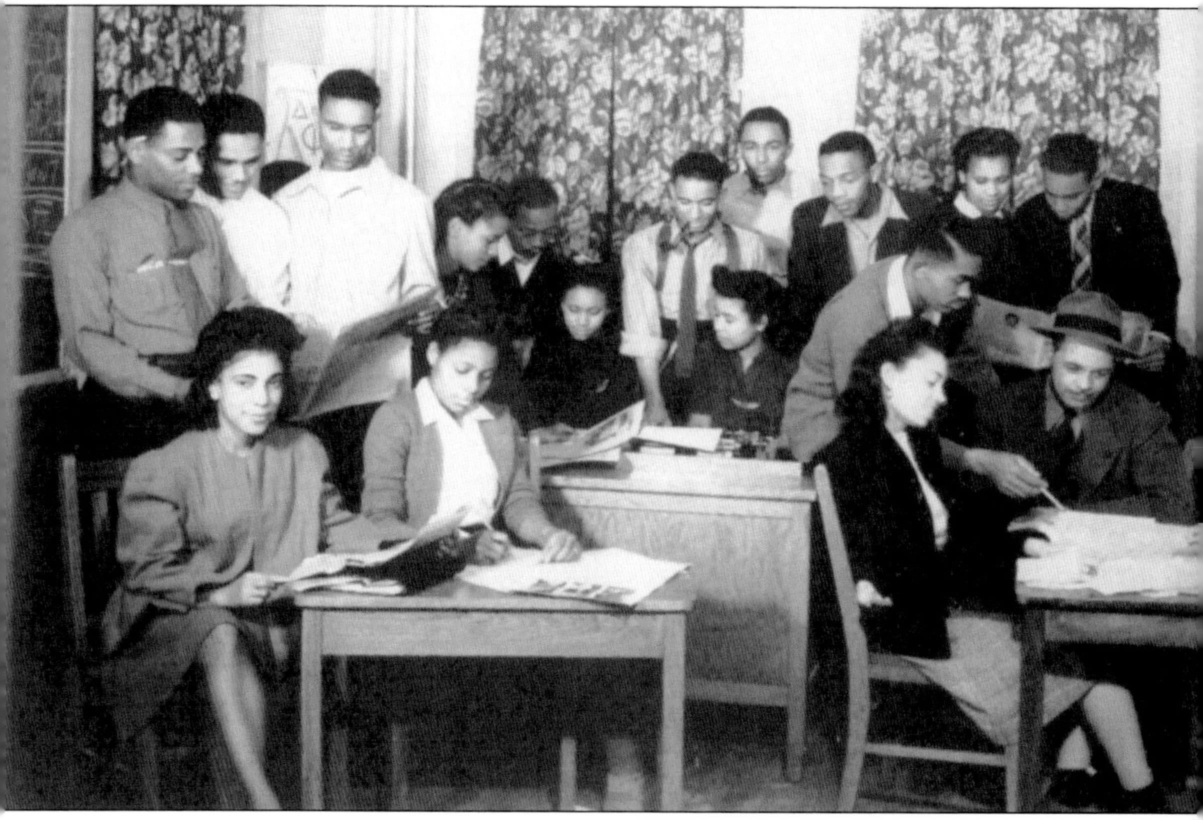

The Lincoln University staff for the school newspaper, named the *Clarion*, is pictured in this 1942 photograph. Included among the student staff are department editors, reporters, artists, photographers, stenographers, and business staff. The newspaper was started in 1932 to serve as an organ of intelligent student opinion and to establish high standards of conduct, scholarship, and sportsmanship. The newspaper is still in continuous publication.

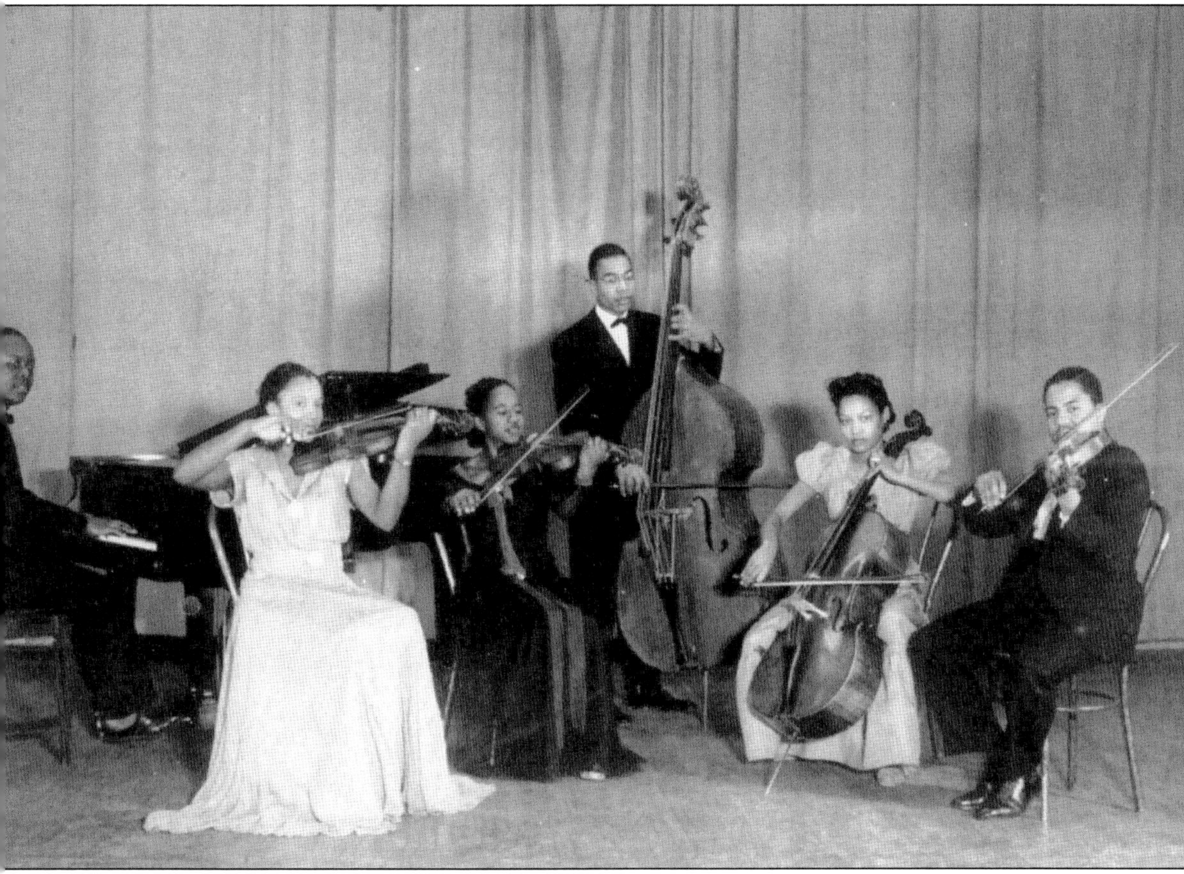

The Lincoln University String Ensemble in 1942, composed of a select group of musicians, appeared at frequent intervals throughout the year on recital programs, at banquets, and in the community. The musicians in this year's group are Margaret Ann Motin, Rubye C. Harris, Mable Lewis, Madestella Copeland, and Wendell Marshal. The ensemble was directed by Rubye C. Harris, whose training included undergraduate work at Oberlin Conservatory and graduate work at Northwestern University and the Chicago Musical College School of Music. Harris held a master of science degree in music education.

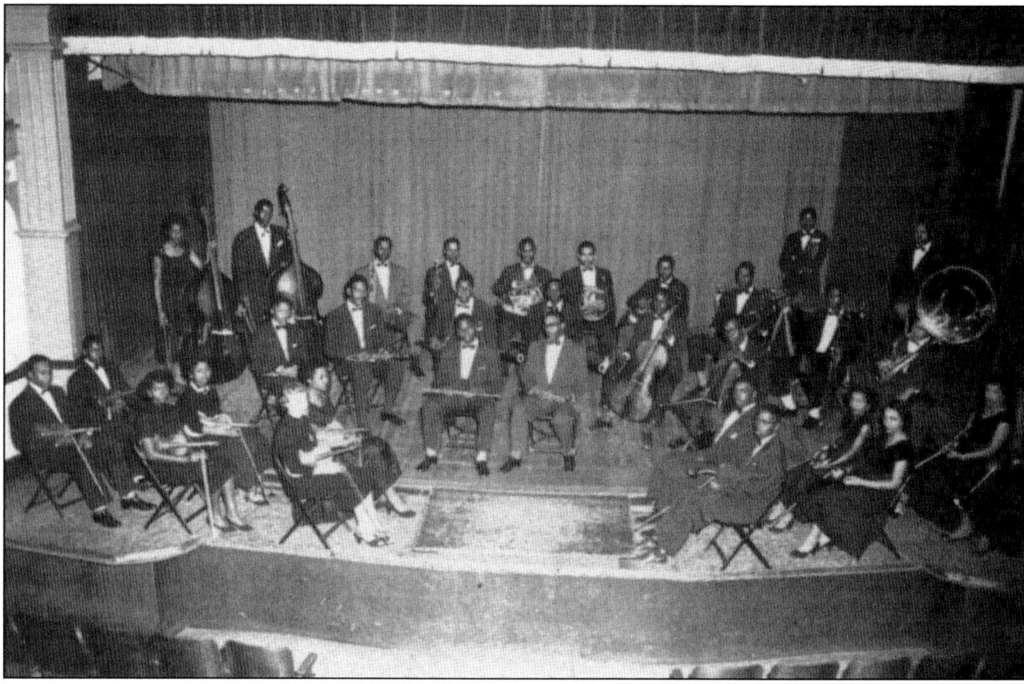

Lincoln University in the 1950s had a 28-piece concert orchestra under the direction of Marshall Penn. One of the violinists (Bobby Daniels) returned to Lincoln University in the late 1980s as vice president of student affairs and professor of education.

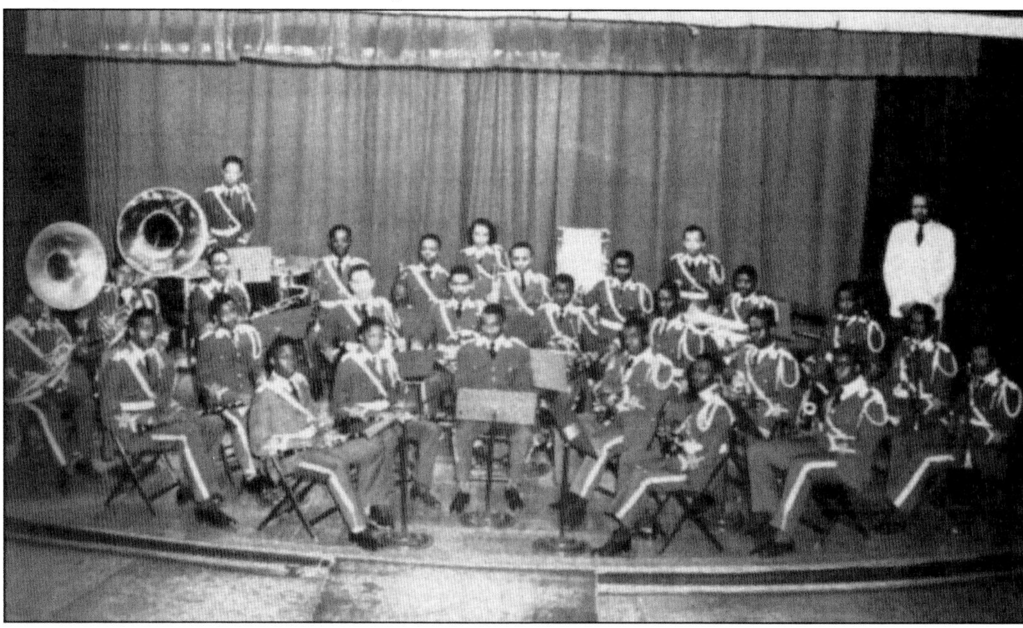

Lincoln University in the 1950s had a 25-member concert band under the direction of Marshall Penn. Bobby Daniels, who played sousaphone in the band, later received a doctorate from the University of Chicago, and Robert Mitchell, who played horn, stayed on to teach at the university, retiring in the late 1990s as professor of music. For years Mitchell directed both the university choir and vocal ensemble.

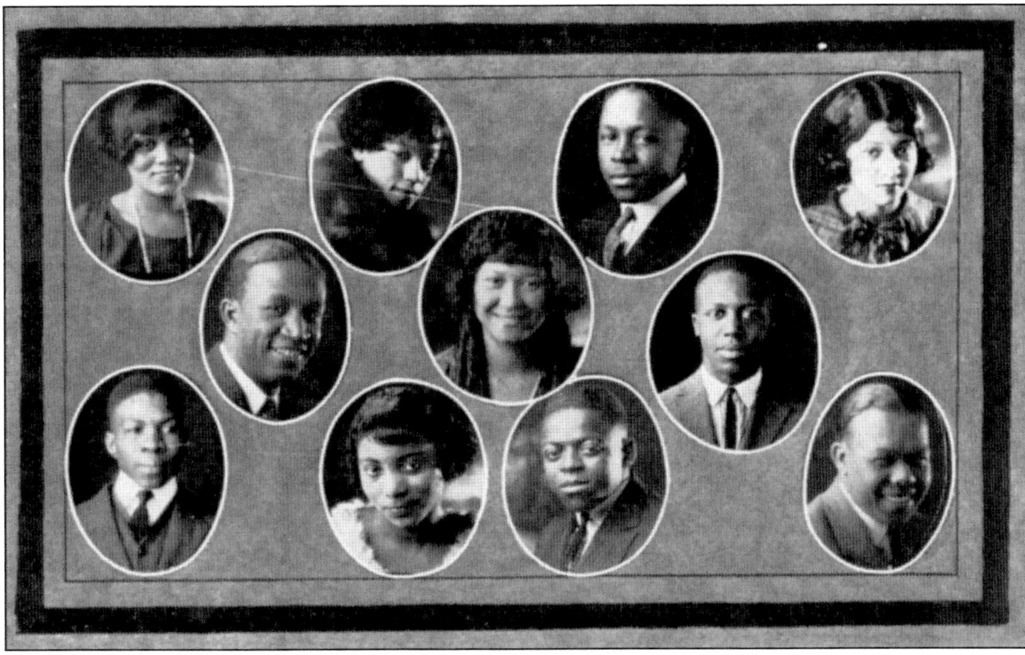

The Jubilee Singers in 1925 were a group that attempted to keep alive black spirituals and folk songs.

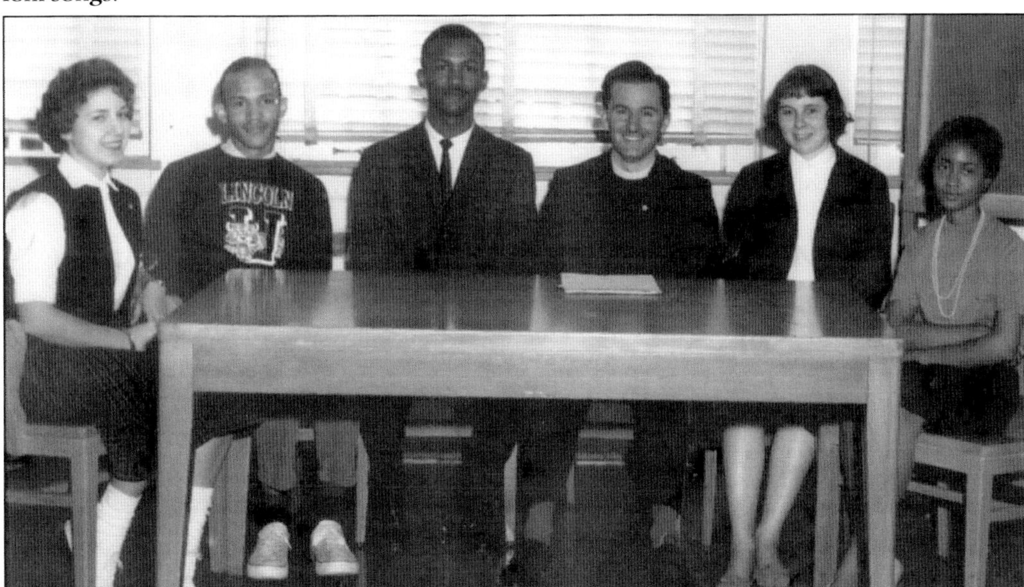


The Tau Sigma Rho Debating Society was organized in 1934 with the purpose being to stimulate student thought, to make students more conversant on significant topics, and to develop material for the varsity debating team. The members were selected from university-wide tryouts. Each year varsity debating keys were awarded to members of the team who participated in two or more major debates. The society was under the supervision of a committee led by Cecil A. Blue of the Department of English. The members of the 1938 debating society shown in the photograph include Harold Holliday, Jesuita Hughes, Jamae Teer, Ollie Lee Tutt, Mallalieu Woolfolk, and Alvin Rose, chairman.

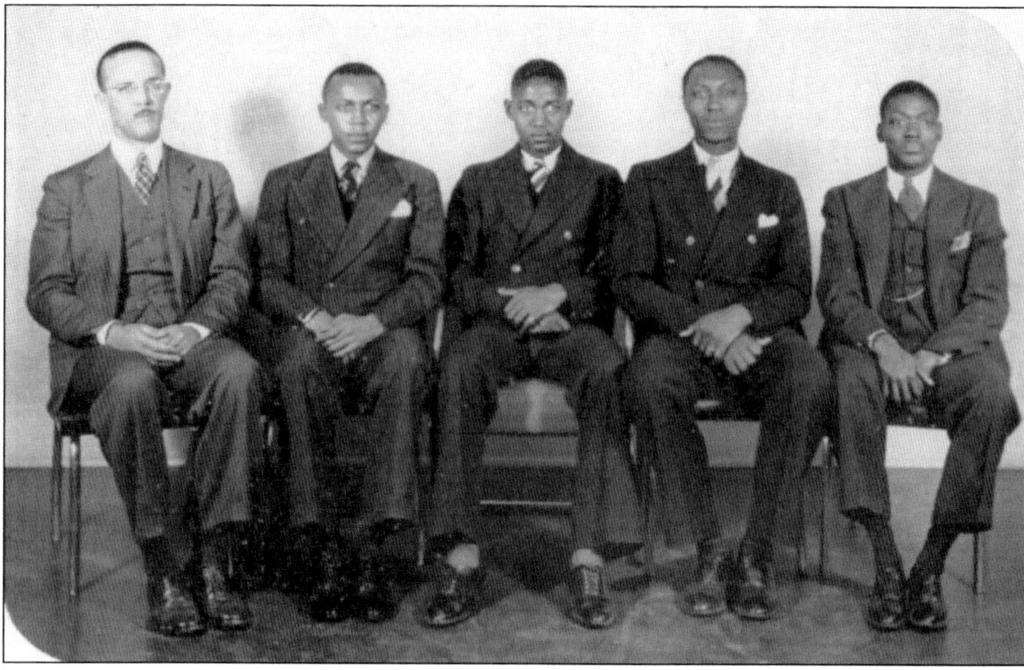

Prof. Cecil A. Blue (far left) is shown with four members of the Tau Sigma Rho Debating Society in 1938.

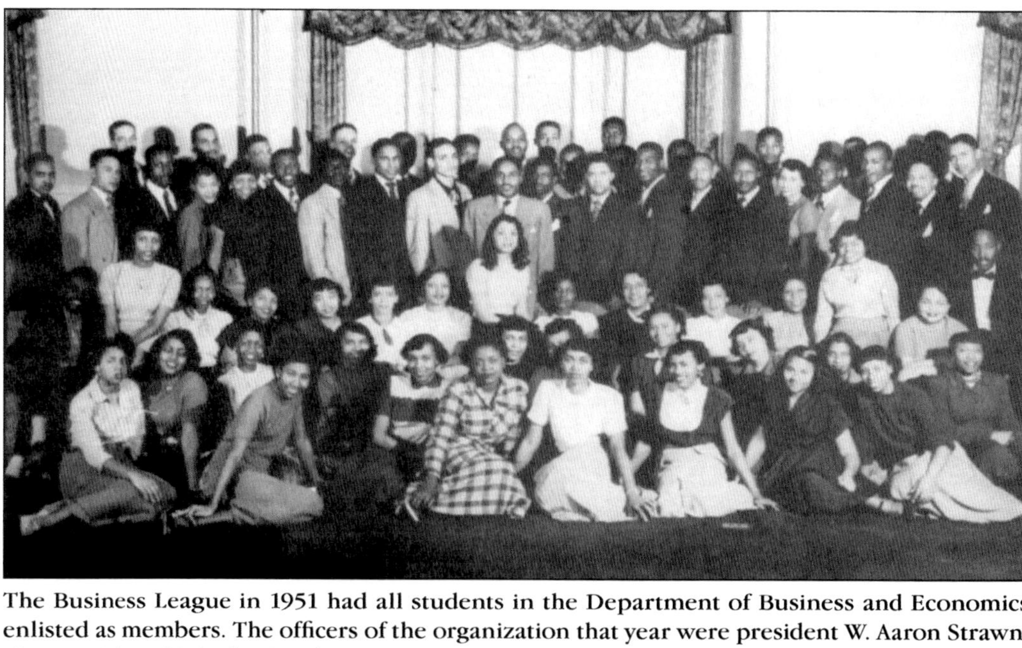

The Business League in 1951 had all students in the Department of Business and Economics enlisted as members. The officers of the organization that year were president W. Aaron Strawn, vice president Malcolm Smith, secretary Lovenia Kelley, and treasurer Wallace McLeon. The sponsor was Prof. H. Monroe Purnell.

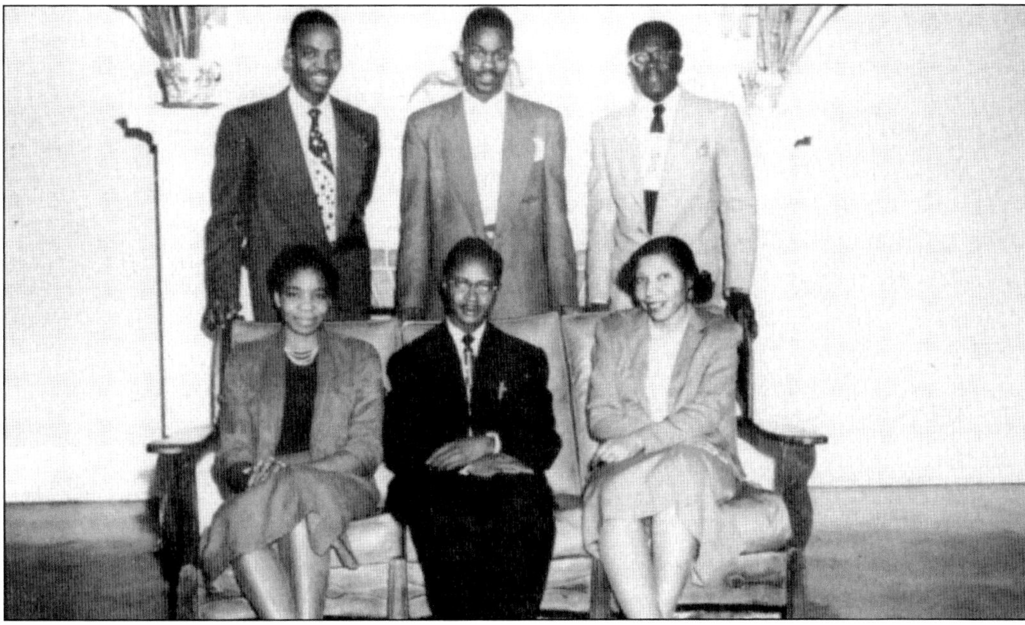

The Foreign Students Association was organized in 1950 to help foreign students become adjusted to their new environment and "to foster better international relations and brotherhood." Shown here from left to right are (first row) Oyibo Akwuba (Nigeria), Benjamin Dennis (Liberia), and Thelma T. Gorham (sponsor); (second row) Roderick Cole (Sierra Leone), Conrad Carrington (Canada), and Peter Nuamah (Nigeria). Members not in the picture included Rennar Etta (Nigeria), James Oliviere (Trinidad), and J. Albert Richardson (Bermuda).

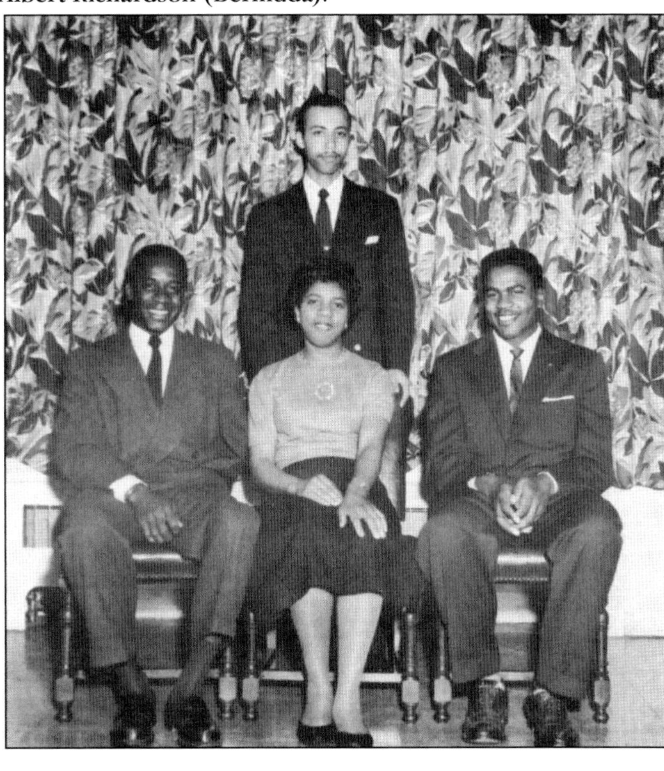

The Student Judiciary Court (1957) heard and passed judgment on any student case referred to the court by the office of the deans. The court chairman served as the chief justice.

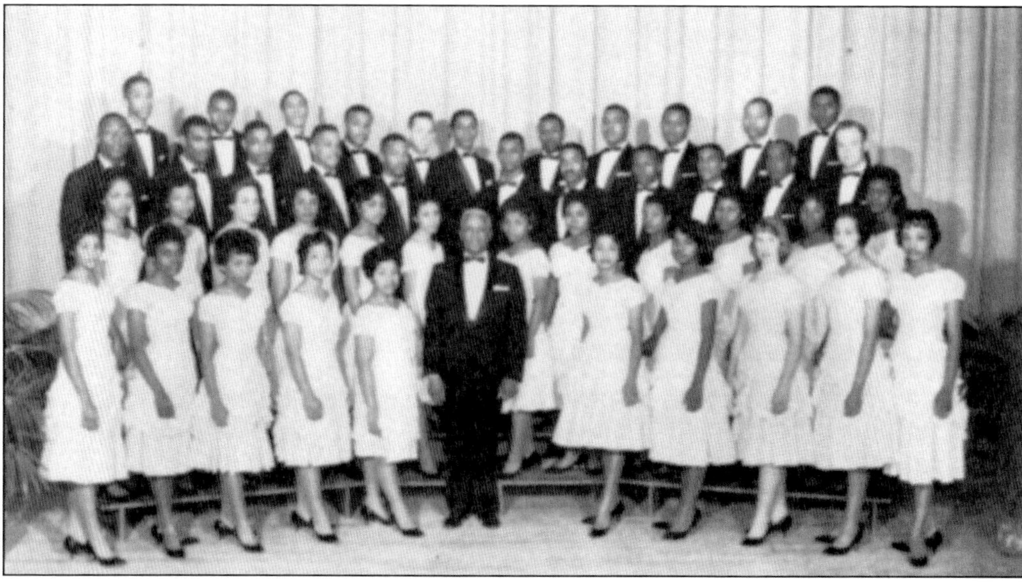

The Lincoln University Concert Choir, shown here, is an abbreviated version of the 100-plus-voice Lincoln University Choir and consisted of select voices devoted to the performance of a cappella literature. This choir made numerous appearances off-campus each year to nearby and distant points. At the center is Dr. O. Anderson Fuller, the choir director.

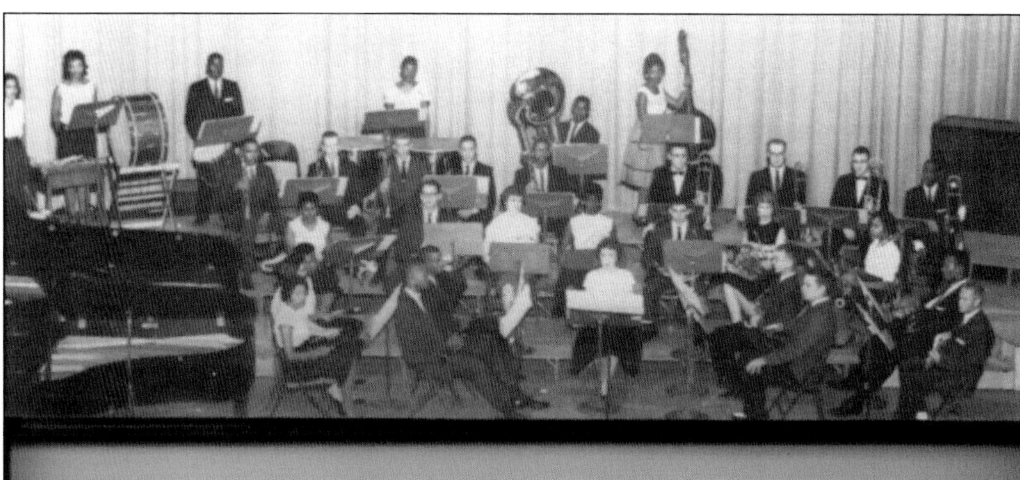

The Lincoln University Orchestra is pictured here in the 1960s.

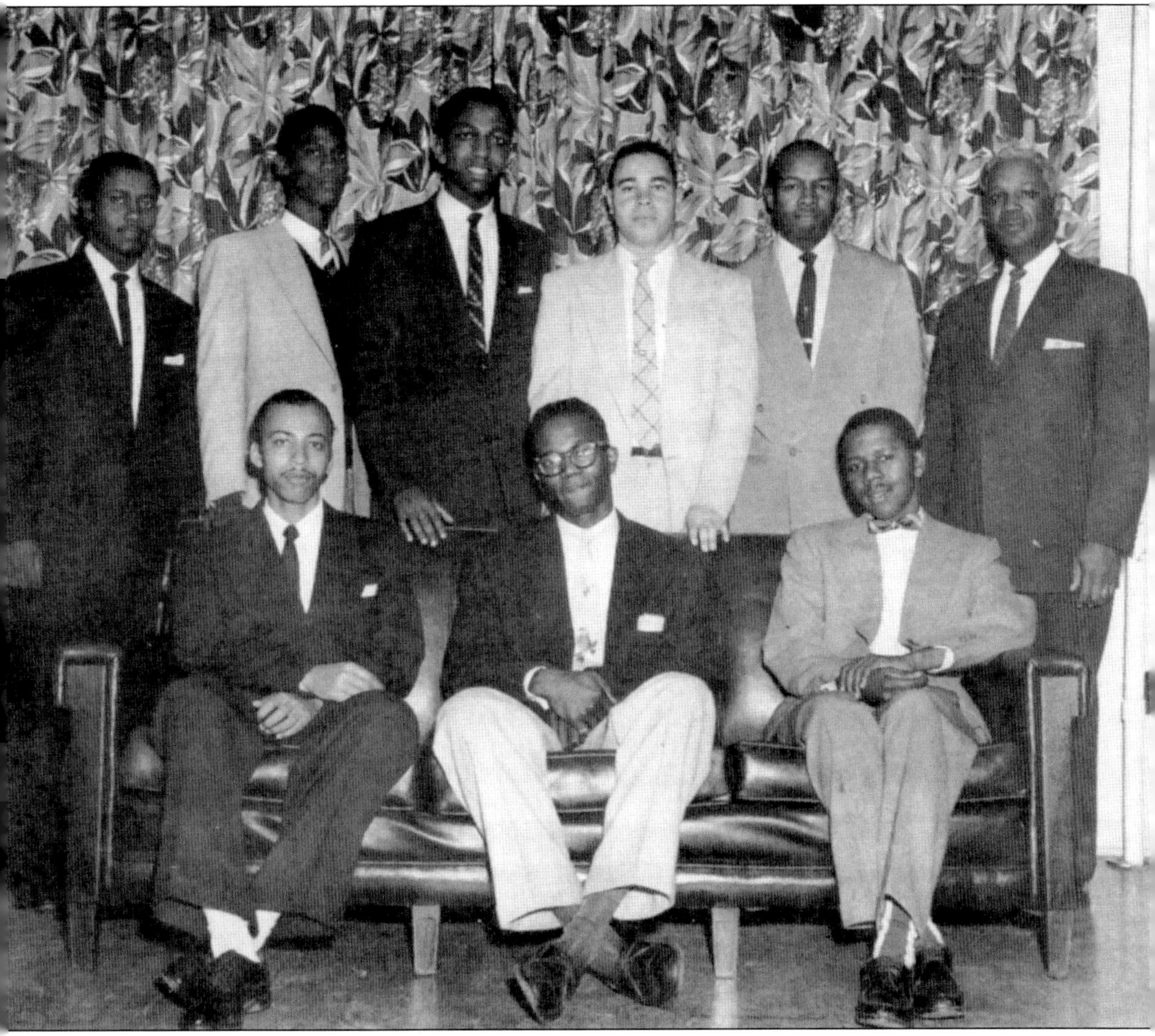

The Phi Mu Alpha Sinfonia national honorary music fraternity had a chapter on the campus with a purpose of forming a brotherhood of students in music. In this 1968 photograph, from left to right are (first row) Shellie Bowers, Alfred Weatherspoon, and Bobby Daniels; (second row) Joe Ray, John Price, Tom White, Robert Mitchell, and Marshall Penn and Dr. O. Anderson Fuller, who were fraternity sponsors.

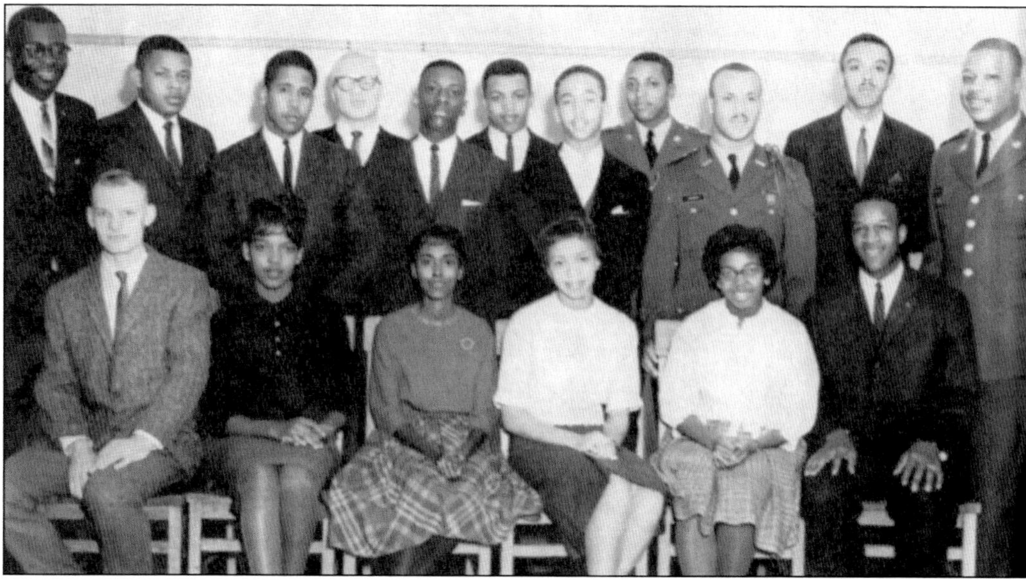

The Student Government Association outgoing president, Willard Pitts, is shown here with members of the student council in 1961. From left to right are (first row) Keith Smallwood, Lillian Carter, Virgie Bland, Frankie Hurt, Wilma Lyghtner, and Willard Pitts; (second row) Joe Mattox, Hugh Flowers, Theodore Groves, Elijah Moore, Charles Ledbetter, Guy Marbury, Robert Leigh Allen, and Robert L. Eddington; (third row) Wiley Rogers, William Hunt, and John Howard.

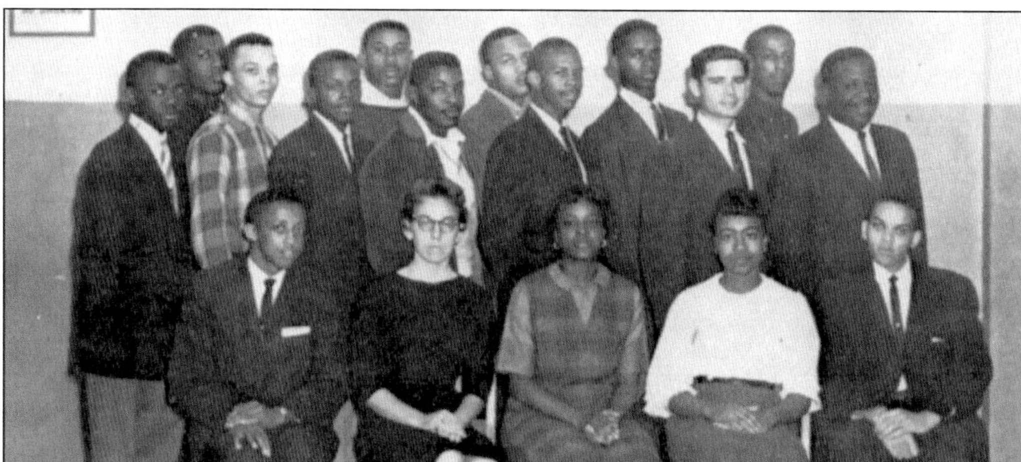

In this photograph of the Lincoln University chapter of the National Association for the Advancement of Colored People (NAACP), from left to right are (first row) James L. Cates, Marilyn Cloren, Betty Sagan, Wilma Barbee, and Don Holt; (second row) Isaiah Martin, Lawrence Hurst, John Scott, Gregory Adams, Markham Stansbury, Joseph Cloren, and Walter Jackson; (third row) Thomas Whitten, Russell Ford, Thomas Guyton, Artis M. Johnson, and Walter Todd.

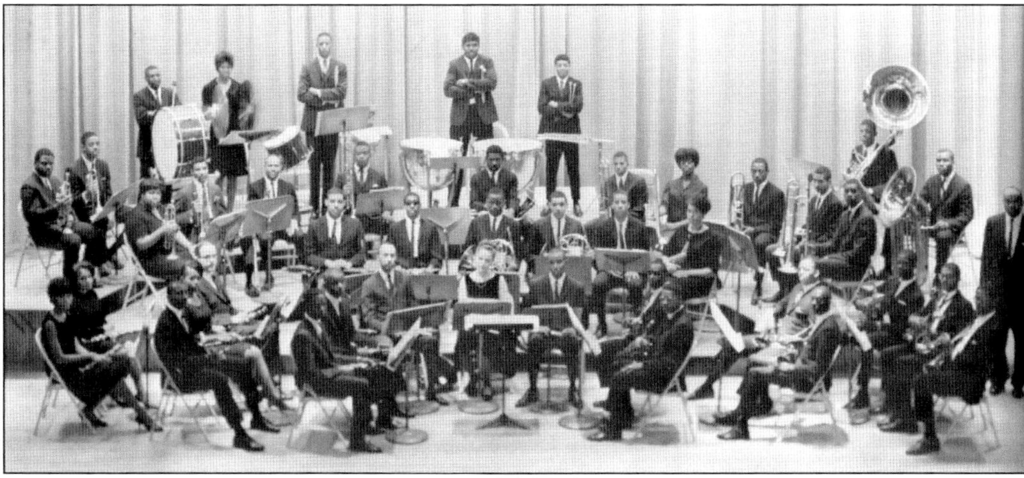

The Lincoln University Symphonic Band in 1966 was a talented group of musicians under the direction of Marshall Penn.

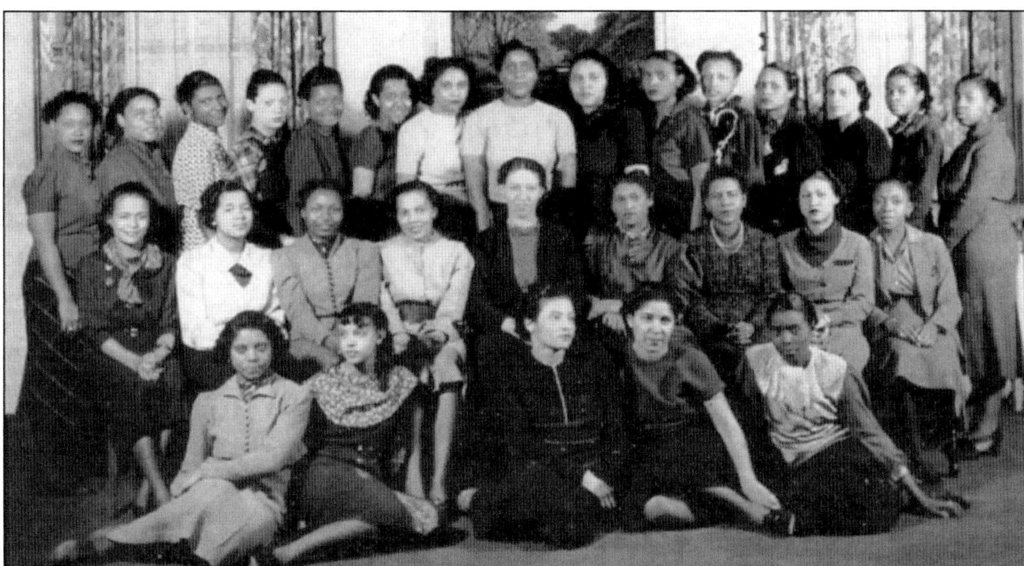

The Cora Winchell Club was founded at Lincoln University in 1931 by students in the Department of Home Economics. The club was organized for the purpose of promoting interest in the field of home economics, developing good leadership and fellowship among its members, and to bring a closer relationship between the department and the home and community. Any student enrolled in home economics courses was eligible for membership. In this photograph of the 1938 club there are 29 members.

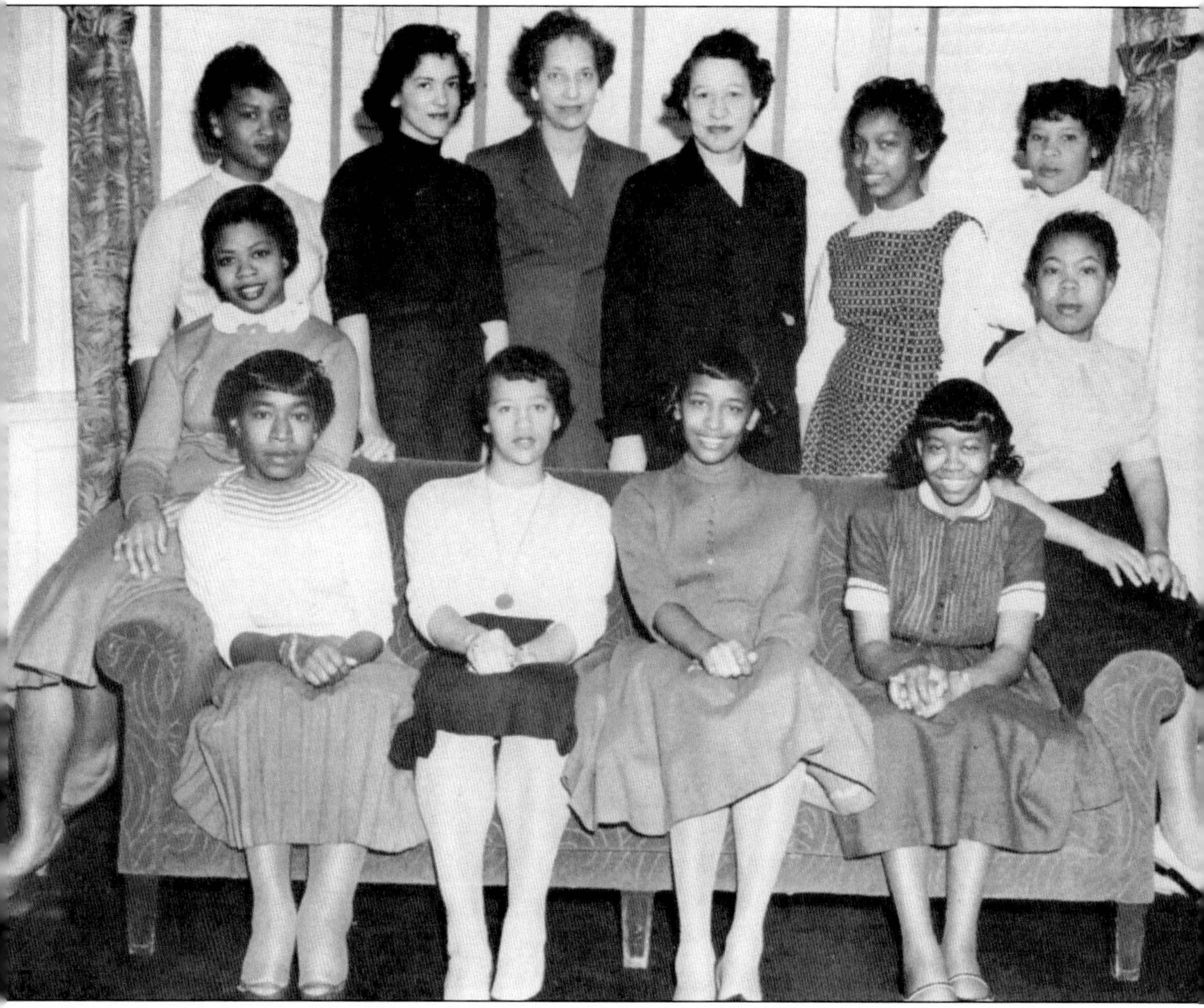

The Cora Winchell Club is shown in this 1968 photograph. Members of the organization include Carrie Allen, Mildred Bess, Joyce Boyd, Mary Bradley, Shirley Carter, Ruth Clinton, Ruby DuVall, Marylyn Nay, Dorothy Samuels, Mary Scott, Gloria Shanks, Dorothy Turner, Juanita Turner, Erniece White, and Monteel Wilson. Maria Hammonds and Myrtle Mitchell served as club sponsors.

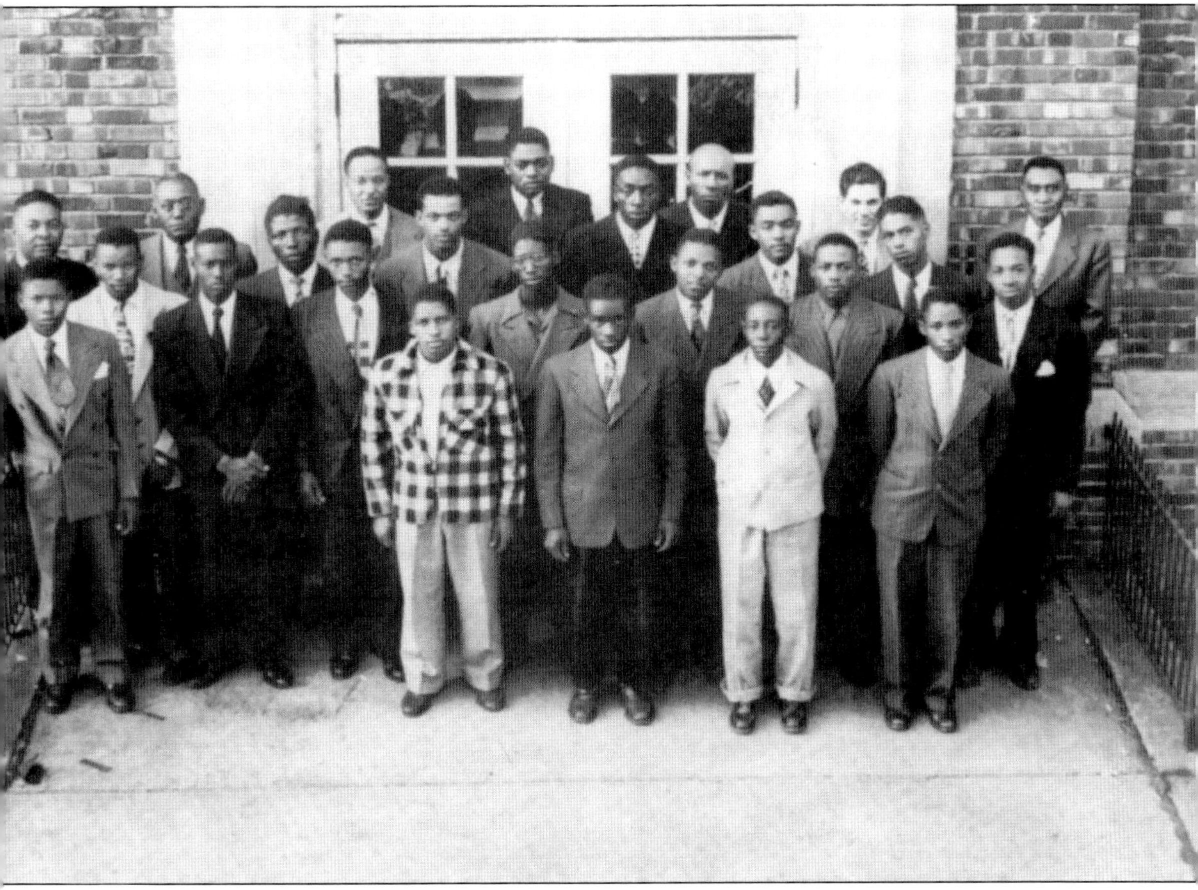

This is the first meting held at Lincoln University of delegates to the Missouri Association of New Farmers of America. Dr. James N. Freeman, head of the Lincoln University Department of Agriculture, served as the state advisor for the organization.

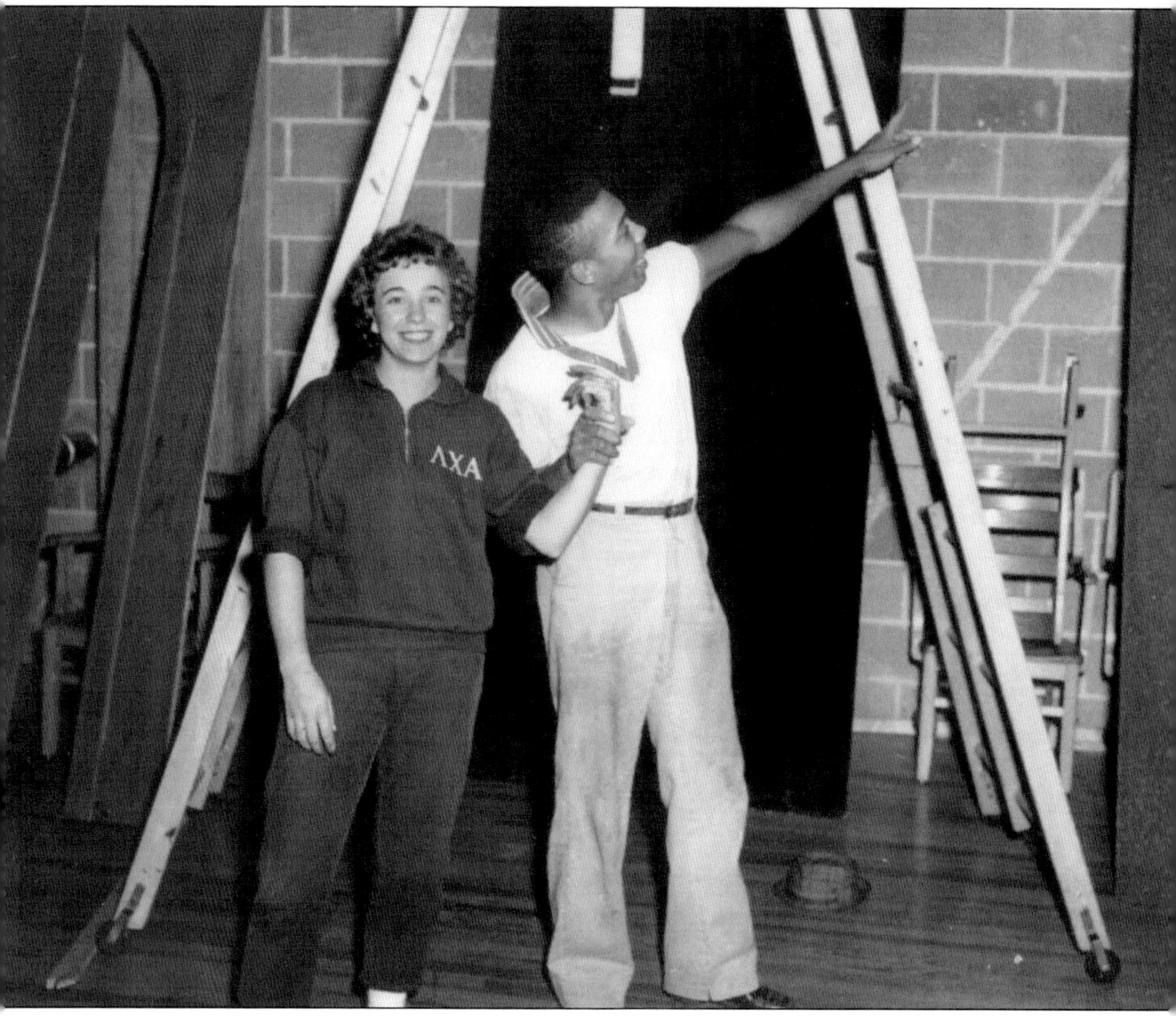


The Stagecrafters in 1960 were preparing for a play. In this photograph, Judy Murrel is completely unattentive to what Murphy Woodcox is pointing out to her. They were participants in the Summer Theatre Series.

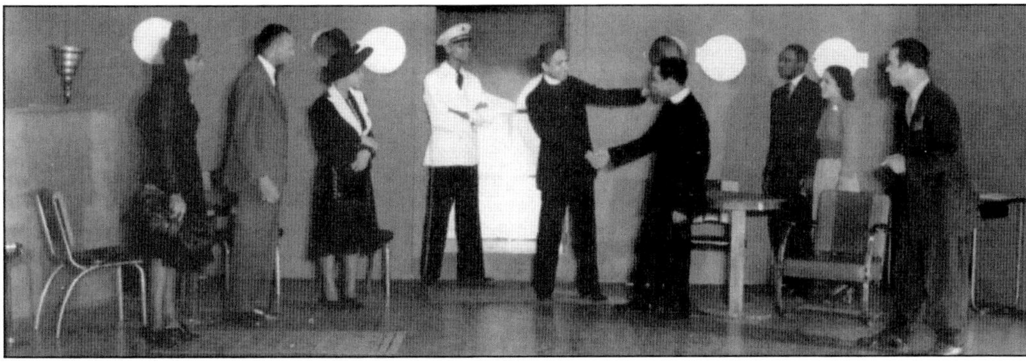

The Stagecrafters in this 1942 production of *Outward Bound* had superb performances turned in by Bettye Wilson as Mrs. Cliveden-Banks and William Crump as Mr. Lingley. Other cast members were William Estes, Birdie Hairston, Roberson King, Jack Gibson, Thomas Bonner, Dorothy Agins, and Charles Brown.

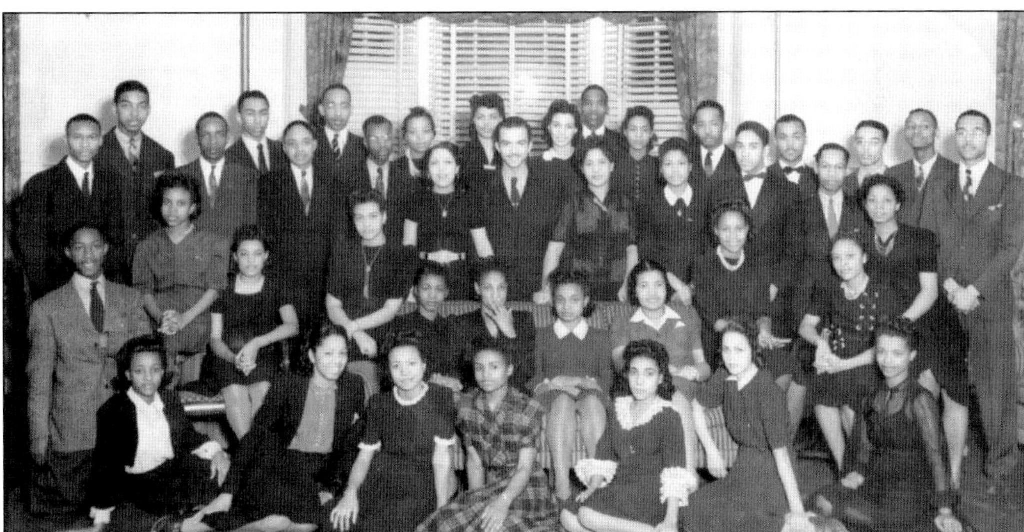

The Stagecrafters, pictured here in 1942 under the direction of Thomas D. Pawley, were a very large group.

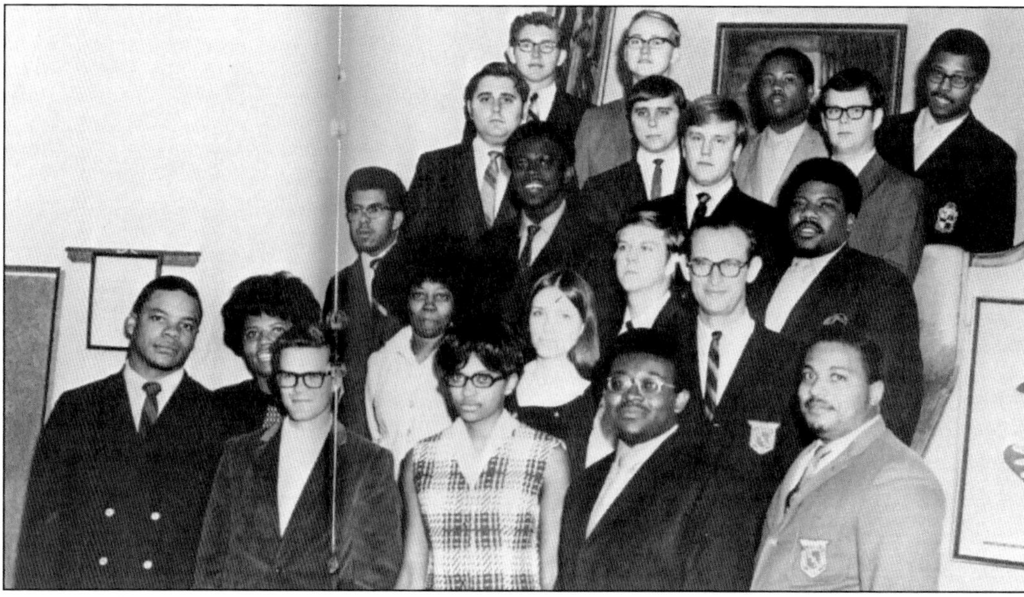

Phi Beta Lambda was a business fraternity whose purpose was to acquaint business administration, economics, and accounting and business education majors and minors with aspects of the business and financial community. The fraternity sponsored a special lecture series by businesspersons as one of its projects. In 1970, members include Jeff Wyatt (state president), Mike Purcell (treasurer), Charles Watkins (vice president), Wayne Shipley (president), Linda Wyatt, Pam Brown, Sharon Lock, Wayne Linhardt (sponsor), Jerry Wilhoit, Theodore Thomas, Byron John, George Abrams, Terry Rehma (public relations), Charles Fitzpatrick, Ron Schubert, Claude Burns, Ed Pendleton, and David Hartman.

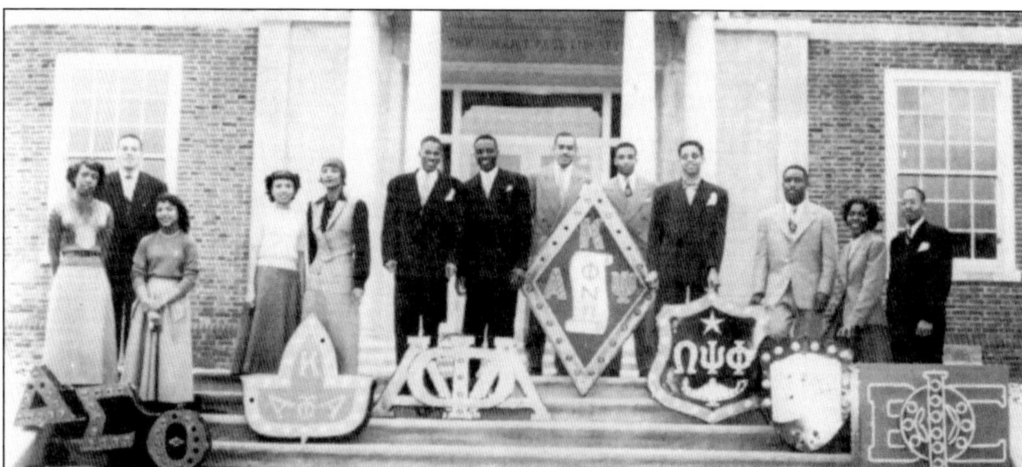


The Lincoln University Pan-Hellenic Council began in 1936 as an organization to form a coordinating unit between sorority and fraternity activities through indirect activities that promoted friendliness and good fellowship among Greek letter organizations. Additionally the council monitored rush week, pledging, and initiation practices. The council held constructive forums and convocations to promote Greek letter harmony. The organizations represented in the photograph include Delta Sigma Theta, Alpha Kappa Alpha, Alpha Phi Alpha, Kappa Alpha Psi, Omega Psi Phi, Sigma Gamma Rho, and Phi Beta Sigma.

# *Four*

# Campus Scenes

During a two-decade span (1950–1970), the annual homecoming celebration held in the month of October was an anticipated event. Campus organizations took considerable time, effort, and money to create colorful decorated floats for the homecoming parade that preceded the traditional football game. The floats were a source of school pride. Another fixture at homecoming was to have entertainment from a top-notch entertainer to headline during the homecoming dance event. Most of the time the artist was an up-and-coming individual or group that showed great promise but had not yet hit the top of the entertainment chart.

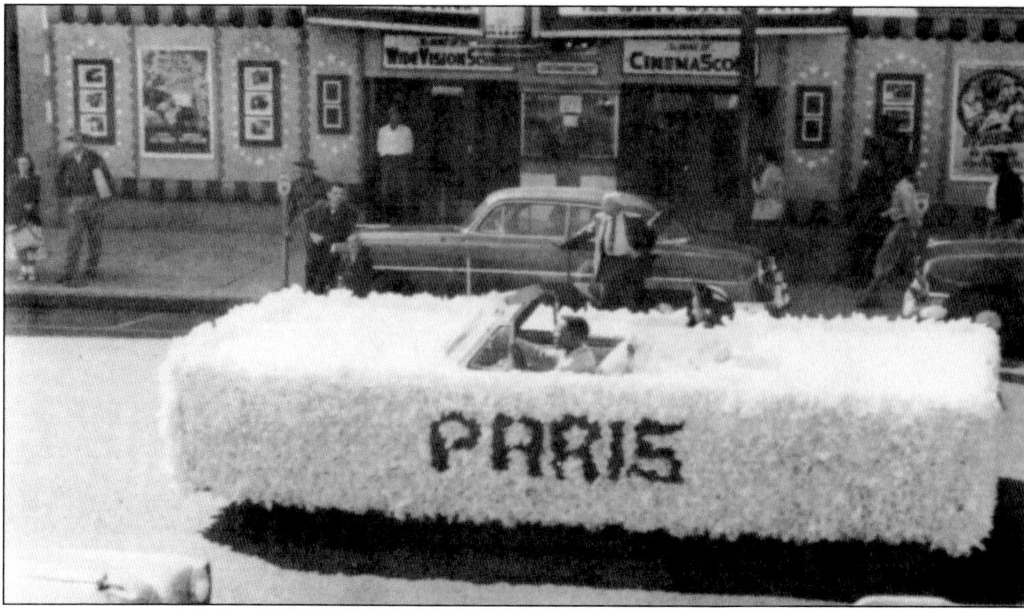


This 1968 homecoming float titled "Paris New Look" took second place in the float competition.

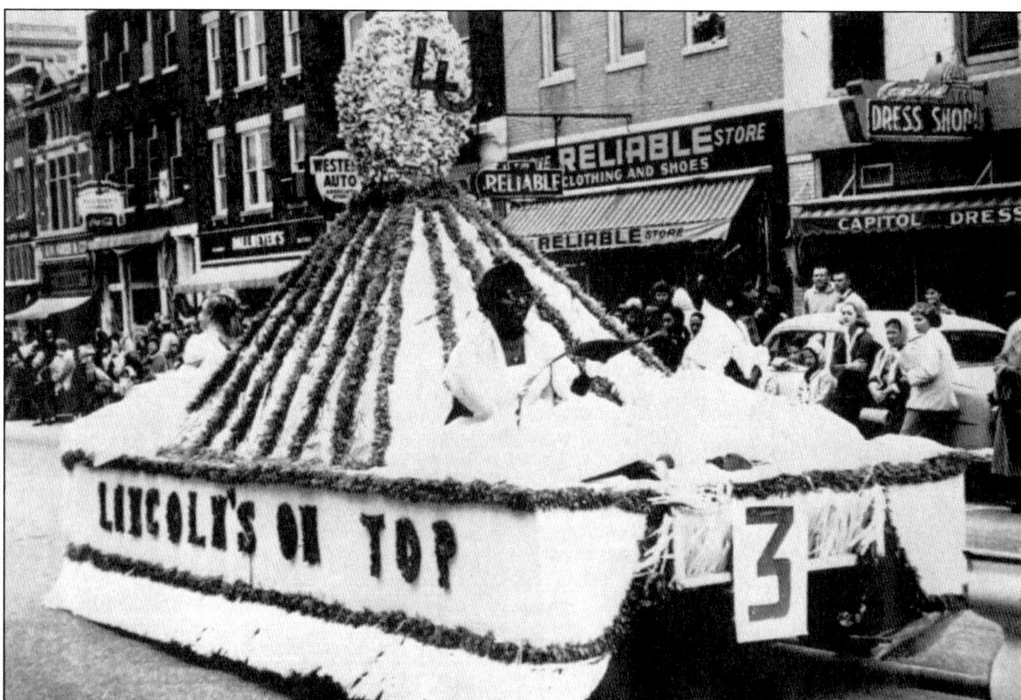


In the 1960s, groups participating in the Lincoln University annual homecoming parades took a lot of time and effort to build very colorful floats. The "Lincoln's on Top" float was an elaborate one for the homecoming queen and her court.

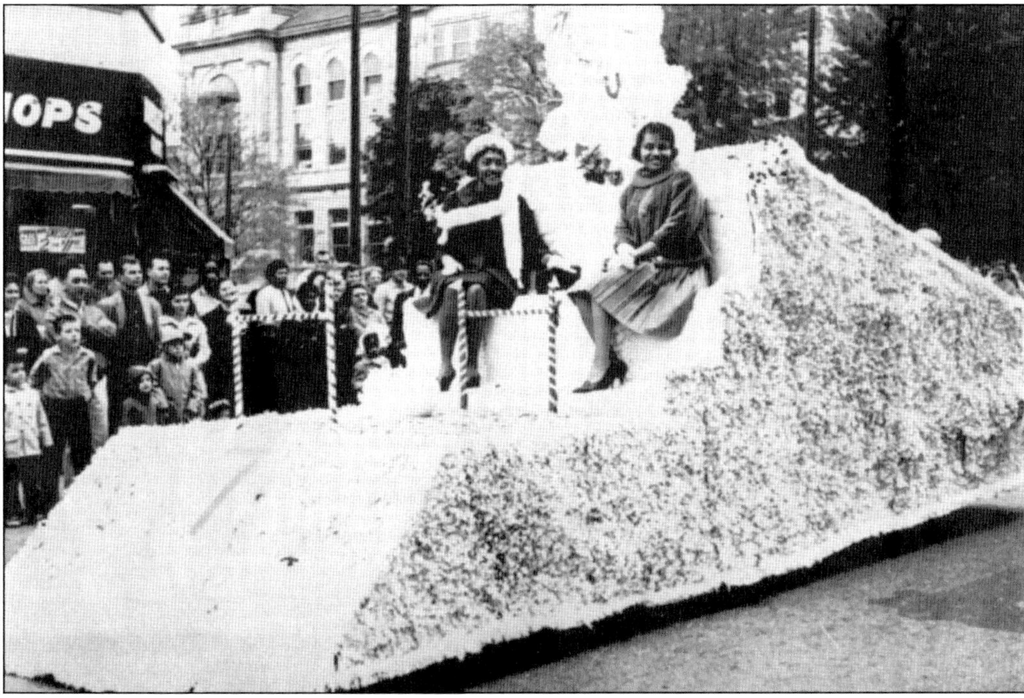


Pictured here is a 1960s homecoming float for the queen and her court.

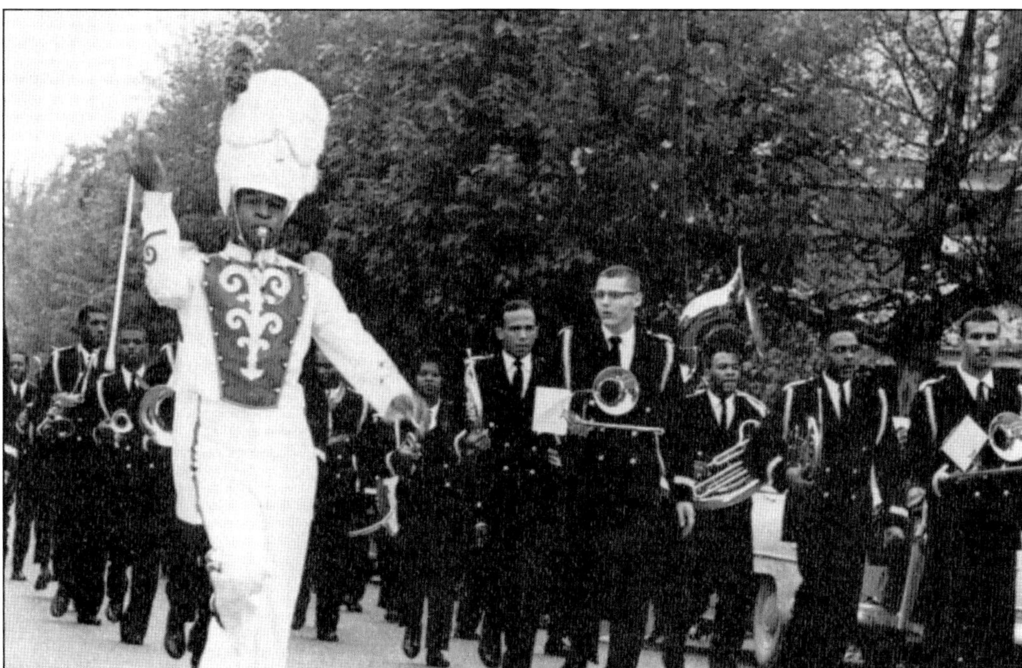

The Lincoln University marching band marches in a homecoming parade that goes through the downtown section of Jefferson City. Willard Pitts, a versatile journalism junior, struts at the head of the Lincoln University band members in new uniforms minus their hats and jacket shields that did not arrive in time for the event.

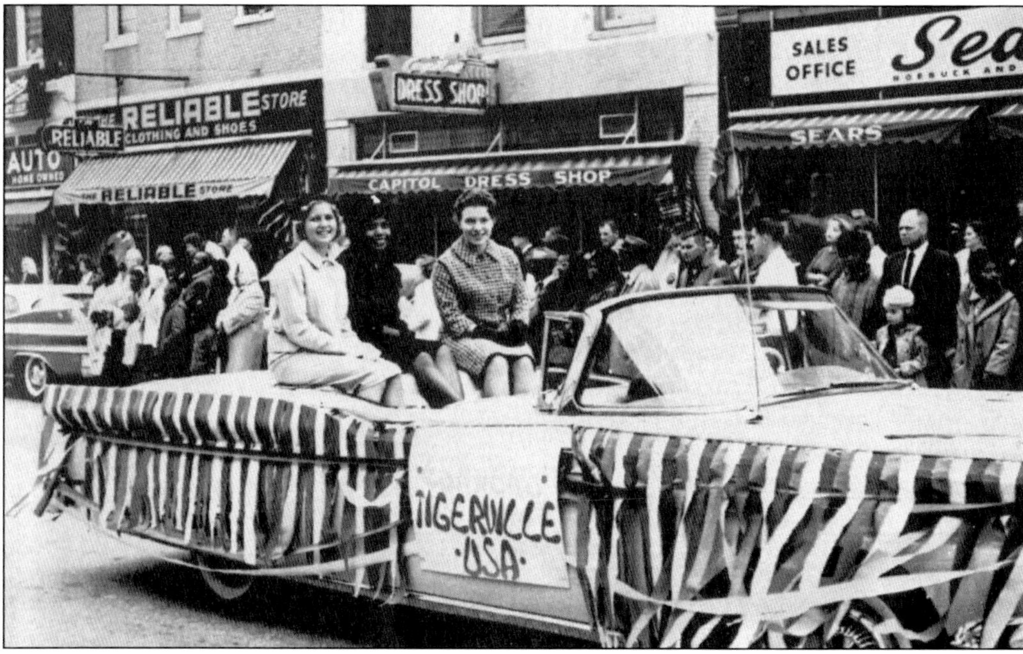


This homecoming float carried the Lincoln University queen and her court. This was one of 20 floats related to the "Tigerville, USA" homecoming theme that year. This float, sponsored by the ROTC, won first place in the float competition. Parade participants were the Lincoln University marching band, ROTC drill team, Jefferson City and Helias High School bands, and the Kemper Military Band and Drill Team.

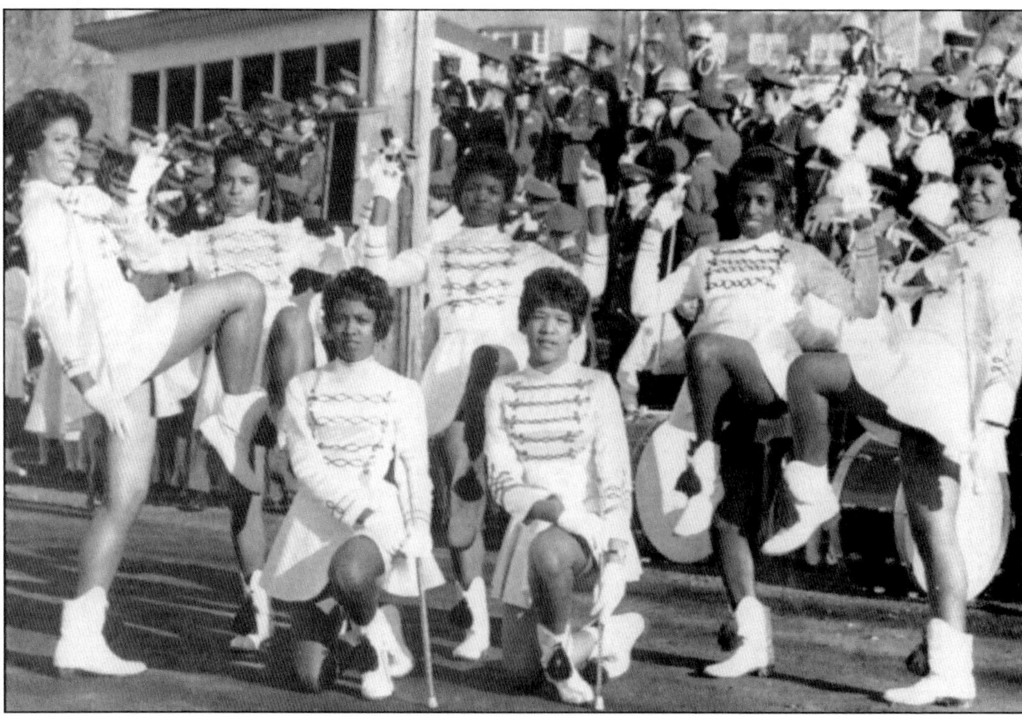

The 1961 Lincoln University Majorettes pose during a homecoming parade.

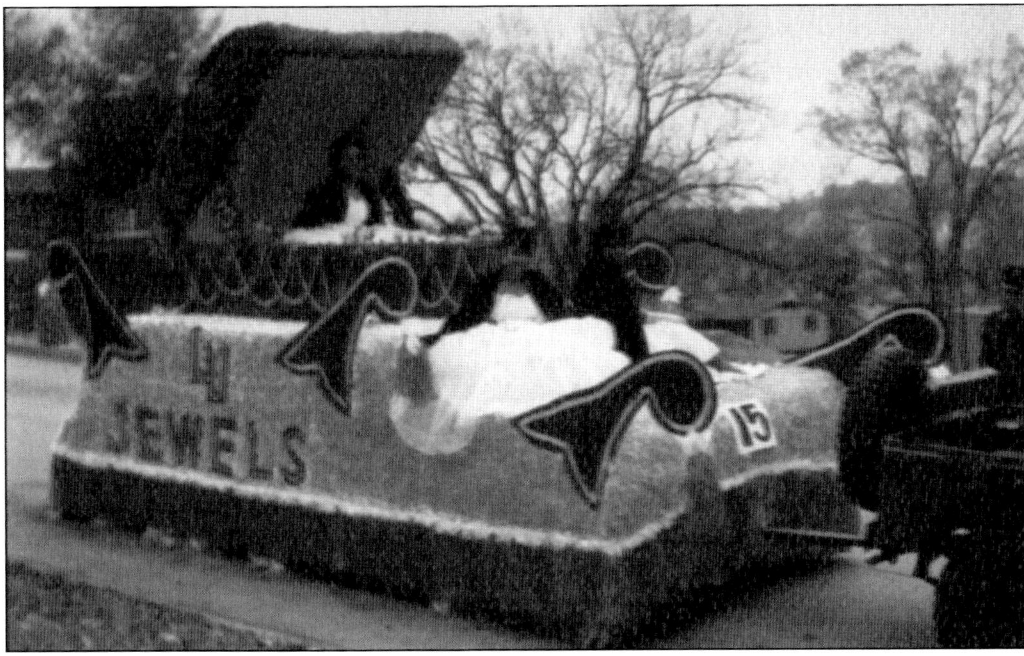


This 1960s homecoming parade float was very well decorated and carried the homecoming queen and a member of her court. It was titled "LU Jewels" and was unique in that the individuals were riding in a jewelry box. A lot of imagination went into designing floats for parades in the era of the 1960s.

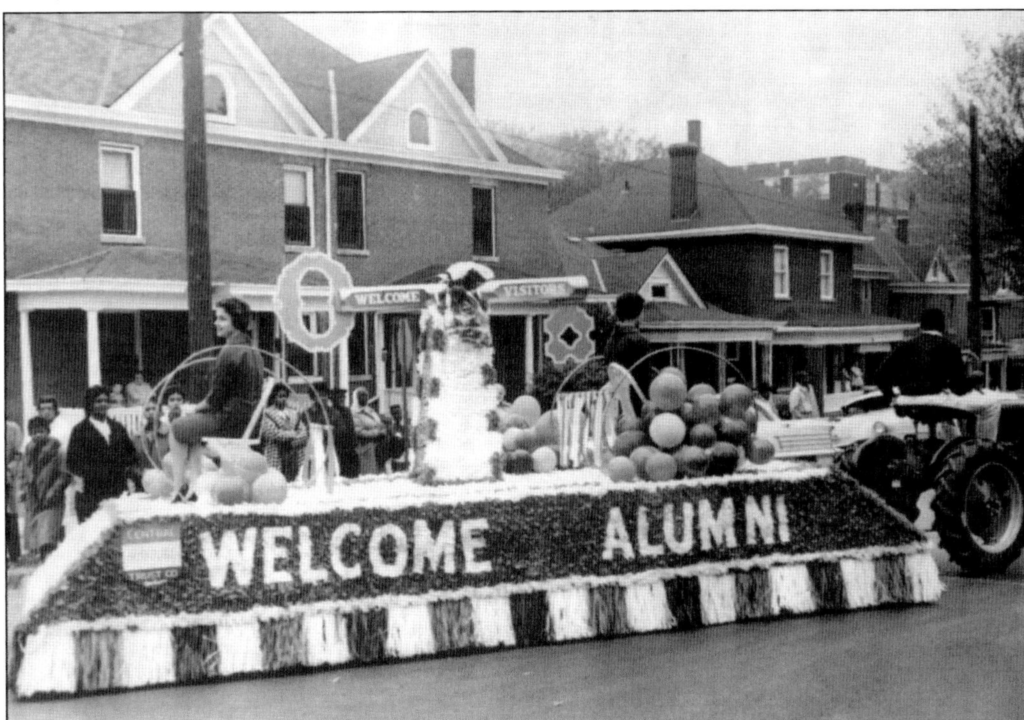


A brightly decorated float in the 1960 homecoming parade welcomes alumni to the event.

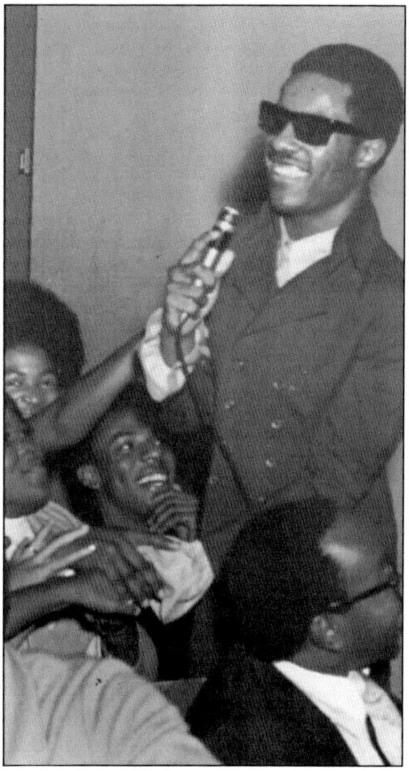

Homecoming events at Lincoln University over the years attracted top-name entertainers. This was particularly true in the 1950s, 1960s, and 1970s. Included among the artists who have played on campus are Stevie Wonder, Ray Charles, George Shearing, Duke Ellington, Dave Brubeck, and the Fifth Dimensions. One of the members of the latter group is a Lincoln University alumnus. This photograph shows a young Stevie Wonder performing at a 1960s annual homecoming.

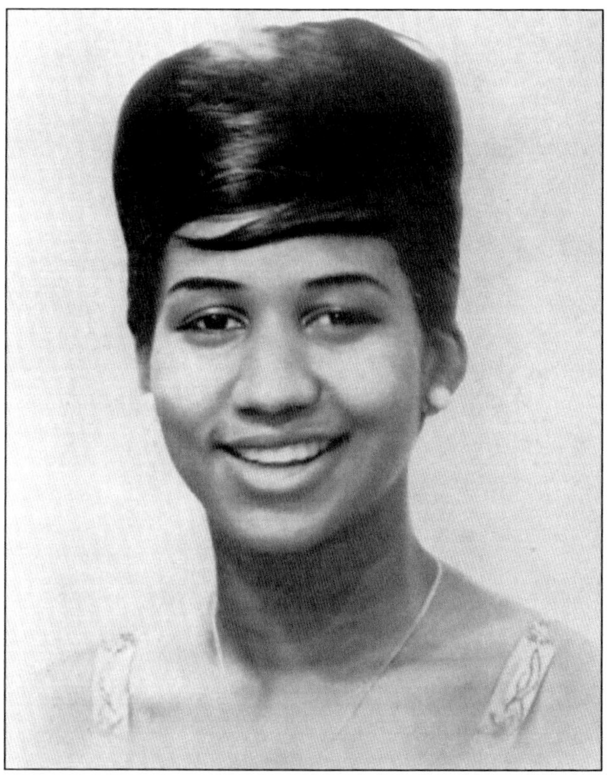

The 1963 homecoming weekend was enhanced by a student council concert that featured Aretha Franklin in concert. Franklin appeared the night after Miss Lincoln's coronation in Richardson Auditorium. The 19-year-old gospel jazz singer was an up-and-coming recording artist with the Columbia Recording Company.

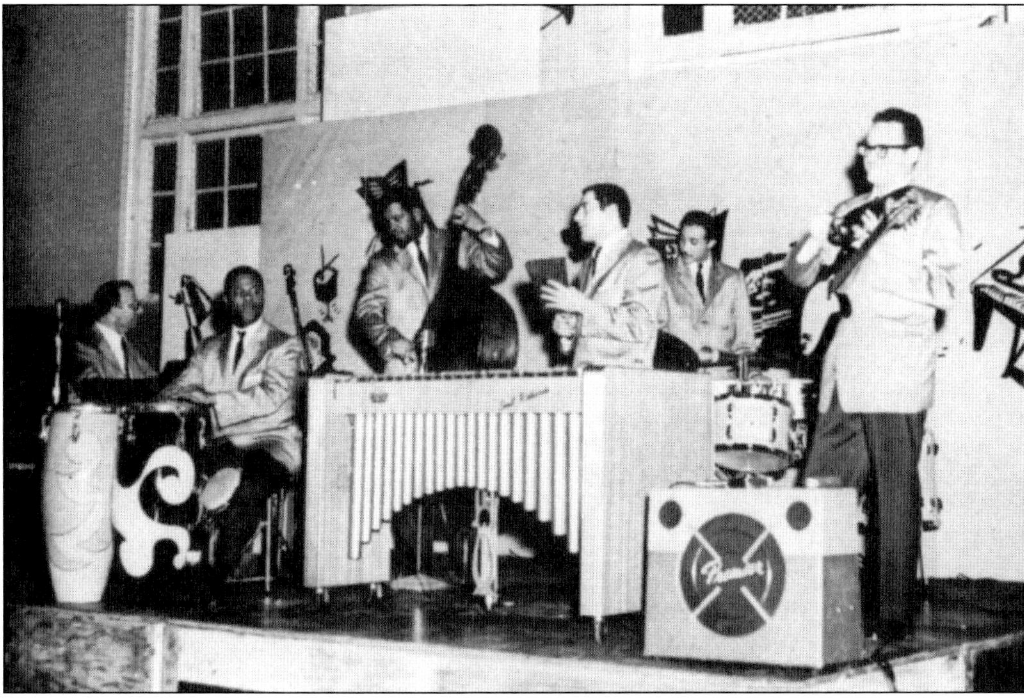

In 1958, the famous George Shearing Quintet played for the homecoming dance in the old gymnasium located in Young Hall.

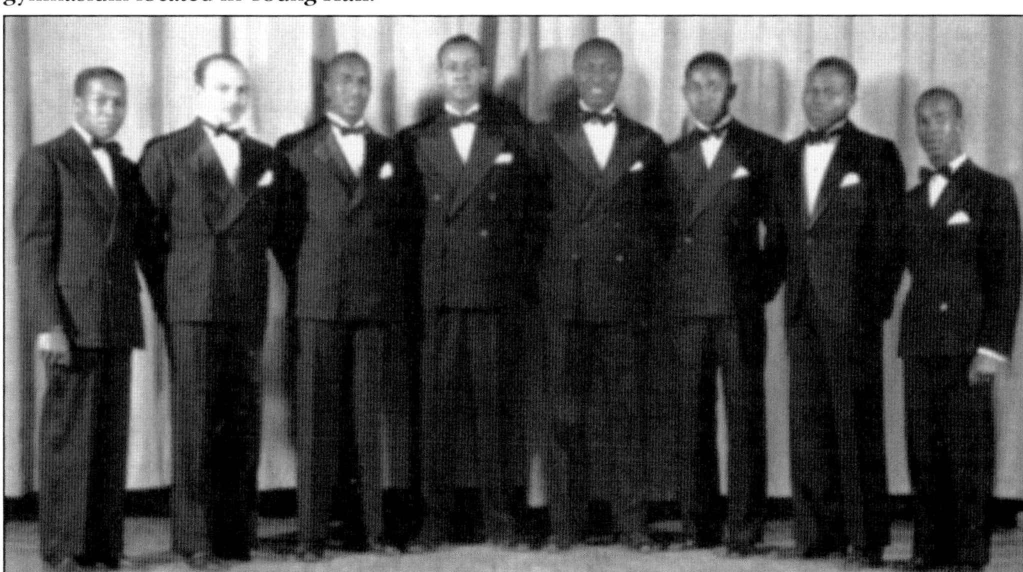

Lincoln University had a men's octet in 1938. Members are, from left to right, William Weddle, James Goble, William Smith, Kenneth Billups, James Teer, Alvin Rose, David Brown, and Jerry White. Both Billups and Rose became noted educators in St. Louis and across the country. Billups was a music educator who taught for many years at Sumner High School in St. Louis and founded a well-known choral group called the Legend Singers. A street in St. Louis near the school where he taught is named after him. Rose obtained a doctorate in sociology and taught at several well-known universities and was well known in sociological research.

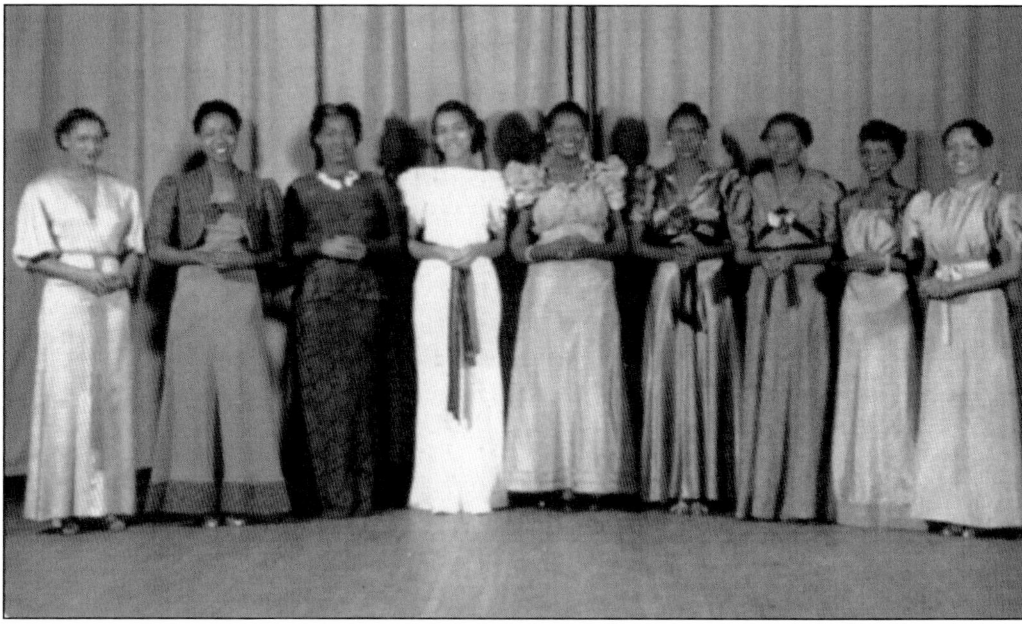

Lincoln University had a women's octet in 1938. Members include, from left to right, Bernice Smith, Gertrude Whitley, Helen Phillips, Ruth Langley, Edna Moore, Alfrenia Young, Marie Wimberly, Cynthia Bolt, and Dorothy Gipson.

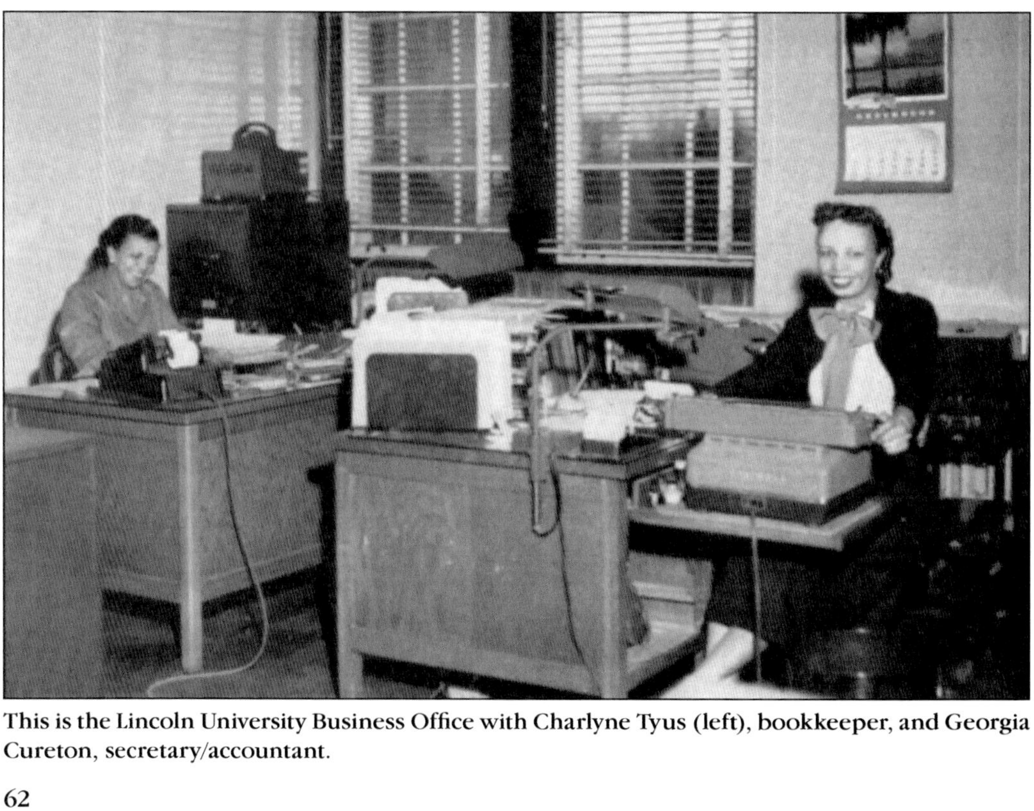

This is the Lincoln University Business Office with Charlyne Tyus (left), bookkeeper, and Georgia Cureton, secretary/accountant.

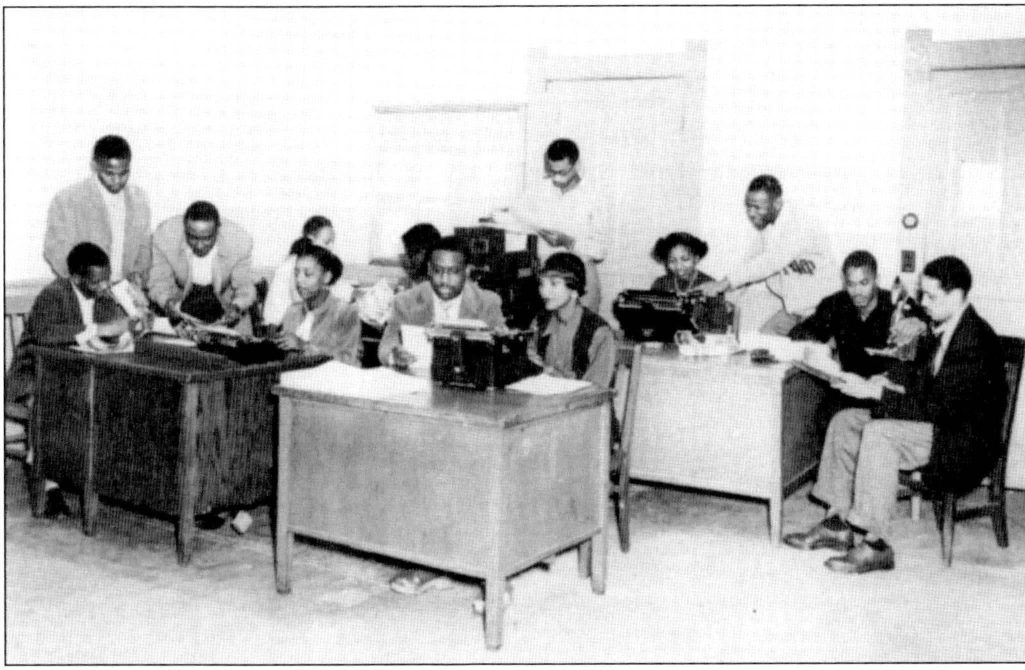

Staff members of the student newspaper the *Clarion* are working hard to meet a press deadline. The individual who is seated second from the right is holding a camera and probably is a news photographer, whereas the other individuals are reporters and copy editors.

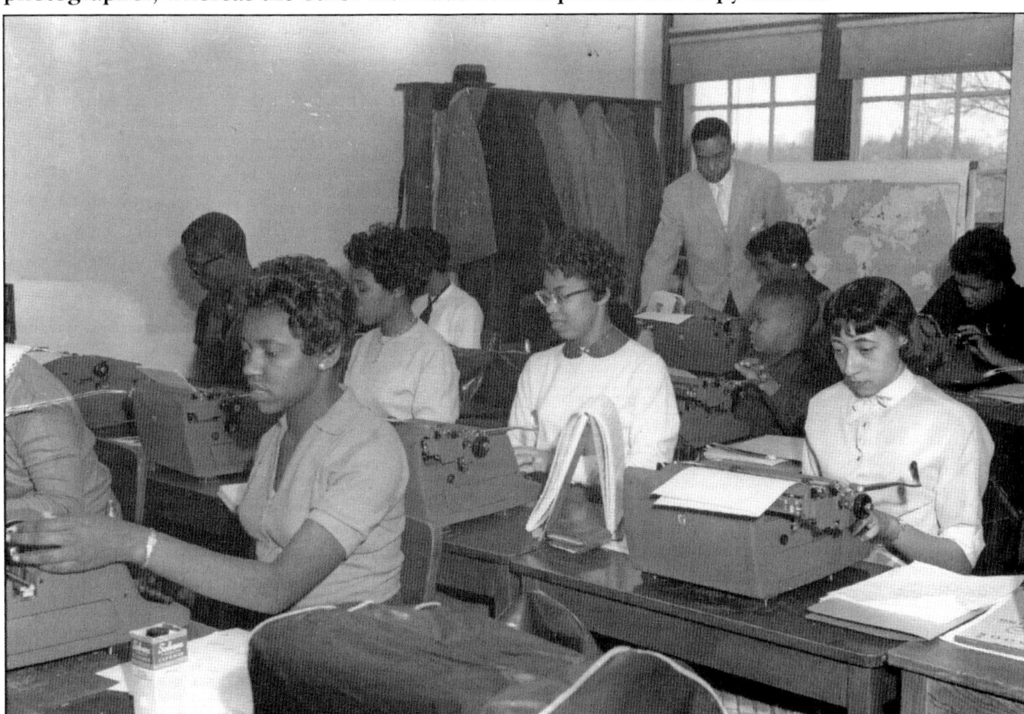

Seen here is a typing class in 1961. The young man in the rear of the picture is probably a visitor and the child of a student in the class.

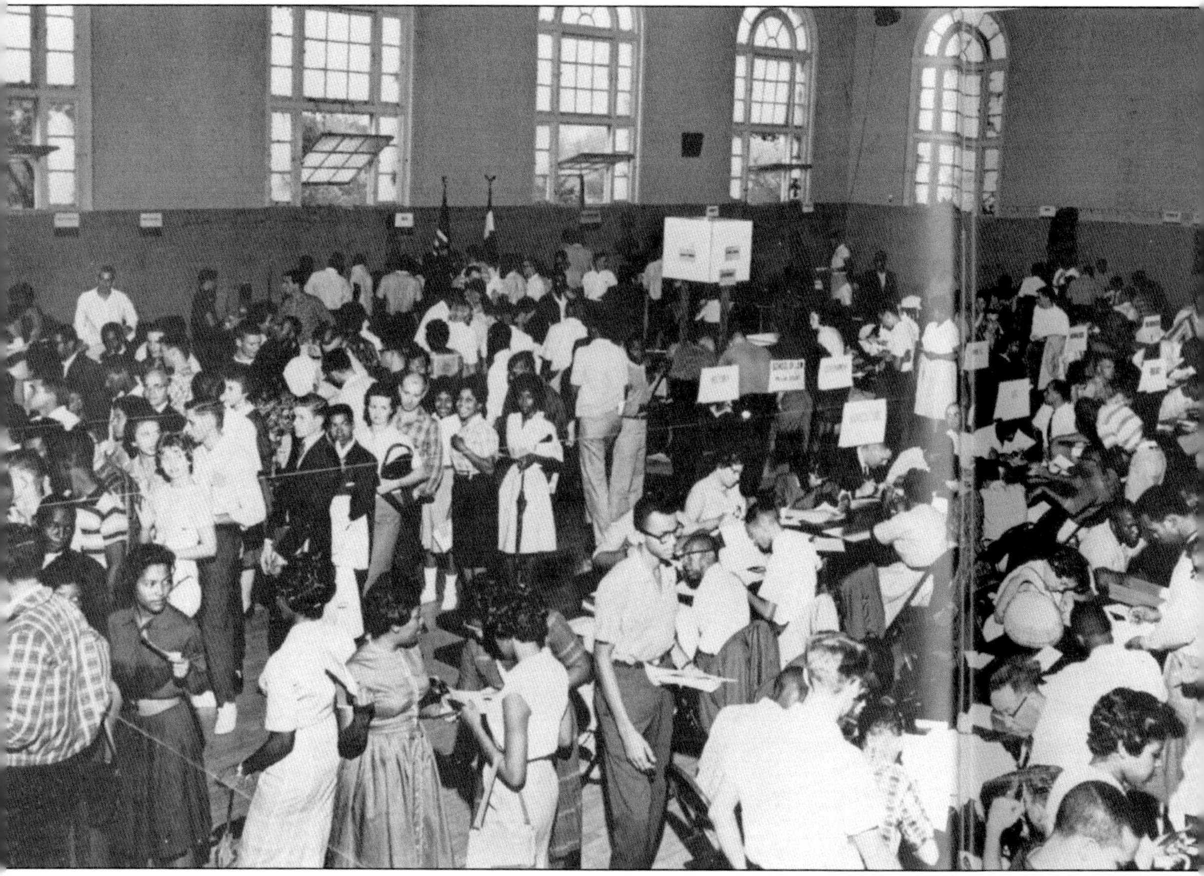

During the 1959–1960 school year registration, the morning hours of the two registration days proved to be the most trying for both students and instructors. Long lines of students usually assembled, and advisors barely had breathing space. This photograph shows a relatively quiet mid-afternoon moment during registration in the old gymnasium in the Young Hall administration building.

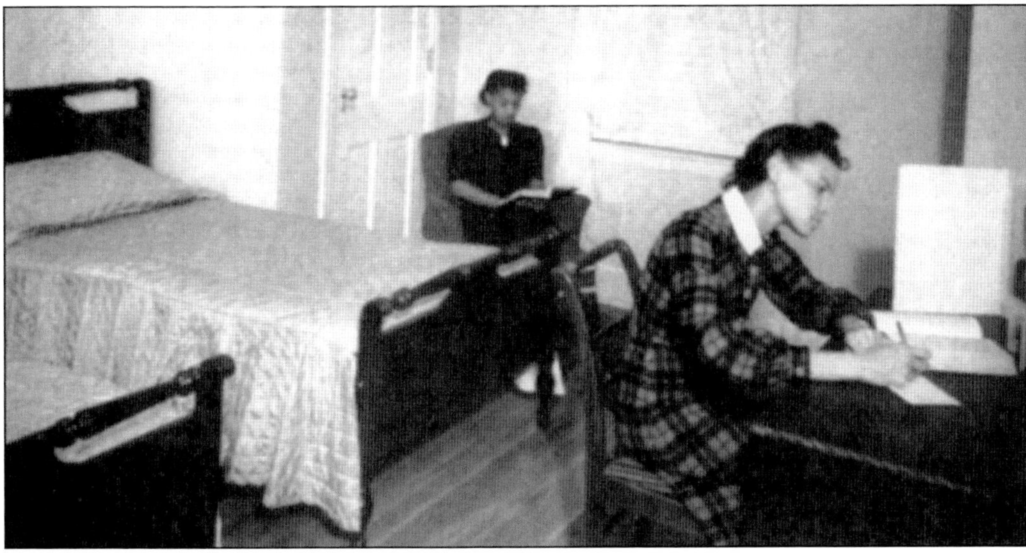

The students in this photograph are studying in the Home Management Cottage, which served as a residence for senior home economics majors. The house consisted of eight rooms, two baths, a kitchen, a living room, a dining room, four bedrooms, and a nursery. Lincoln University students under the supervision of G. Robert Cotton and the mechanic arts staff constructed the house in 1940.

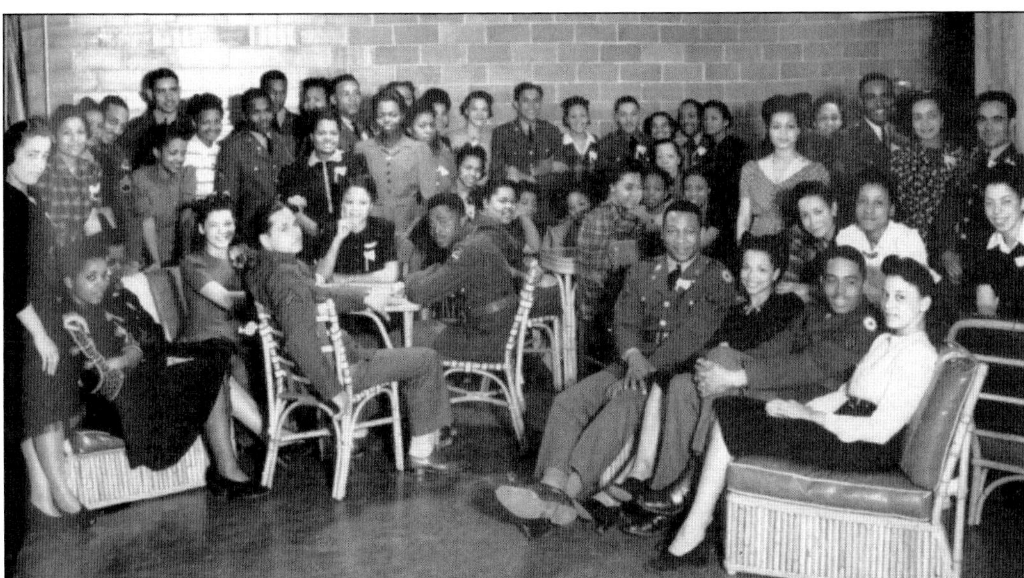

During World War II, servicemen stationed at the Fort Leonard Wood Army Base in Missouri came on weekend passes to Lincoln University for dances and other social events. This picture was taken in 1942 at a get-together on the campus.

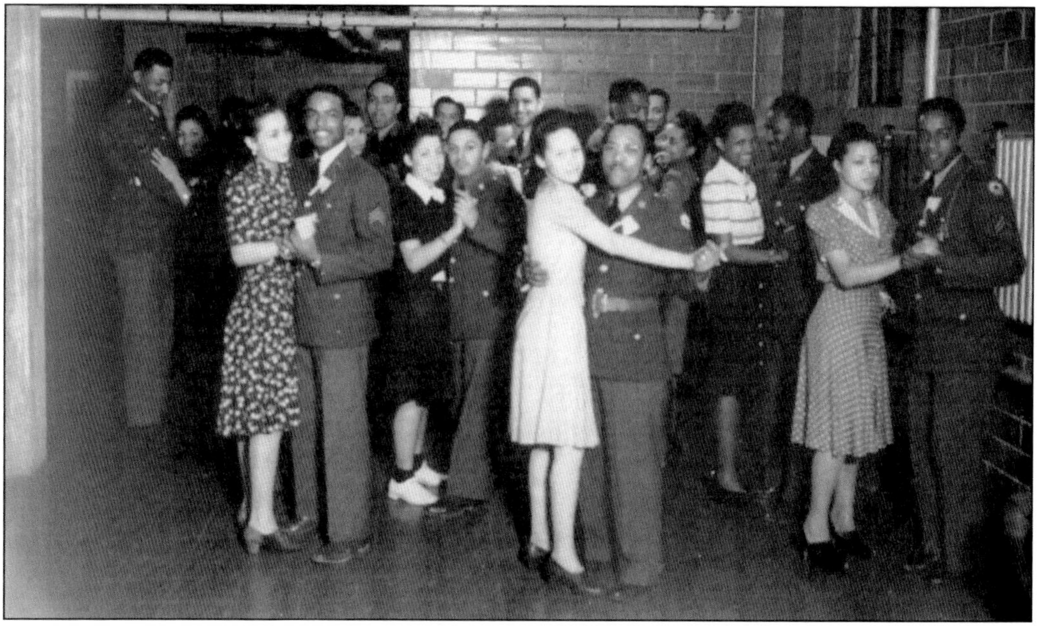

A group of servicemen from nearby Fort Leonard Wood Army Base and Lincoln University females enjoy a night of dancing in 1942.

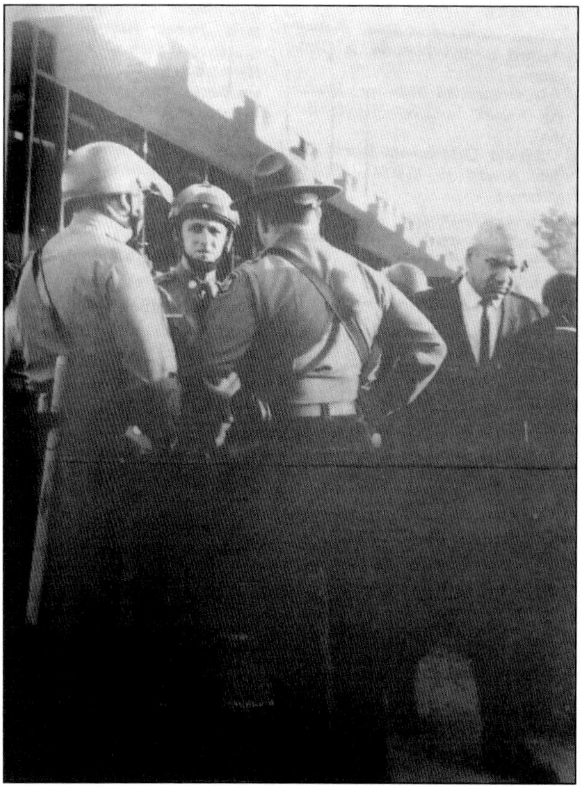

In the late 1960s, the Lincoln University campus was not immune to the student protests taking place on college campuses. A group of Lincoln University students partially destroyed, by fire, the Scruggs Student Center during a local protest. During the demonstration, law enforcement officers from the Jefferson City Police Department, and more than 200 Missouri State Highway Patrol officers and 200 Missouri National Guard troops, converged on the campus to quell the disturbance. Local protestors presented a list of 55 demands divided into administrative, academic, and social concerns. The list the students presented to the administration included a noncensorship policy for the *Clarion* student newspaper.

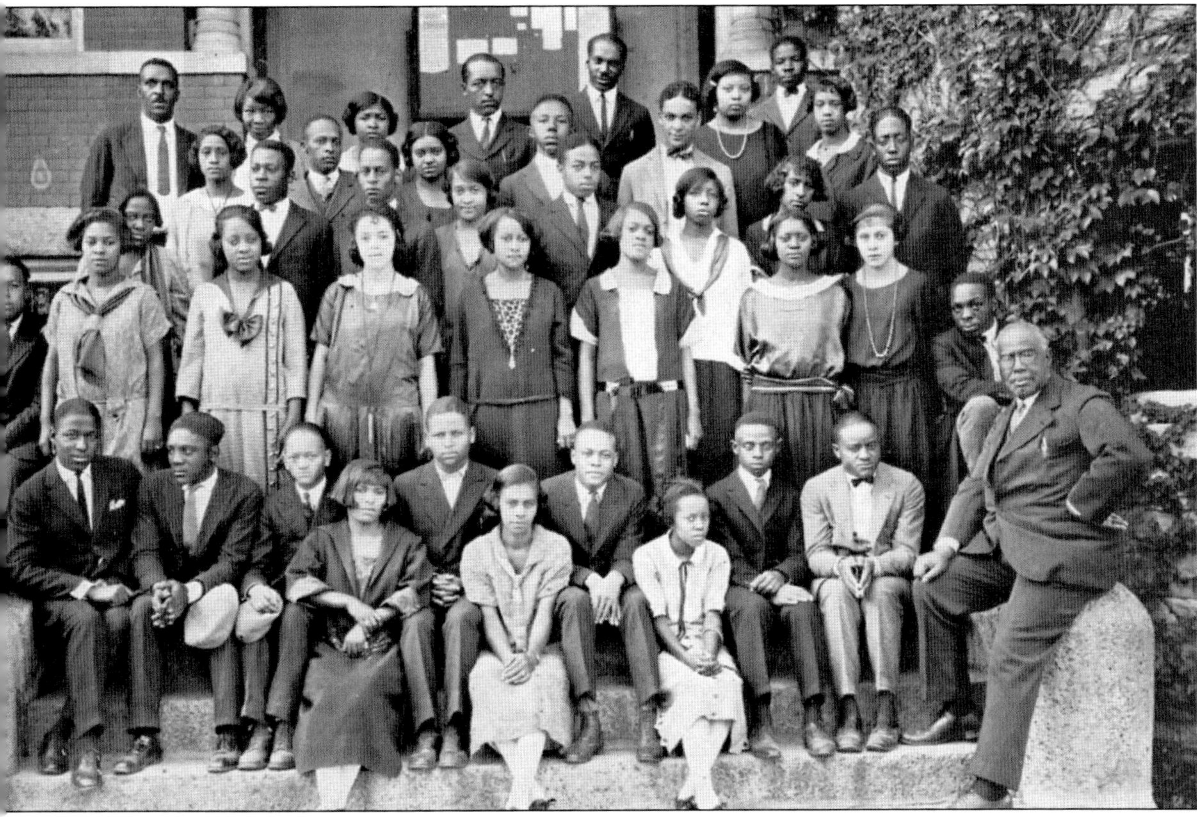

This photograph shows the 1925 sophomore class. The man sitting on the stoop in front on the far right is university president Dr. Nathan B. Young.

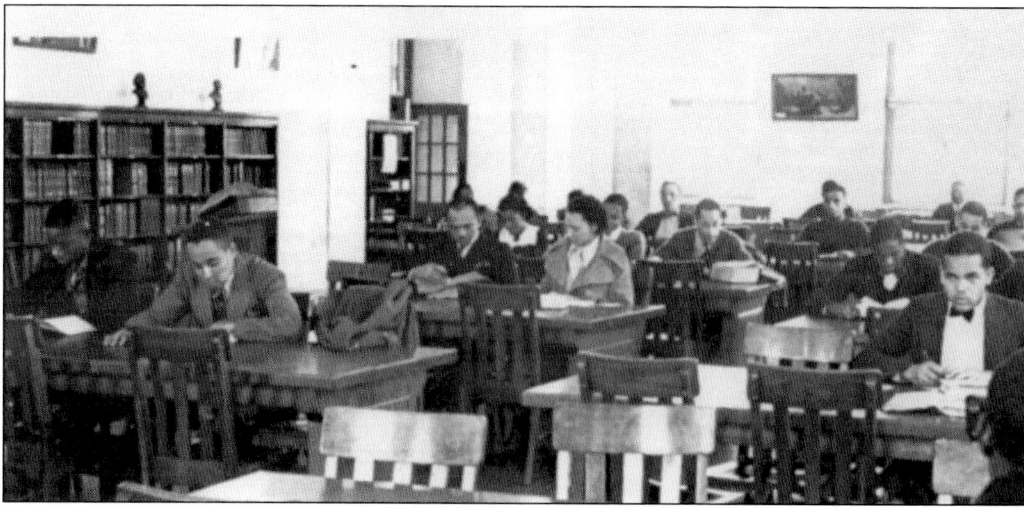

Students study in the Young Hall administration building library prior to the construction of a library only (Inman E. Page Library) in 1948.

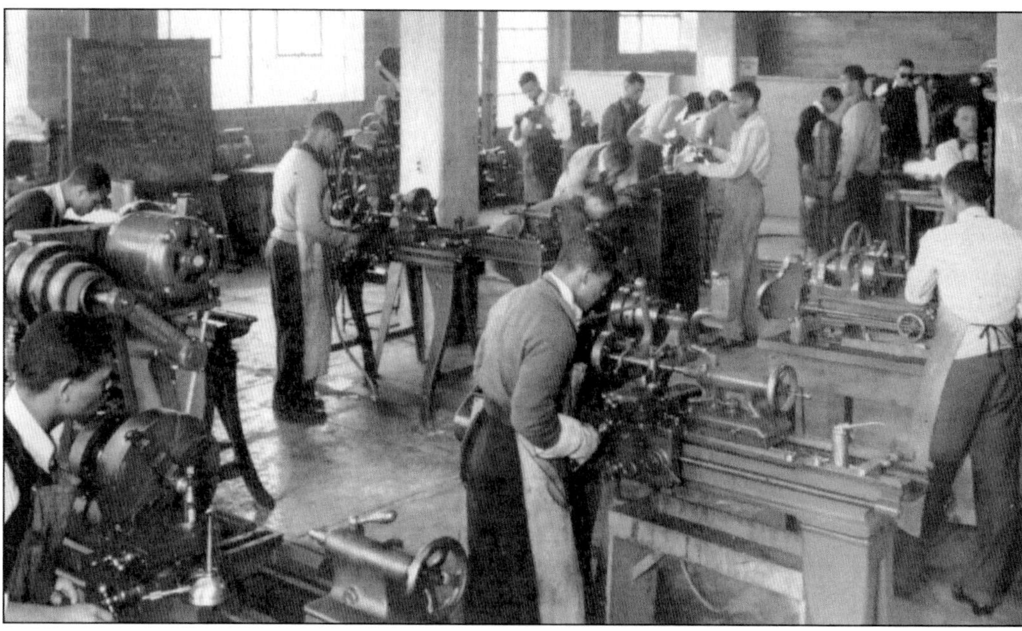

During World War II, Lincoln University was active in many areas in support of the war effort. A program for training technicians in air war production enabled many young men, such as those pictured here, to secure jobs in support of national defense. This is a 1942 class in machine operation.

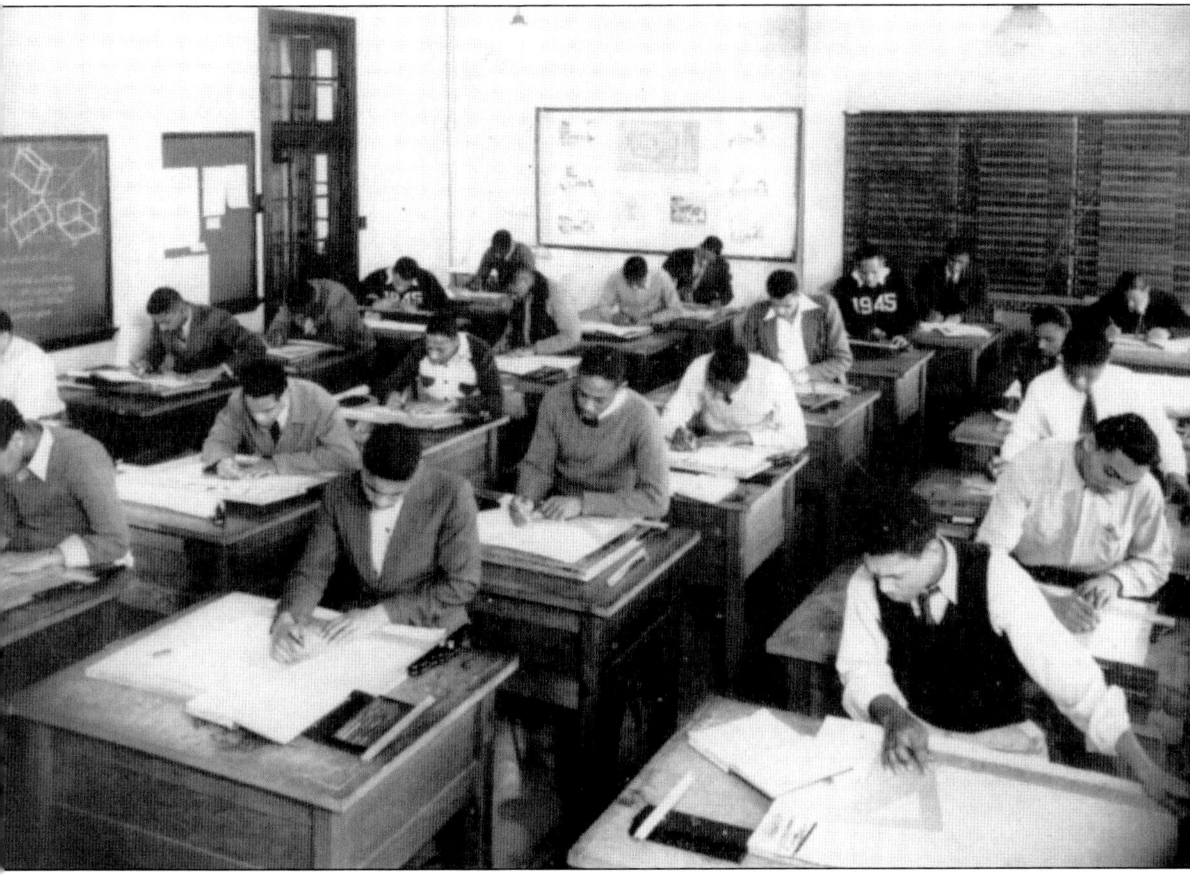


A class in engineering drawing during the 1942 school year is pictured here.

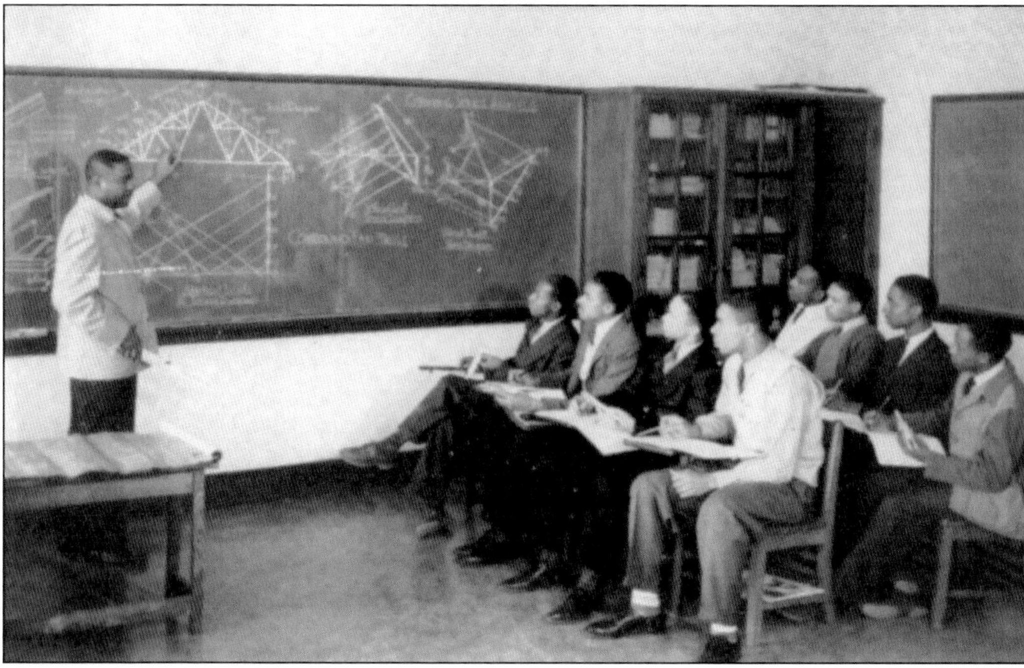

Pictured here is a 1942 building engineering class.

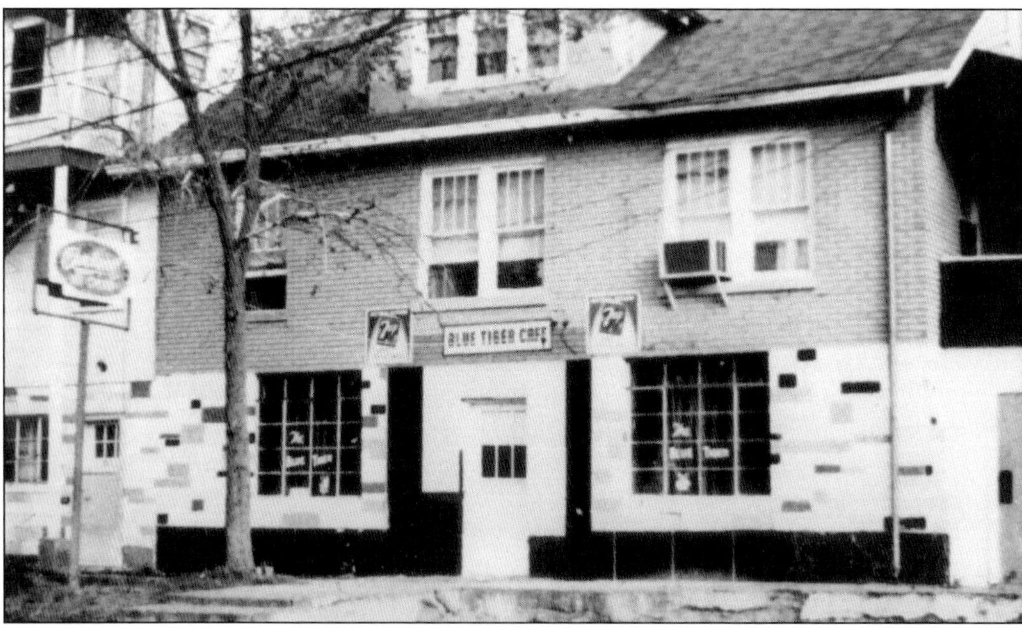


The Blue Tiger Cafe, while not an official campus building, was nevertheless located within the campus complex of buildings. Often called the "greasy spoon" by many students and faculty, the café was built in the 1920s and served an important function because it was one of the few restaurants near the campus that served blacks. The restaurant was a major gathering spot for students to eat and socialize and also offered rooms upstairs for renters. The building was torn down in the fall of 1984 to provide land for the Collier-Hatcher-Parks parking lot at the corner of Atchison and Chestnut Streets.

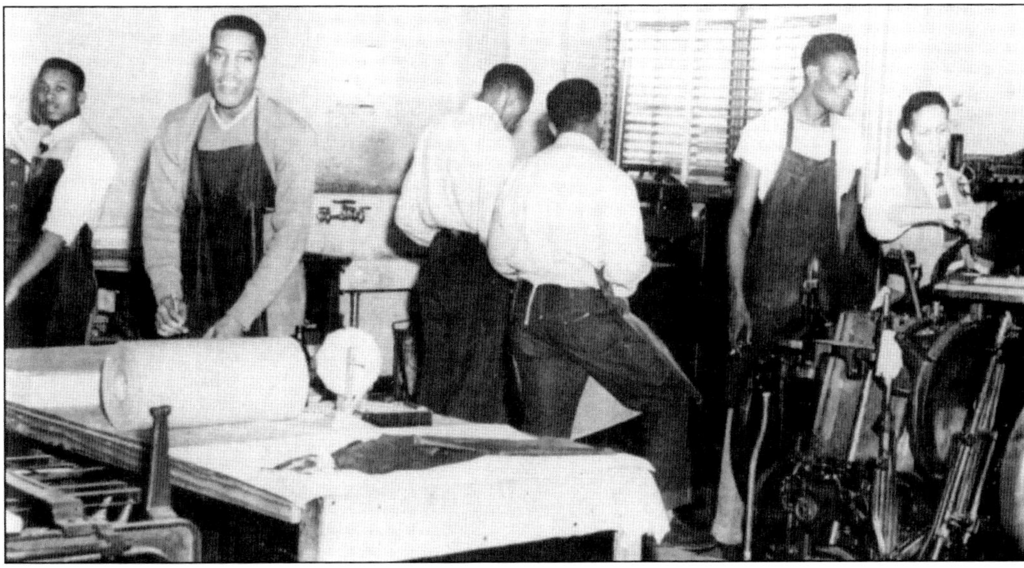

Lincoln University in 1890, under the second Morrill Act passed by Congress, was designated a 1890 land-grant institution and given funds under this program to train students in the agricultural and mechanical arts. The University of Missouri is the state's only other land-grant institution, having been granted that designation under the first Morrill Act passed in 1862. The Lincoln University land-grant status remains intact today. One of the technical courses offered that attracted a large number of mechanical art students in the 1950–1970 time period was printing. Here a group of students is learning that trade.

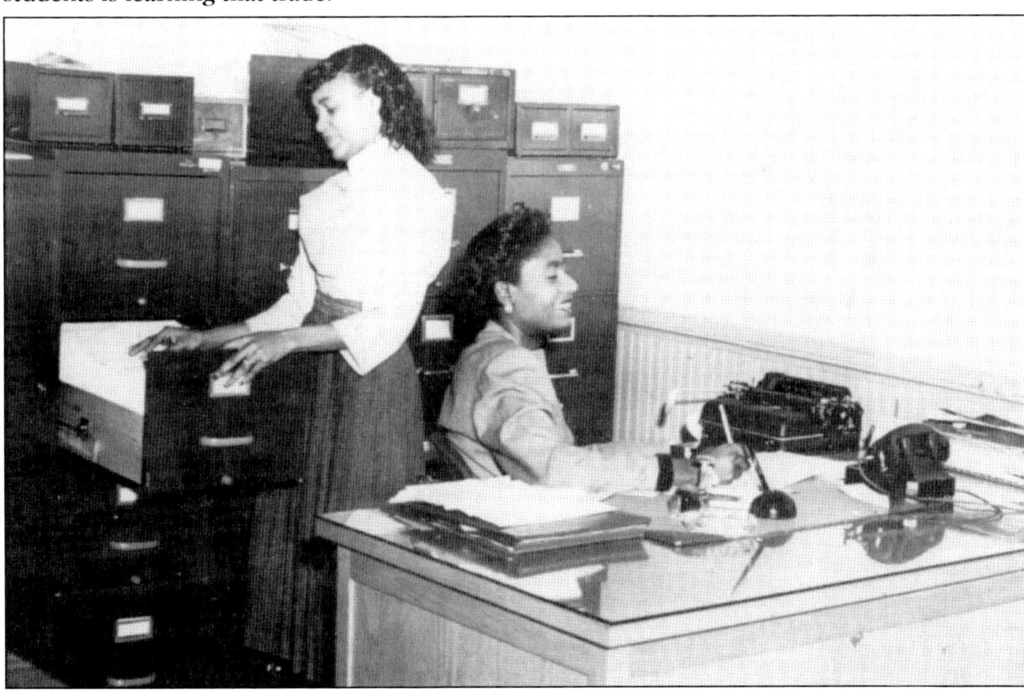

Two Lincoln University students are shown working in a campus office. The person on the far left is Yvonne Starks Wilson, former president of the Lincoln University Board of Curators and currently a Missouri state senator.

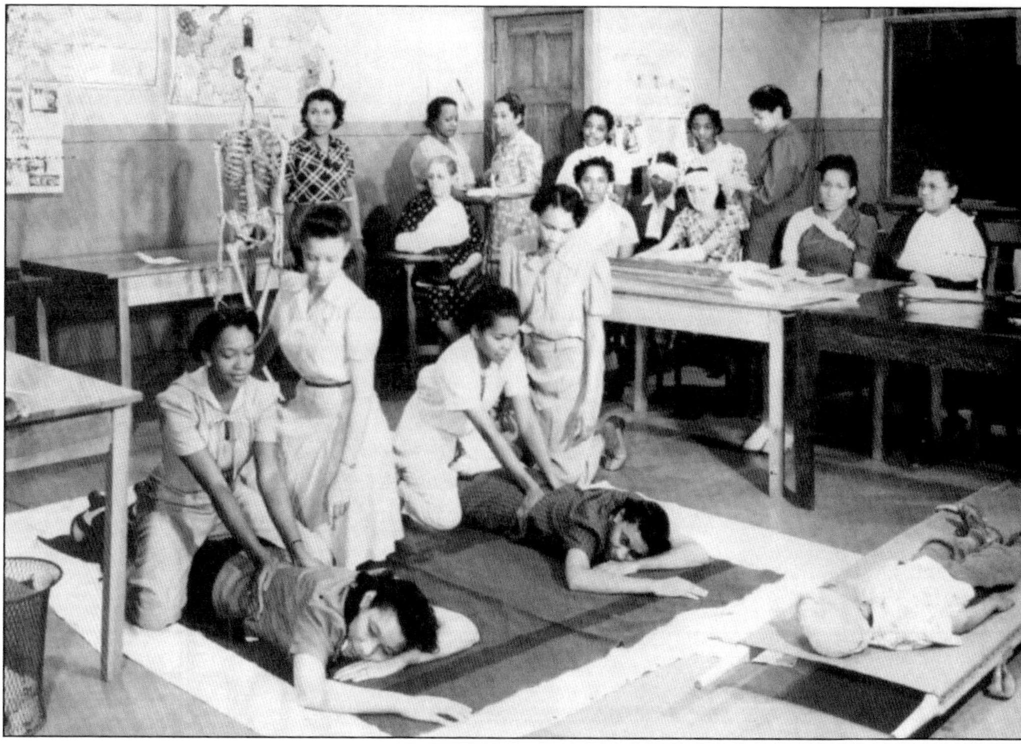
In this photograph, a first aid class practices during the 1942–1943 school year.

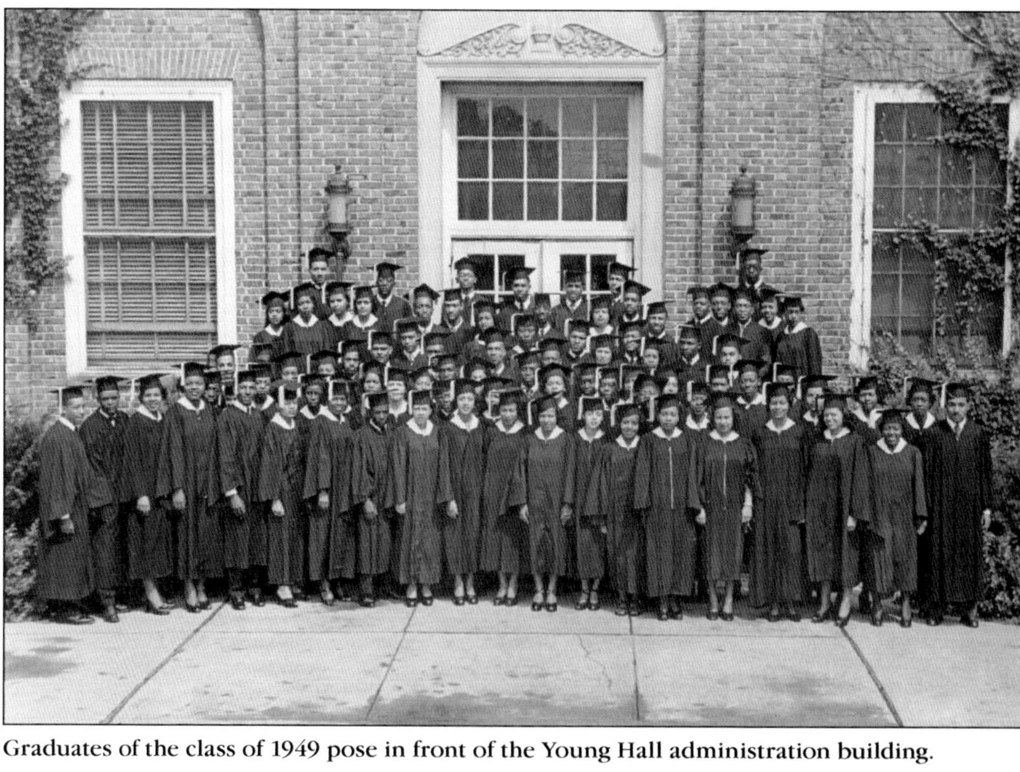
Graduates of the class of 1949 pose in front of the Young Hall administration building.

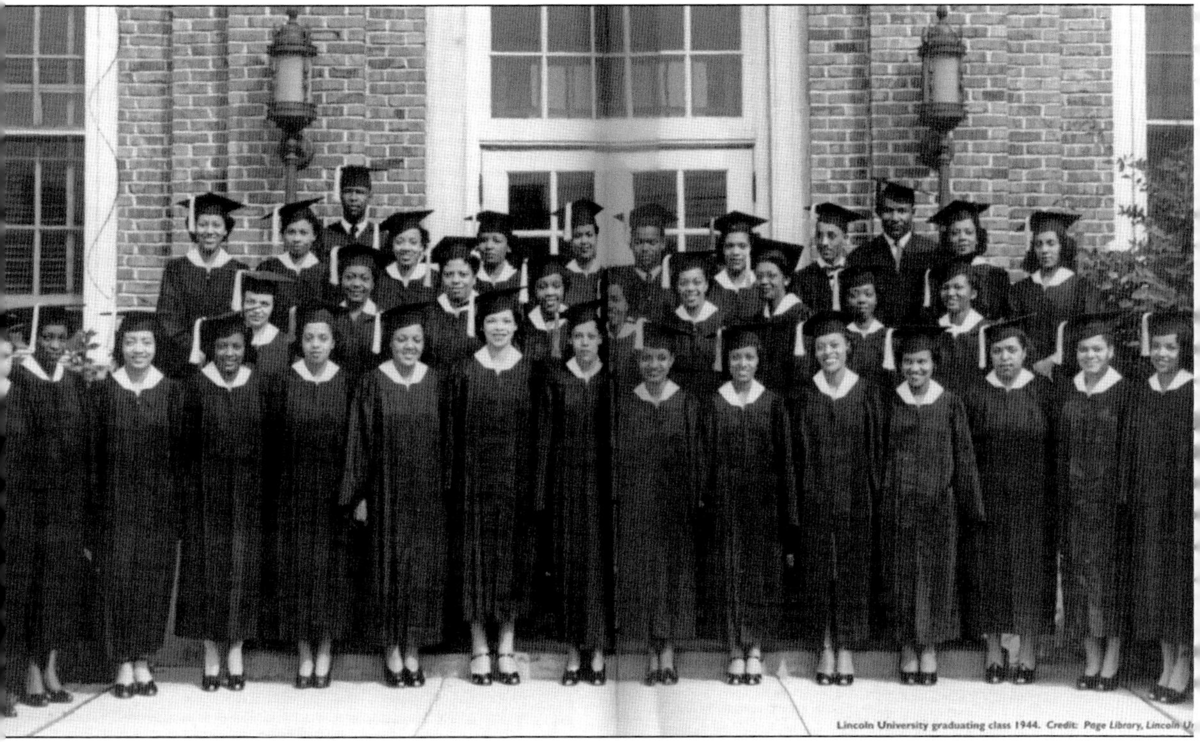


Here graduates of the class of 1944 pose in front of the Young Hall administration building.

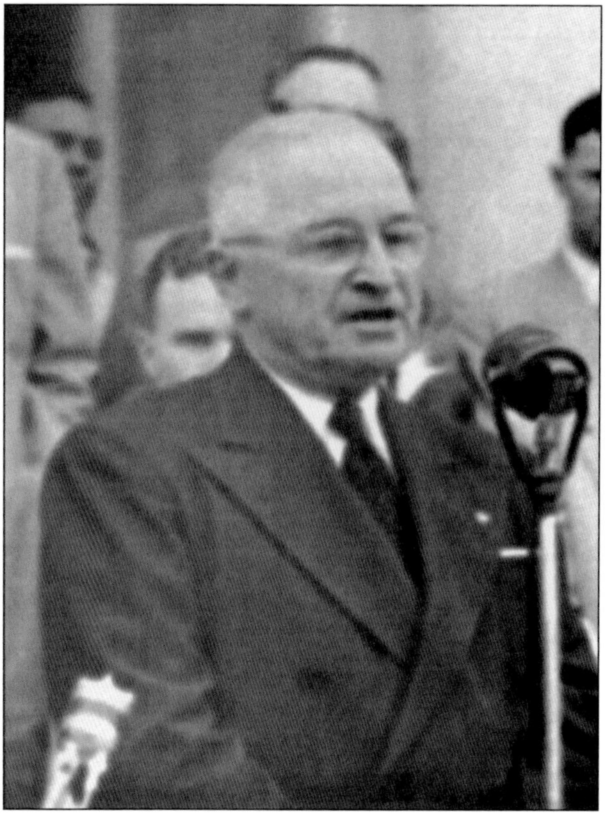

Pres. Harry S. Truman, a native Missourian, visited the Lincoln University campus in 1953. Truman has the distinction of being the only United States president to visit the campus. This photograph shows Truman making a speech on the steps of the former Inman E. Page Library (now Stamper Hall).

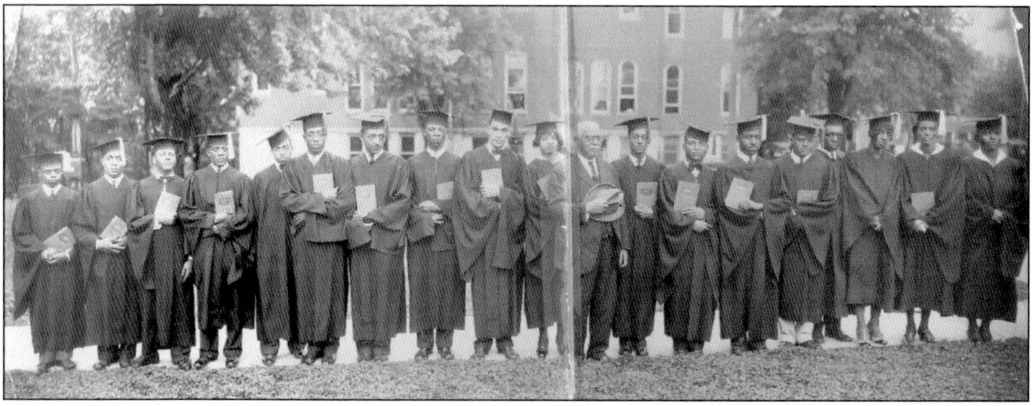

This is a 1920s Lincoln University graduating class. Pres. Nathan B. Young is the man holding the hat.

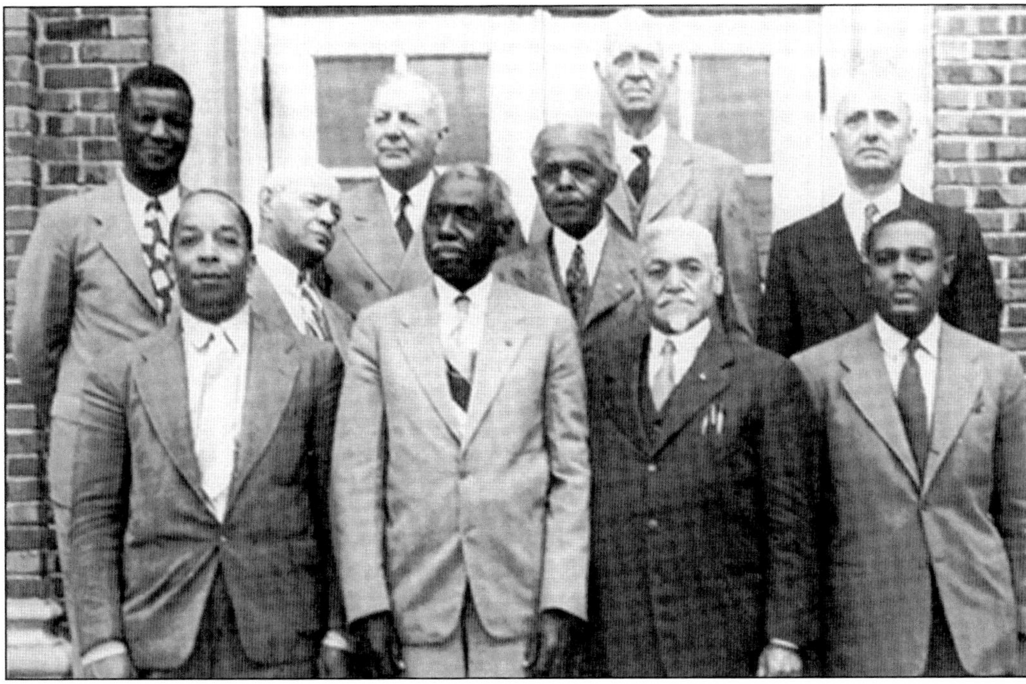

The board of curators in 1946 expressed a concern that Lincoln University would be governed by the best minds available and politics would have no part in the school's administration. Lincoln University president Dr. Sherman D. Scruggs (far left) is shown with members Dr. Harry S. Blackiston (St. Louis), Dr. A. W. Craddock (St. Louis), Cliff G. Scruggs (Jefferson City), Dr. J. Edward Perry (Kansas City), Christopher C. Hubbard (Sedalia), Dr. J. E. Eliff (Columbia), John W. Evans (St. Louis), H. Byron Masterson (Kennett), and G. Cletus Burchette, faculty member and secretary to the board.

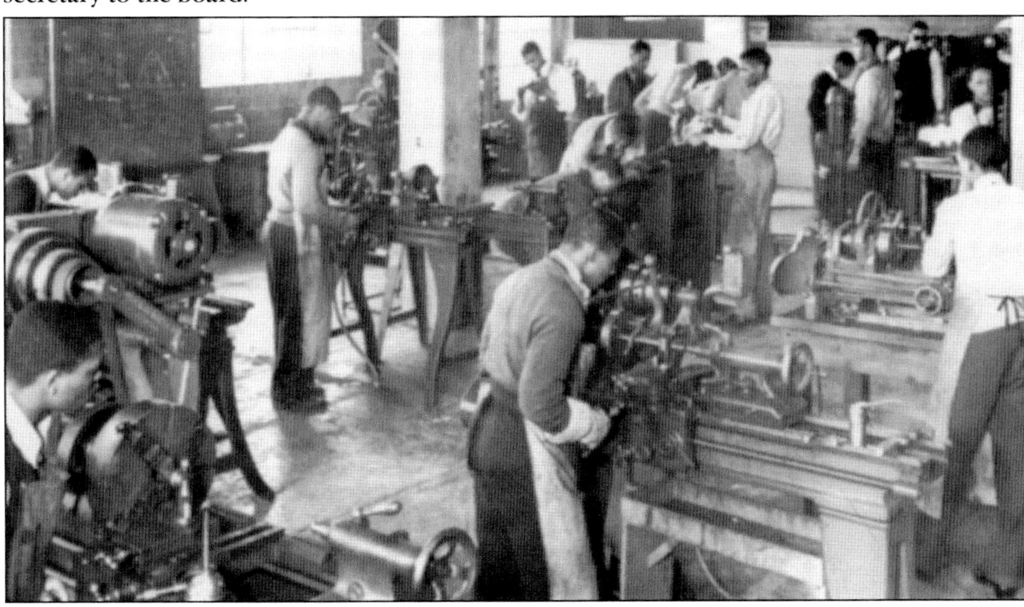

Under Lincoln University's land-grant mission to train students in the agricultural and mechanical arts, several students are shown here in the 1960s learning a mechanical trade.

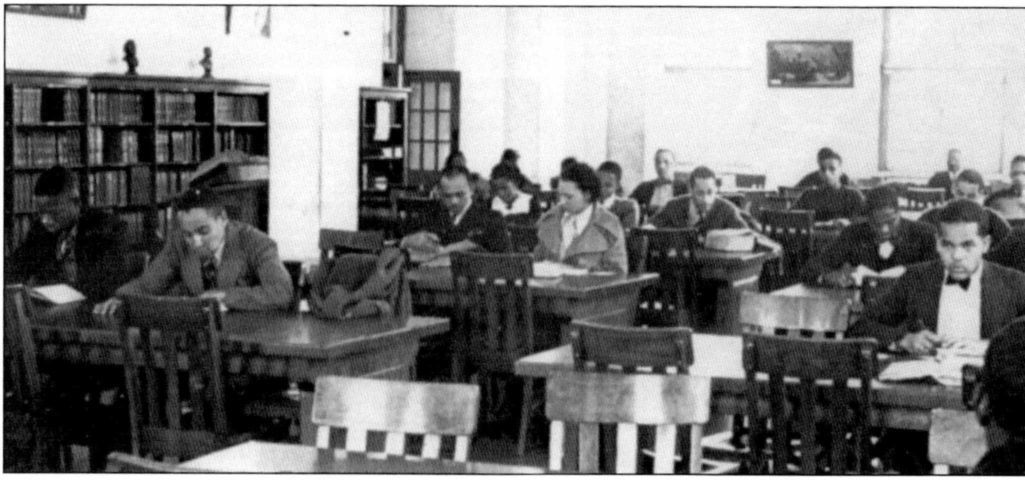

Several Lincoln University students in the 1940s study in the library when it was located in the Young Hall administration building before the first Inman E. Page Library was constructed in 1948.

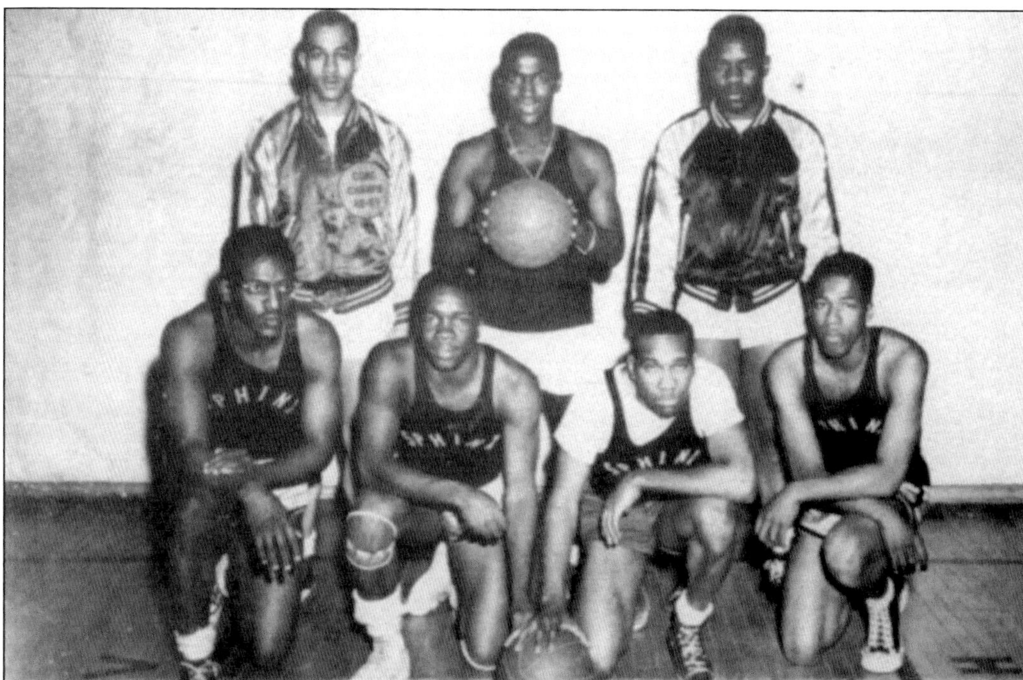

The pledge club of Alpha Phi Alpha fraternity, called the Sphinxmen, played in the intramural basketball program. Seen here from left to right are (first row) Robert Darden, Benny Blair, Fred Clark, and Clement Cooper; (second row) Edward Johnson, Earnest Wyatt, and William Rice.

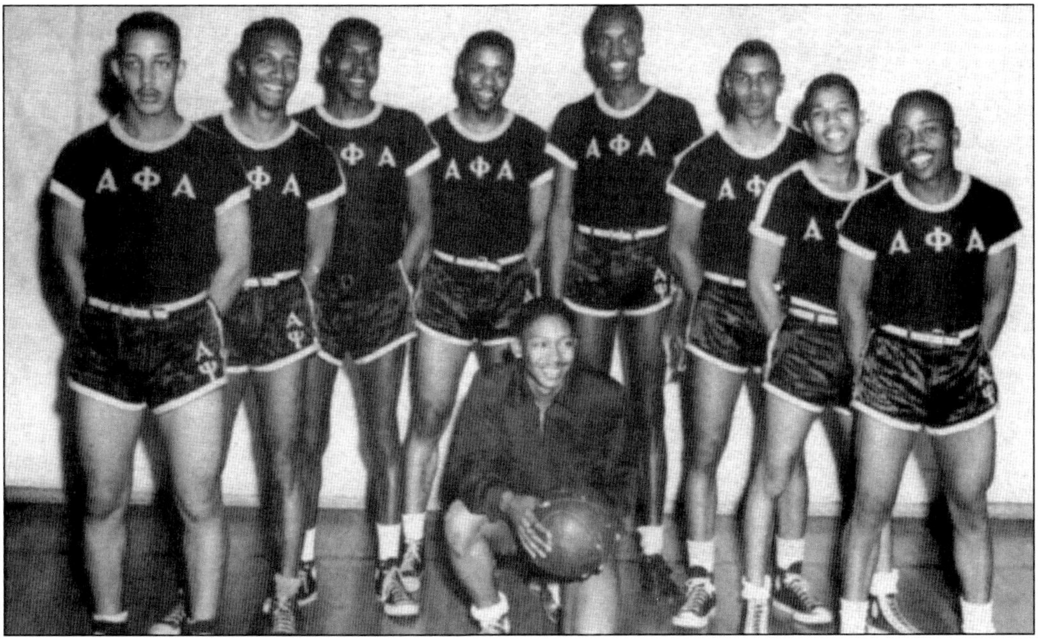


The Alpha Phi Alpha fraternity in 1951 had a basketball team in the intramural sports program. Members standing from left to right are John Franklin, Cleveland Williams, Johnny Gordon, Eddie Madison, Melvin Crouther, Charles Owens, Robert Reese, and Joseph Lewis. Holding the ball is Jack Wright.

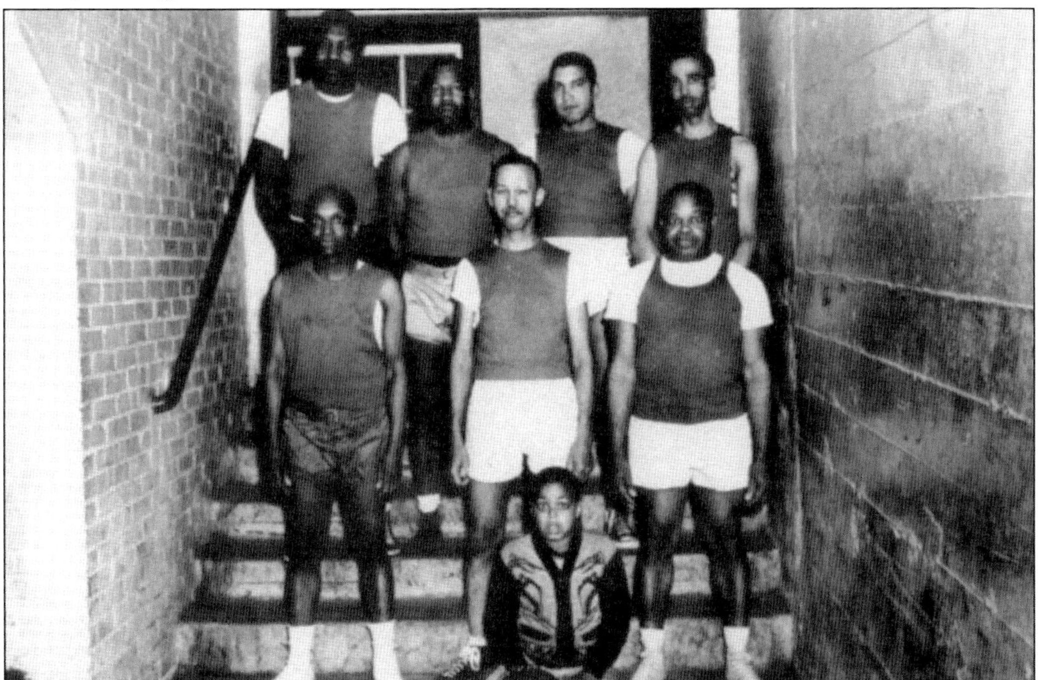

Lincoln University in 1951 had an intramural faculty basketball team. Members are, from left to right, (first row) Willis Pitts, Milton Hardiman, and Alonzo Dent; (second row) Alexander Pitts, Herbert Tucker, Dwight Reed, and Gerald Brooks. Holding the ball is mascot "Skipper" Reed.

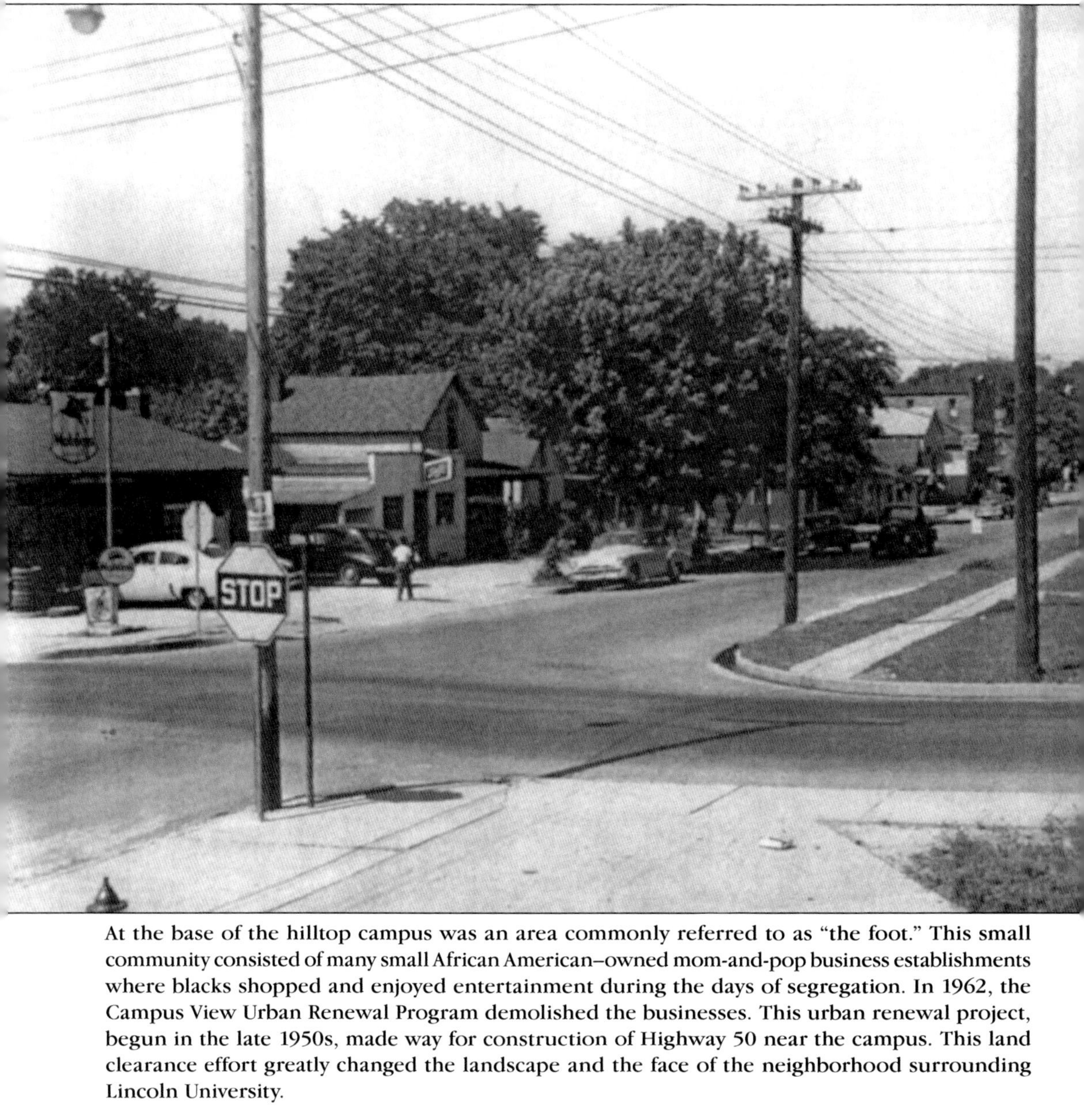


At the base of the hilltop campus was an area commonly referred to as "the foot." This small community consisted of many small African American–owned mom-and-pop business establishments where blacks shopped and enjoyed entertainment during the days of segregation. In 1962, the Campus View Urban Renewal Program demolished the businesses. This urban renewal project, begun in the late 1950s, made way for construction of Highway 50 near the campus. This land clearance effort greatly changed the landscape and the face of the neighborhood surrounding Lincoln University.

# *Five*

# The Black Harvard of the Midwest

Because of the high-caliber scholars Lincoln University was able to attract during the decades of the 1920s, 1930s, and 1940s, the school was often referred to as "the Black Harvard of the Midwest." The movement to assemble such a high-caliber faculty began under the presidency of Nathan B. Young, who in 1920, after assuming the position, quickly concluded that the academic program of the university needed upgrading. In a letter he wrote to the famed black scholar W. E. B. DuBois, Young indicated that his desire was to create "A First-class Institution of Higher Learning in the Middle West." In order to accomplish this goal, Young raised salaries to a level that exceeded that at most black schools and also set in place a program of sabbatical leaves for faculty continuing education. It has been noted that during his tenure the number of professors with graduate degrees tripled within four years. With the faculty development programs in place, Young was able to attract faculty with master's and doctorate degrees from some of the top-rated universities in the country and abroad. He was particularly adept at attracting scholars who had trained at top-rated schools in both the eastern and southern United States. Among the persons recruited by Young and their respective teaching specialties and degree-granting institutions were Sterling Brown in literature (Williams College and master of arts at Harvard College); Norval Barksdale, modern foreign languages (University of Kansas and Dijon University in France); L. Symington Curtis, economics (Harvard College and Columbia University); Thomas Miles, mathematics (University of Pennsylvania); James Dallas Parks, art (Bradley Polytechnic Institute); Harry Blackiston, languages (University of Pennsylvania); Albert A. Kildare, physics (Boston University); Cecil A. Blue, English (Harvard University); and William W. Dowdy, biology (University of Iowa and Cornell University). Both Sterling Brown and Cecil A. Blue, who were two Harvard-trained professors, both became important Harlem Renaissance writers. Brown in particular later became known as one of America's most prolific and creative African American poets.

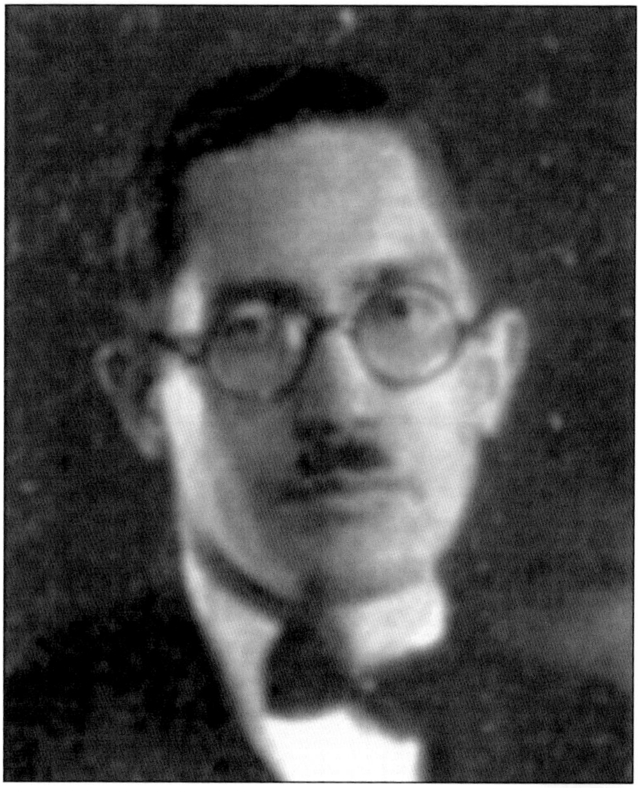

Sterling Brown, a 1922 graduate of Williams College in Massachusetts, immediately enrolled in Harvard University, completing a degree in English from that prestigious institution in 1923. Brown's initial teaching job was at Virginia Seminary in Lynchburg, Virginia, where he taught three years before coming to Lincoln University in 1926. In the cultural enclave of African American Jefferson City, Brown encouraged his students to be observers of their surroundings. As such, he attached himself to hanging out in "the foot" community, which consisted of black-owned business establishments at the lower end of the campus.

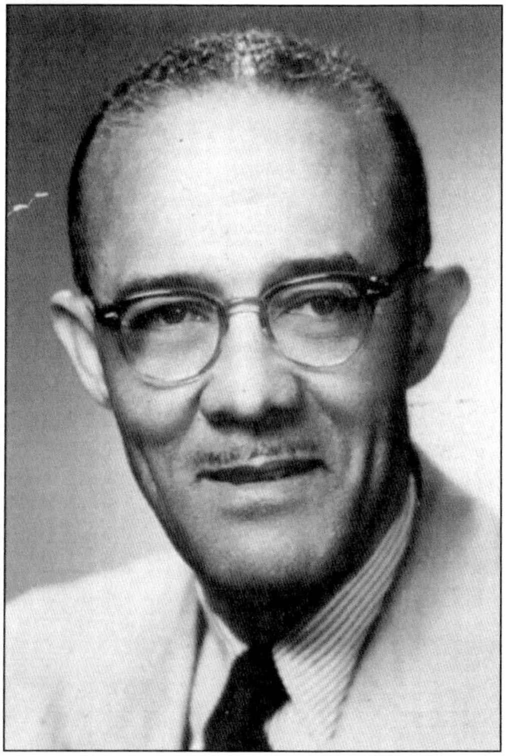

Cecil Archibald Blue, a native of British Columbia, graduated from Harvard in 1926 and initially took a job teaching at Johnson C. Smith College in Charlotte, North Carolina. Blue was in communication with Sterling Brown, who encouraged him to come teach at Lincoln University, so he accepted the challenge. A well-known Harlem Renaissance writer, Blue won a national short-story contest for his story titled "The Flyer." At Lincoln University, he was a demanding teacher and brilliant thinker. One of his great passions was to coach the Tau Sigma Rho Debating Society, which was a skilled debating team that competed against prestigious higher education institutions from all over the United States and on one occasion even served as the host of a debate team from Oxford University.

Dr. Milton G. Hardiman, a Lincoln University graduate, taught French and Spanish at the university for 46 years, as well as teaching the last courses in Latin offered at Lincoln University. Hardiman, whose special interest was French literature of the 17th and 19th centuries, lived one year in France and traveled in Mexico and most of western Europe.

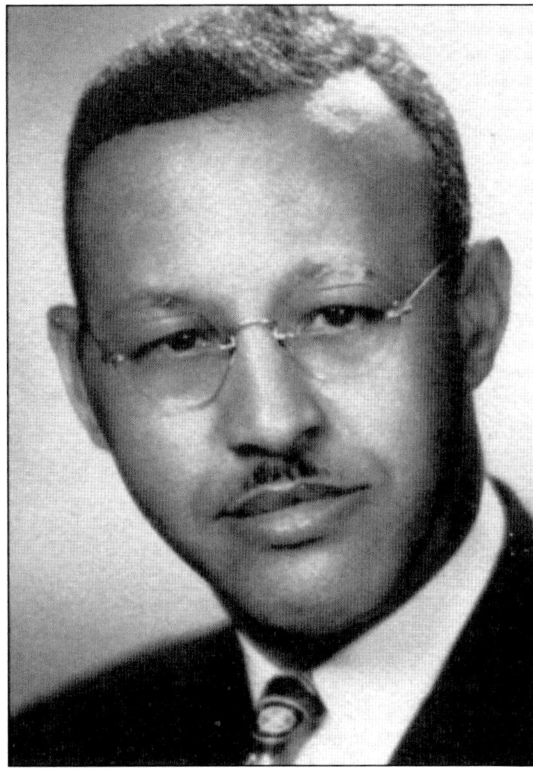

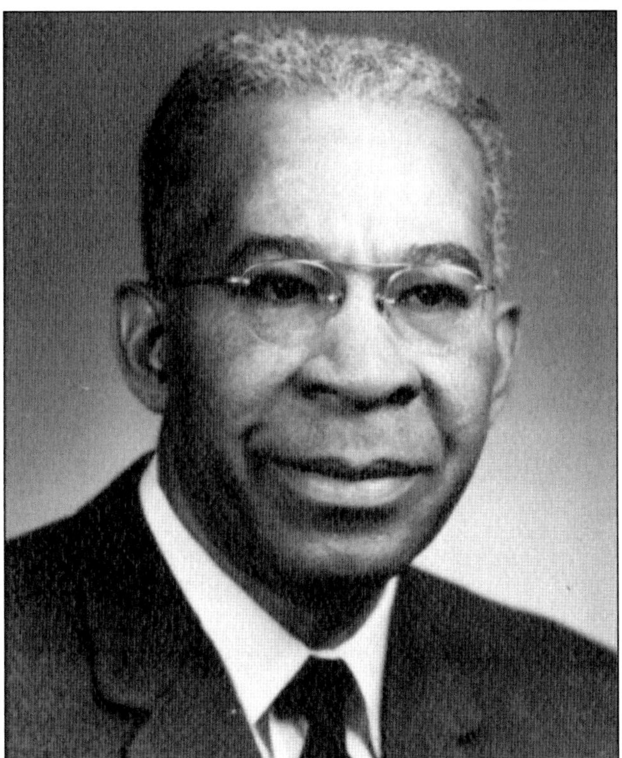

Dr. Oliver Cromwell Cox, a renowned scholar, taught 24 years at Lincoln University. His work in the area of race relations earned him national recognition and called the attention of scholars to ideas of social order and social change. A sociologist by training, many of the five books written by Cox had an economics perspective. He was labeled a Marxist, which he denied, referring to himself as a "borrower" from Marx. It has now come to light, under the Freedom of Information Act, that the FBI kept a file on Cox starting in 1948.

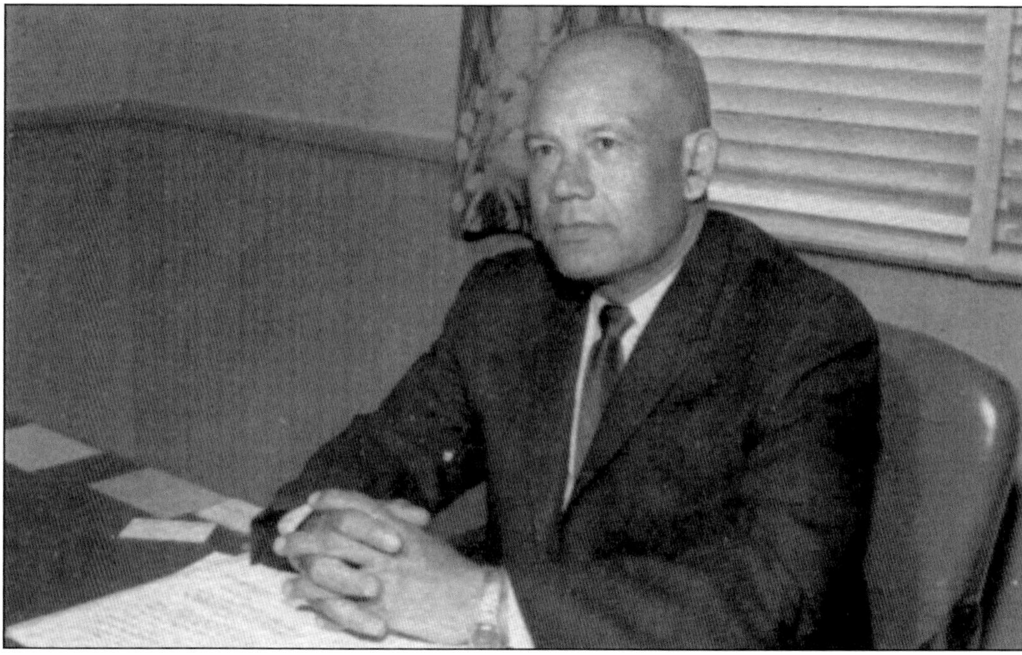

Dr. James H. Seeney taught 35 years at Lincoln University and in 1956 was the first African American to receive the doctor of education degree from the University of Missouri–Columbia. Because of his distinguished teaching record at Lincoln University, he was, in 1992, posthumously awarded the title of distinguished professor of education.

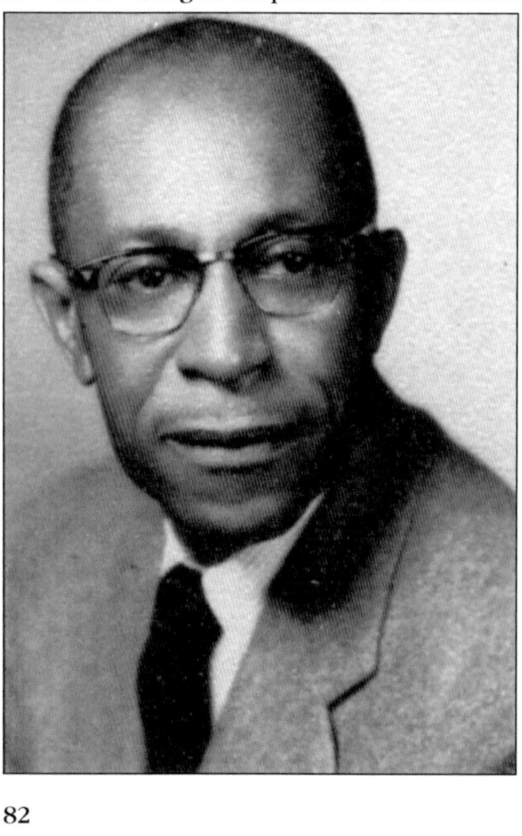

Dr. Lorenzo J. Greene taught at Lincoln University from 1933 to 1972 and was regarded as one of the foremost authorities on African American history in the United States. He was the author of the classic book titled *The Negro in Colonial New England* and was either the author or coauthor of eight books and numerous scholarly articles. However, one of his most notable publications was began in 1947 and titled the *Midwest Journal*. This 150-page, Lincoln University–based publication was a magazine of research and creative writing and gave the university national exposure.

The *Midwest Journal* was published semiannually from 1948 to 1953. The first issue was printed by the Lincoln University Printing Department, and Von Hoffman Press of Jefferson City printed all subsequent issues. The journal was devoted to research and creative writing. The views expressed in the journal did not necessarily reflect those of the editors or Lincoln University. The editorial staff consisted of Lorenzo J. Greene, editor; Cecil A. Blue, Sidney J. Reedy, and Ulysses Lee as associate editors; and business managers J. Errol Miller and Consuelo Young.

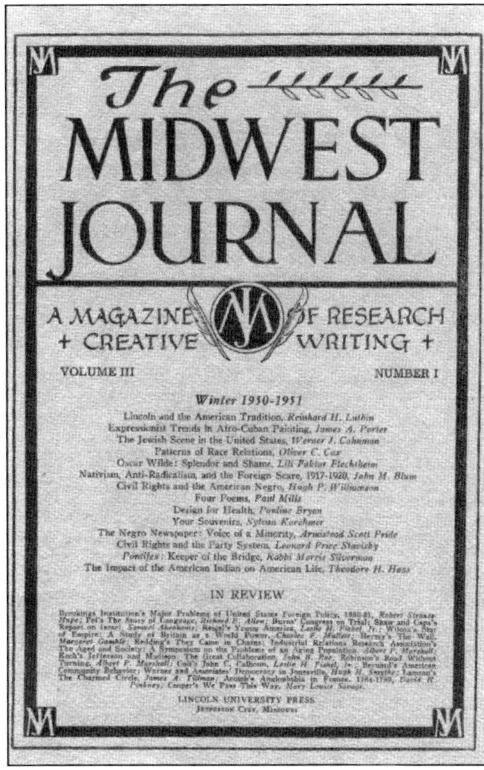

The MIDWEST JOURNAL

A MAGAZINE OF RESEARCH + CREATIVE WRITING +

VOLUME III — NUMBER I

*Winter 1950-1951*

Lincoln and the American Tradition, *Reinhard H. Luthin*
Expressionist Trends in Afro-Cuban Painting, *James A. Porter*
The Jewish Scene in the United States, *Werner J. Cohnman*
Patterns of Race Relations, *Oliver C. Cox*
Oscar Wilde: Splendor and Shame, *Lili Faktor Flechtheim*
Nativism, Anti-Radicalism, and the Foreign Scare, 1917-1920, *John M. Blum*
Civil Rights and the American Negro, *Hugh P. Williamson*
Four Poems, *Paul Mills*
Design for Health, *Pauline Bryan*
Your Souvenirs, *Sylvan Karchmer*
The Negro Newspaper: Voice of a Minority, *Armistead Scott Pride*
Civil Rights and the Party System, *Leonard Price Stavisky*
*Pontifex*: Keeper of the Bridge, *Rabbi Morris Silverman*
The Impact of the American Indian on American Life, *Theodore H. Haas*

IN REVIEW

LINCOLN UNIVERSITY PRESS
Jefferson City, Missouri

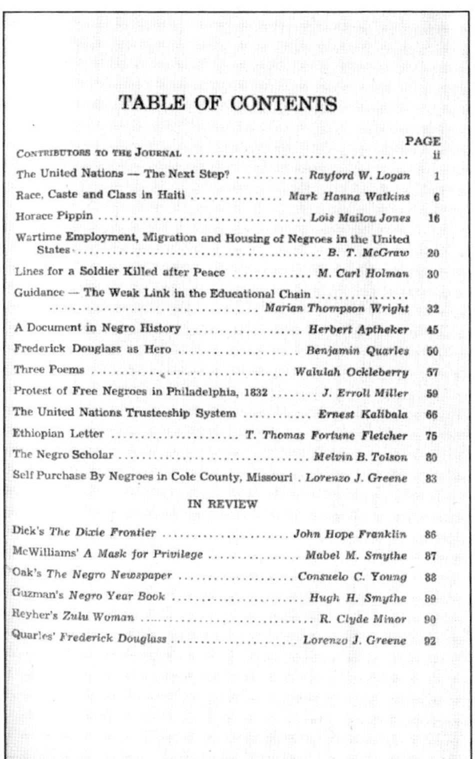

TABLE OF CONTENTS



The table of contents from one edition of the *Midwest Journal* shows that it had a wide variety of articles, essays, and book reviews ranging from international and national to local perspectives. Examples of each of the latter-mentioned variations in the materials included in the publication are international, "Race, Caste and Class in Haiti" and "The United Nations Trusteeship System"; national, "Wartime Employment, Migration and Housing of Negroes in the United States"; and local, "Self Purchase By Negroes in Cole County, Missouri."

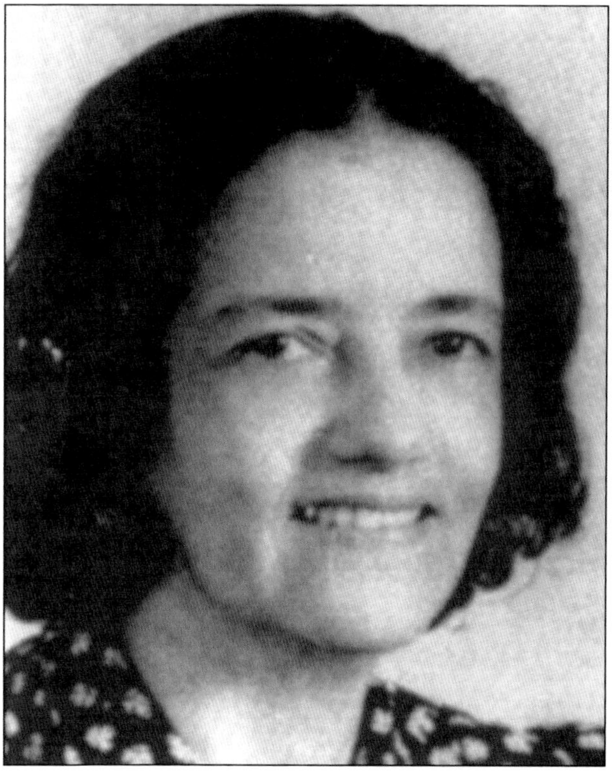

Dr. Hazel McDaniel Teabeau joined the Lincoln University English faculty in 1937, teaching at the university until 1962, except for brief leave periods to complete work for both her master's and doctorate degrees. She was the first black woman to enter the University of Missouri–Columbia, completing the doctorate degree in speech with an exceptional academic record. Teabeau as a teacher possessed an extensive knowledge of the English language, how to read to understand, how to write to communicate, and how to speak with influence.

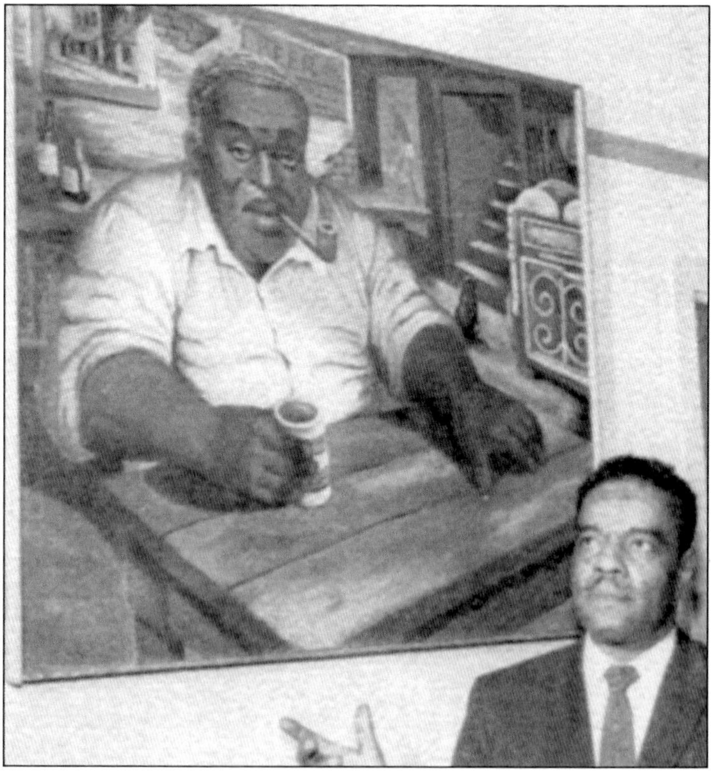

James Dallas Parks taught art at Lincoln University for 49 years. He is one of the few university employees who could trace their family association with Lincoln University to the founders, since he was the nephew of John Draine, who assisted with starting the Lincoln Institute in 1866. Parks also knew Logan Bennett, a Jefferson City founder who the school honors every year. Parks was well known as an artist and had his works exhibited at the Nelson Gallery in Kansas City, the St. Louis City Art Museum, Howard University, Tuskegee Institute in Alabama, and many other places.

Renowned artist Thomas Hart Benton is seen here painting with Parks.

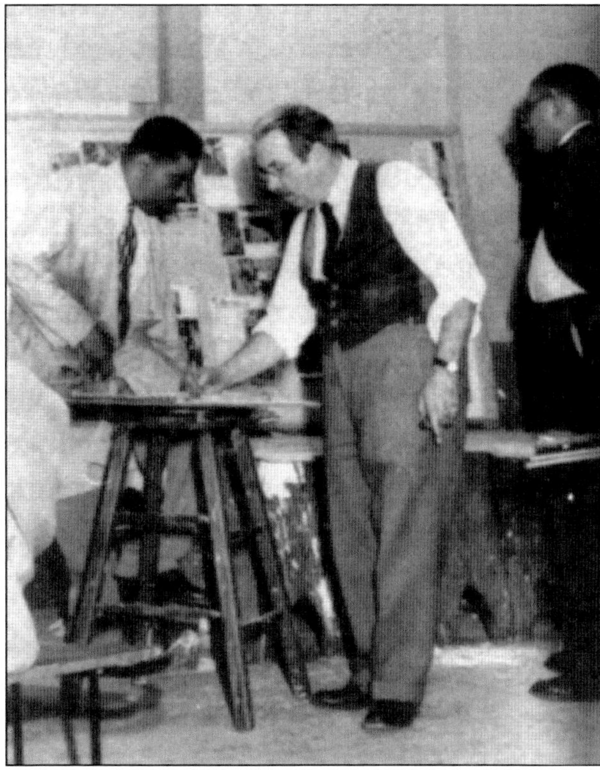

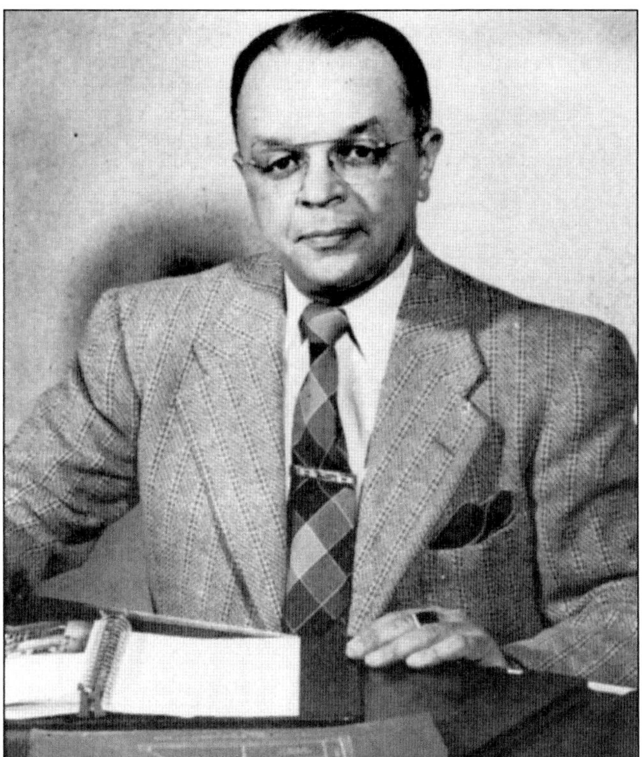

Dr. Armistead S. Pride served Lincoln University for almost 40 years as a professor, dean of the School of Journalism, and later as the head of the renamed Department of Journalism. He was the founder of the Headliner Awards program that recognized journalists who had done outstanding reporting on minority issues. This event later became known of as the Unity Awards in Media program. A Fulbright scholar, Pride was considered by many academicians to be the dean of black journalism because he spent his professional life researching and writing about the black press. Pride also served as a visiting professor throughout the United States and around the globe because of his expertise in black journalism.

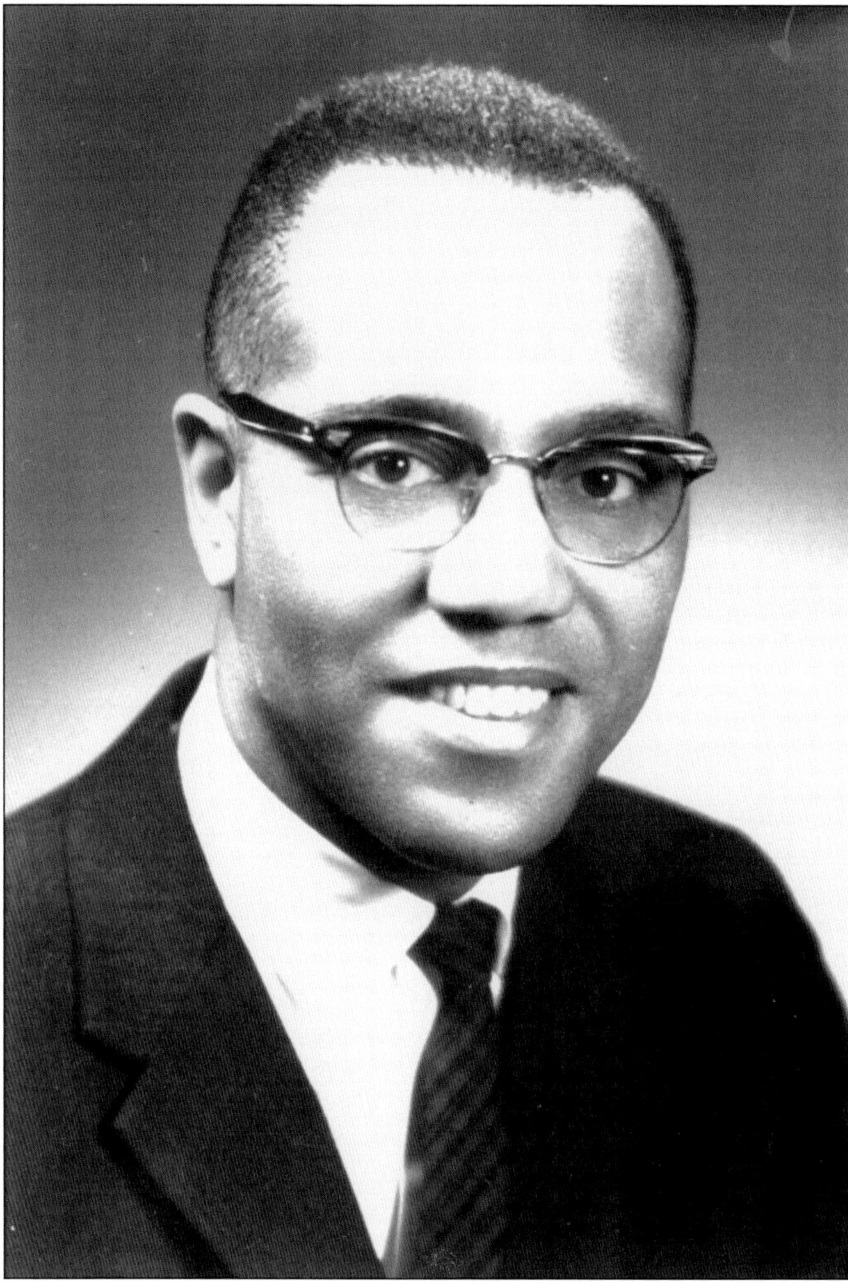

Dr. Thomas D. Pawley, a graduate of the University of Iowa, came to Lincoln University in 1940. During his tenure at the university, Pawley was a major force in the area of drama and theater, beginning in the early 1940s as the university advisor of the Stagecrafters organization. While at Iowa, four of his plays were produced, and at Lincoln University, two of Pawley's plays, *F.F.V.* and *The Tumult and the Shouting*, were staged. He served as president of the National Association of Dramatic and Speech Arts and, along with William R. Reardon, coedited the book titled *The Black Teacher and the Dramatic Arts: A Dialogue, Bibliography and Anthology*. In the 1980s, the board of curators honored Pawley with the title he currently holds as curators' distinguished professor of speech and theater.

This is another profile of James D. Parks, renowned Lincoln University art professor and artist.

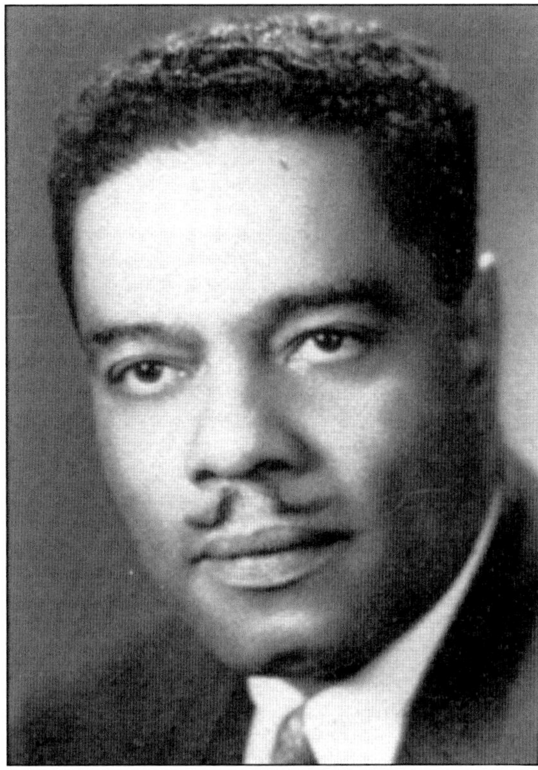

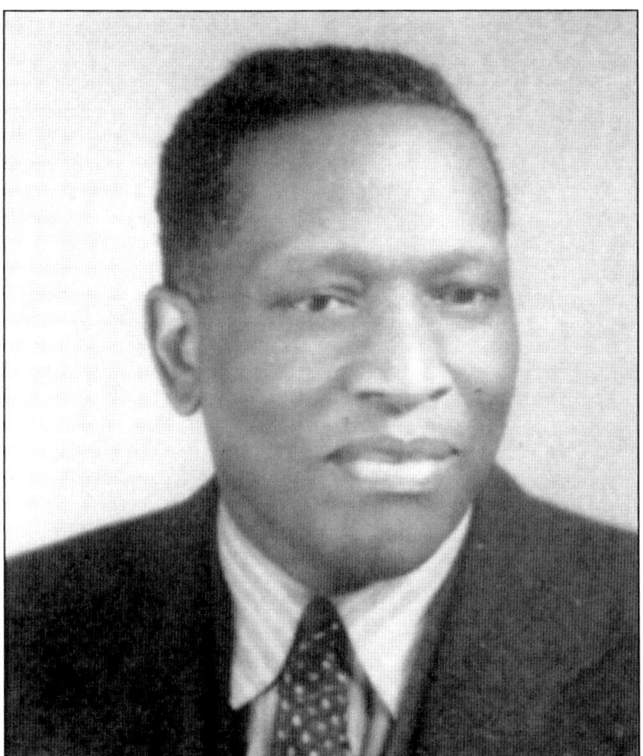

Dr. W. Sherman Savage, a historian, taught for 40 years at Lincoln University. He wrote a thorough and comprehensive book titled *The History of Lincoln University* along with several shorter supplements that dealt with historical facts on the university. He was born in Wattsville, Virginia, and graduated from Howard University in Washington, D.C., with a bachelor of arts degree in 1917, coming to teach at Lincoln University in 1921. Upon arriving at the university, through the urging of Pres. Nathan B. Young, the young professor pursued graduate work at the University of Oregon, where he earned a master of arts degree in 1925, becoming that school's first African American graduate. He continued his studies at Ohio State University, receiving a doctorate in history in 1934.

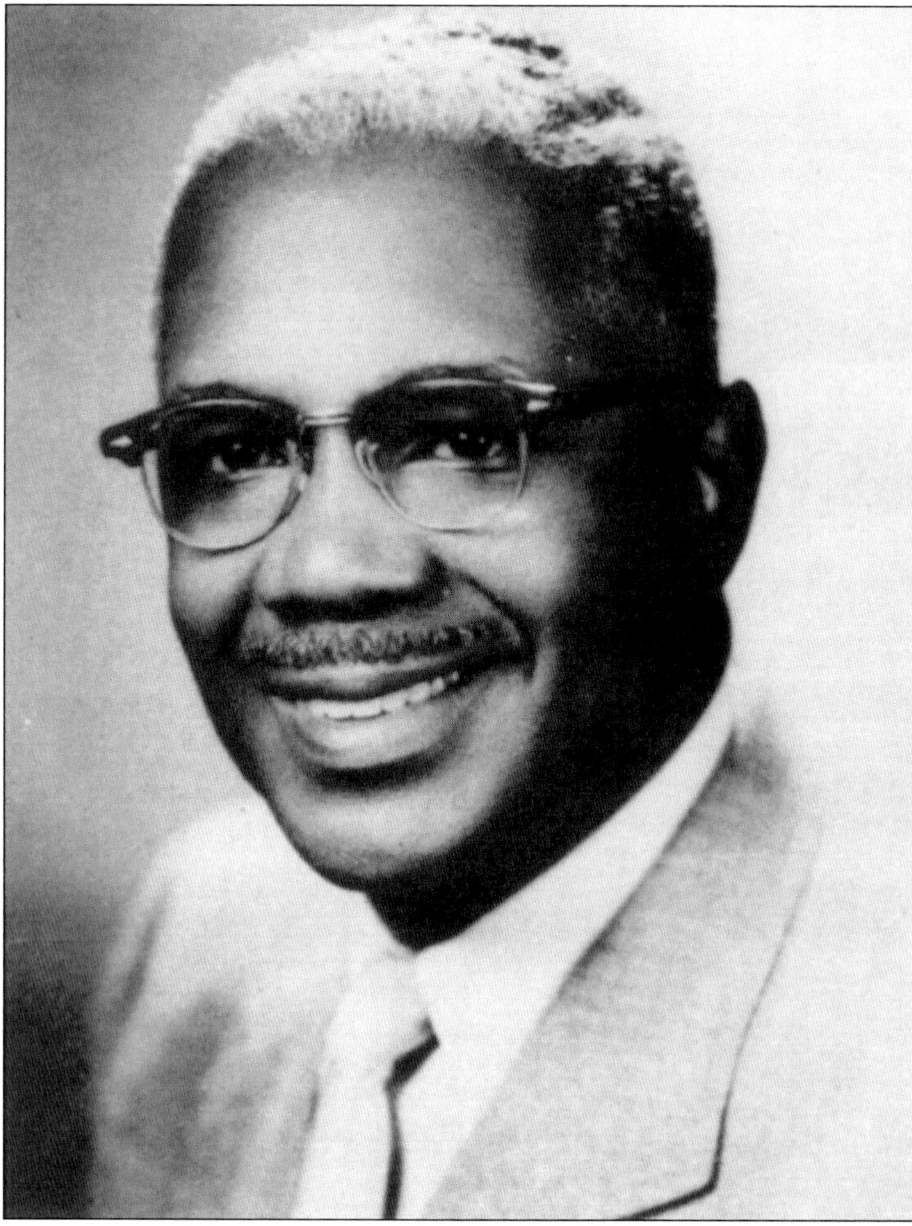

Dr. O. Anderson Fuller received a bachelor's degree from historically black Bishop College, where his father served as dean. He later studied at the New England Conservatory, where an instructor there told him about the University of Iowa. It was there that Oscar Anderson Fuller was one of only 8 or 10 black students in the university's enrollment of approximately 5,000 in the early 1930s. After college, Fuller briefly taught at two historically black institutions—North Carolina Agricultural and Technical University and Prairie View State University. Fuller came to Lincoln University to teach in 1942, after receiving his doctorate at Iowa where he was the first black person in the country to be awarded the doctorate in music. Fuller guided the Lincoln University music program to accreditation from the National Association of Schools of Music. Under his direction, the music faculty grew from 3 to 10 members in seven years. The number of majors grew from 9 to 115 in the 32 years he taught before his retirement in 1974.

# *Six*

# The Schools of Law and Journalism

The Lincoln University School of Law resulted from a discrimination lawsuit, which questioned the lack of legal training for African Americans in Missouri. The state did not allow blacks to attend its state-supported law school. Instead, Missouri paid tuition stipends for residents of color to attend out-of-state schools, although African American lawyers were allowed to practice law in Missouri once they graduated and passed the state bar examination. Lloyd L. Gaines, a Mississippi native who grew up in St. Louis and was an honors graduate of Lincoln University with a bachelor's degree in history, applied in 1936 for admission to the School of Law at the University of Missouri. Denied admission to that law school because of his race, Gaines filed suit in the state courts and finally the United States Supreme Court. The latter court ruled 6–2 in December 1938 in Gaines's favor and ordered the University of Missouri to either admit Lloyd Gaines or provide another suitable alternative. As a consequence, the state legislature created the Lincoln University School of Law, which operated out of the old Poro Beauty College building in St. Louis. The law school opened in September 1939 with 31 students enrolled. Unfortunately Lloyd Gaines mysteriously disappeared in 1939 and never attended the institution. However, once established, the school became a member of the American Association of Law Libraries in December 1939, was approved by the Missouri Board of Law Examiners in February 1940 and by the American Bar Association in October 1942, and was elected to membership in the Association of American Law Schools in December 1941. This is the highest rating a law school can attain. Few law schools presented such a progressive record of accreditation in such a short period of operation. By 1954, the total number of law students enrolled in the Lincoln University School of Law program was 12, which was 6 less than the 18 students in the previous year. Therefore, the expense of maintaining a law school for so few students was a drain on the meager resources of the university.

The Lincoln University School of Journalism was created because an African American journalist named Lucile Bluford sought to attend graduate school at the prestigious University of Missouri School of Journalism but was denied admission in 1939. Rather than forcing the admission of Bluford, who had earned an undergraduate degree in journalism with honors in 1932 from the University of Kansas in Lawrence, the Missouri General Assembly moved to create a separate journalism school at Lincoln University. The school opened in 1942 under the leadership of Dr. Armistead S. Pride, who had a master of science degree in journalism and a doctorate in the field from Northwestern University. The Lincoln University School of Journalism for many years was the only journalism school for black students in the country. When the Supreme Court ordered school desegregation, the school was downsized to a department in the Lincoln University College of Arts and Sciences for efficiency in administration and better utilization of the arts program. Additionally the number of enrolled students in the School of Journalism had dwindled to only six majors in 1954. This was not enough students to allow it to keep its designation as a stand-alone school of the university.

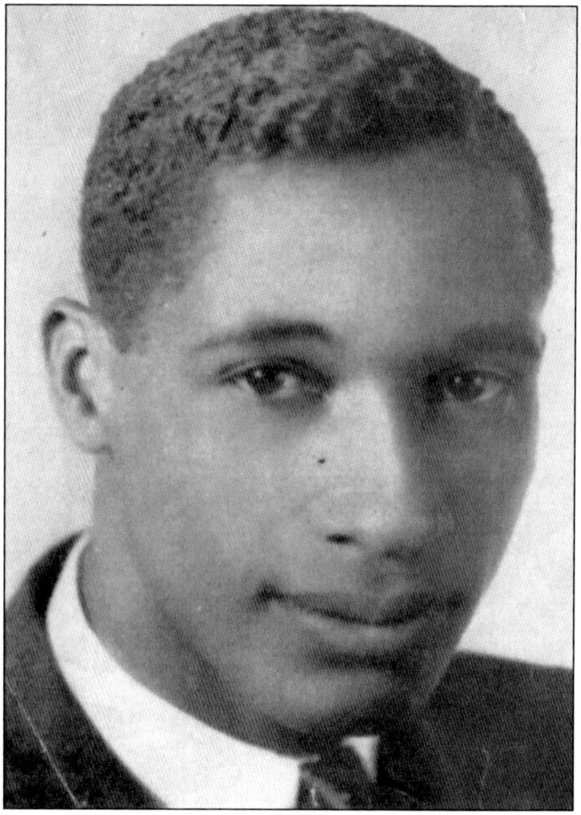

Lloyd L. Gaines was the key figure in one of the most important court cases in the civil rights movement. A Mississippi native who grew up in St. Louis, Gaines graduated with honors from Lincoln University. He then applied to the University of Missouri–Columbia School of Law. Sy Woodson Canada was the registrar who denied Gaines admission solely because of his skin color. Gaines sued in the now famous *Gaines v. Canada* case of 1938. The Supreme Court ruled that the university must either admit Gaines or the state should establish a separate law school for blacks. Gaines never entered the University of Missouri–Columbia School of Law or the segregated one set up by the State of Missouri, which passed a bill providing $275,000 for Lincoln University to establish a law school. Gaines was discouraged by the state's response to the court ruling and moved north and earned a master's degree in economics from the University of Michigan before mysteriously disappearing in 1939.

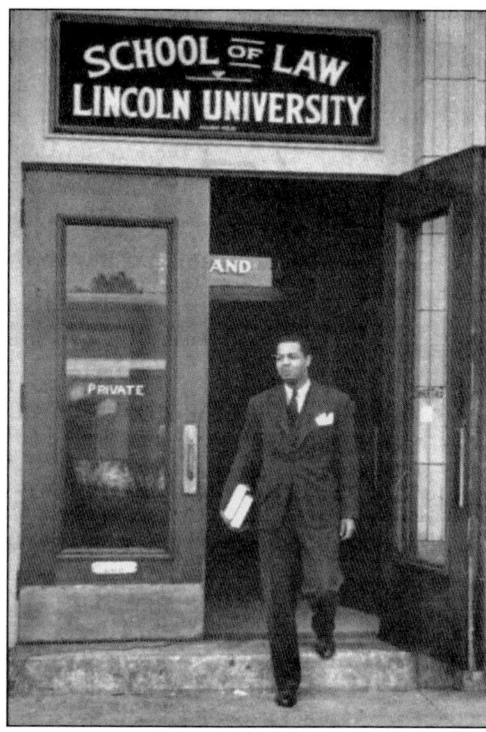


The Lincoln University School of Law was located in St. Louis rather than on the Jefferson City campus because university officials believed that student enrollment would be better in an urban-centered program. Additionally the university felt that the St. Louis location offered students opportunities to meet with practicing lawyers and proximity to two white university law schools, whose faculty might be available as part-time lecturers. The first dean of the law school was W. D. Taylor, formerly acting dean of the Howard University Law School. Pictured leaving the school is freshman Julian Rogers of Detroit, Michigan.

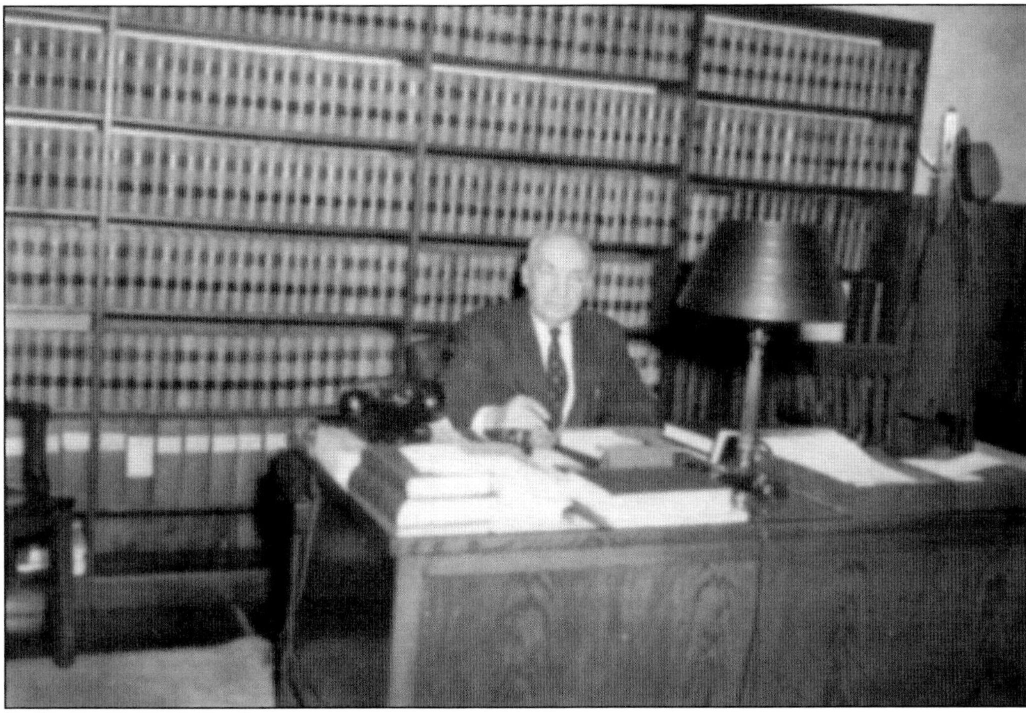

Attorney Daniel W. Bowles served as acting dean of the Lincoln University School of Law in 1954–1955.

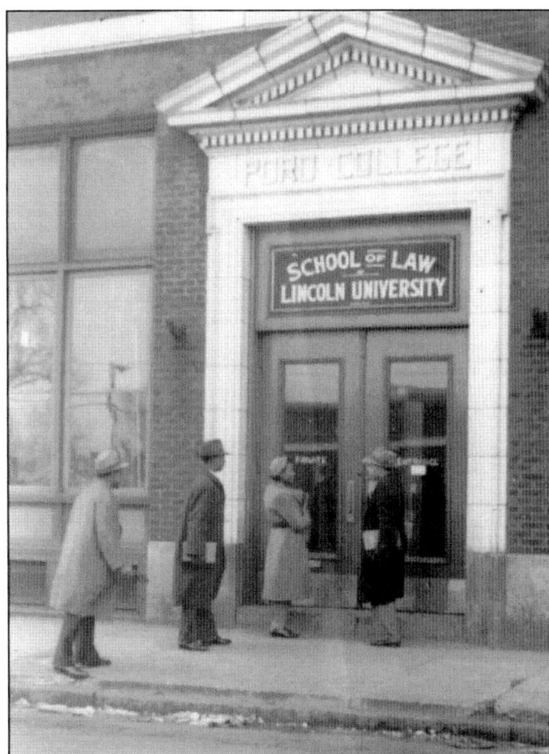


Students linger at the entrance of the Lincoln University School of Law located in the Poro Beauty College building. The law school was established in 1939 and closed in June 1955 after the law passed to integrate schools in Missouri.

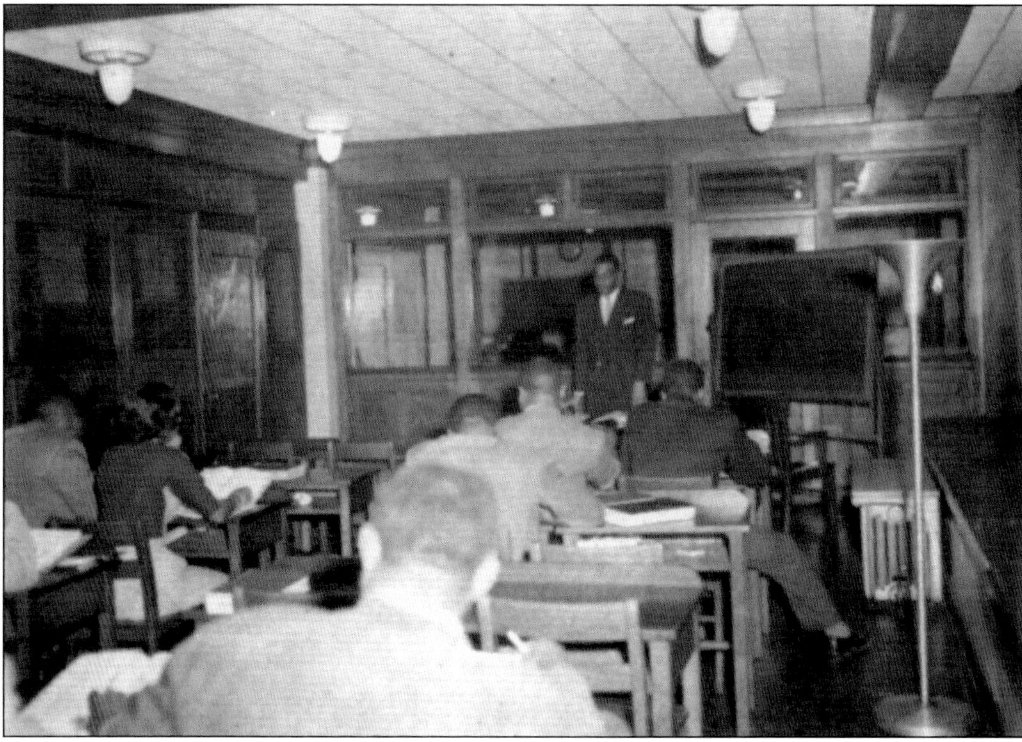

Law students in a class at the Lincoln University School of Law are pictured here.

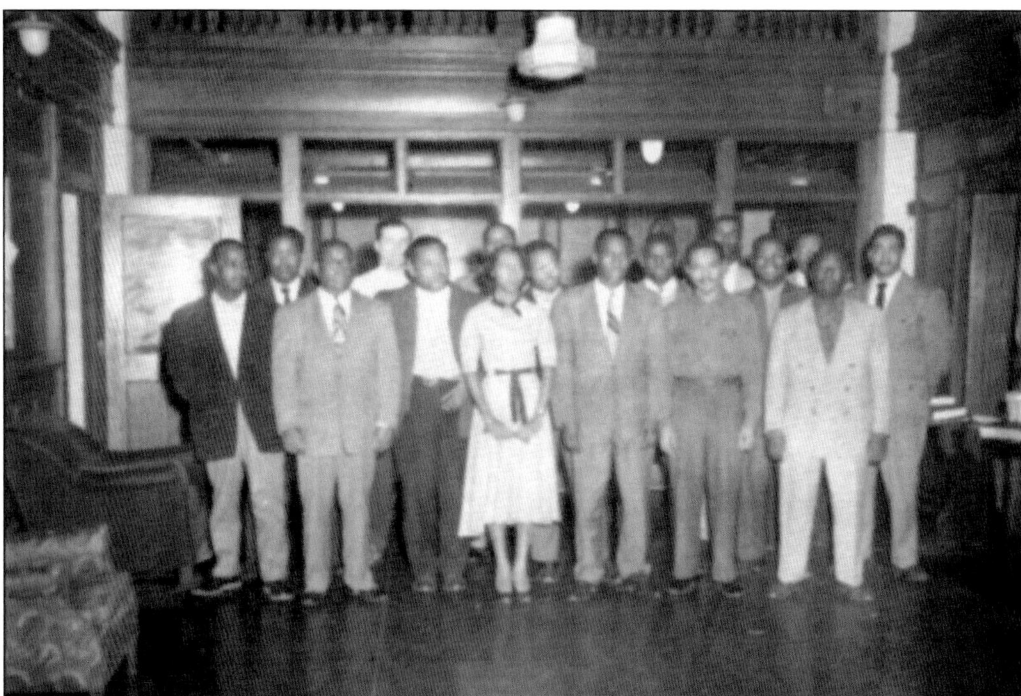

Law students pose for a picture.

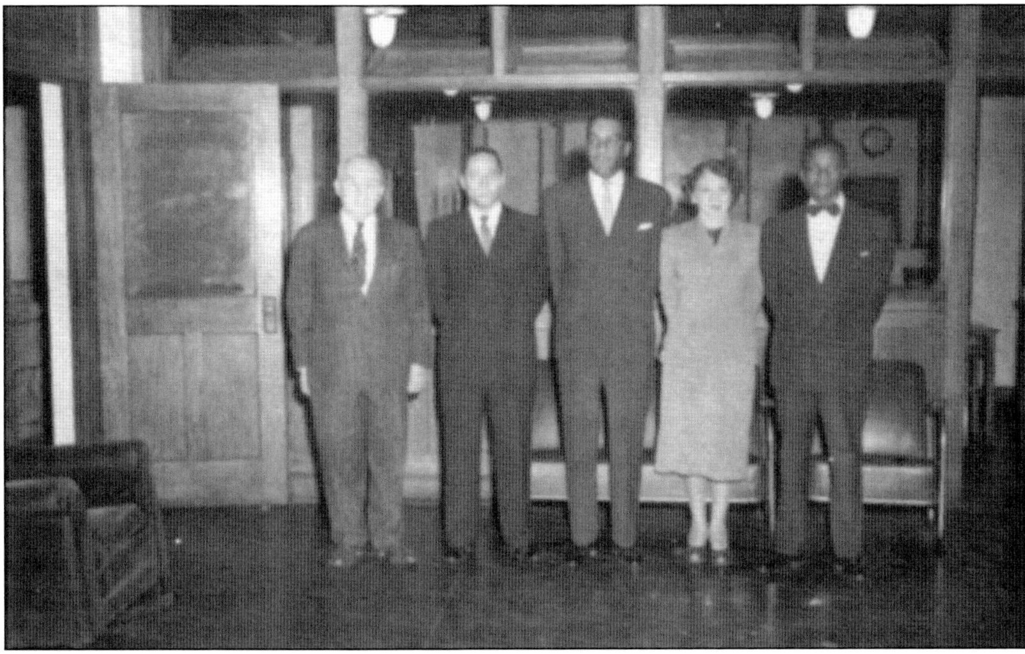

A group of law school faculty poses for a picture. The person in the photograph on the far right is attorney Joseph S. McDuffie, who received both his undergraduate and law degrees from Lincoln University and practiced law in St. Louis. When not employed by the university, McDuffie served two separate terms on the Lincoln University Board of Curators.

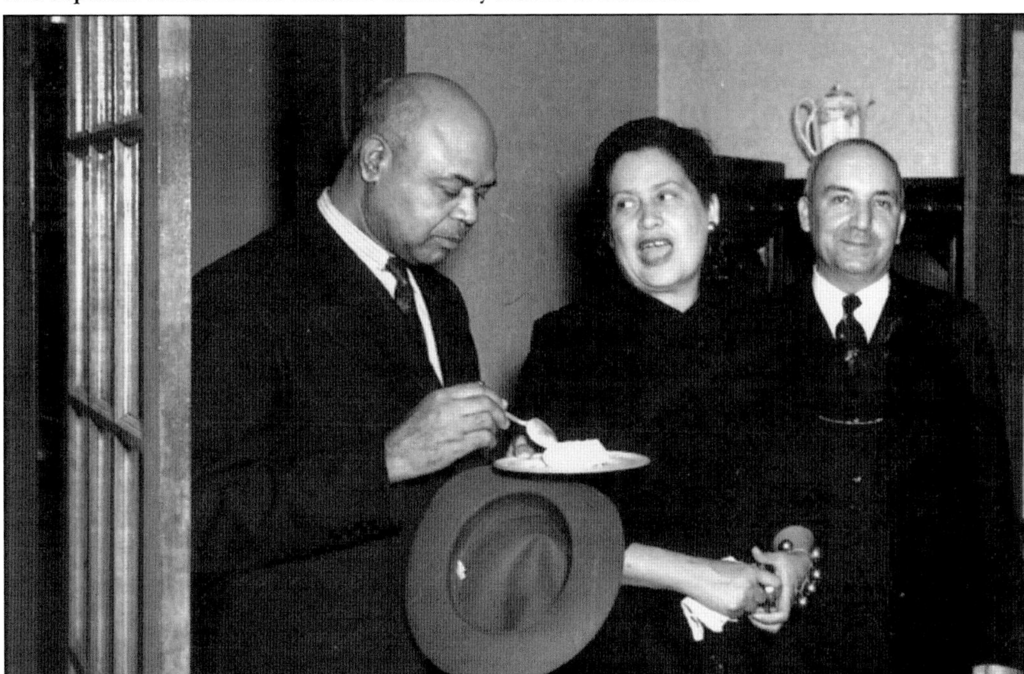

Pictured here are attorney Daniel W. Bowles and his wife with an unidentified man (holding his hat). Bowles was as associate professor of law and acting dean in 1940–1941.

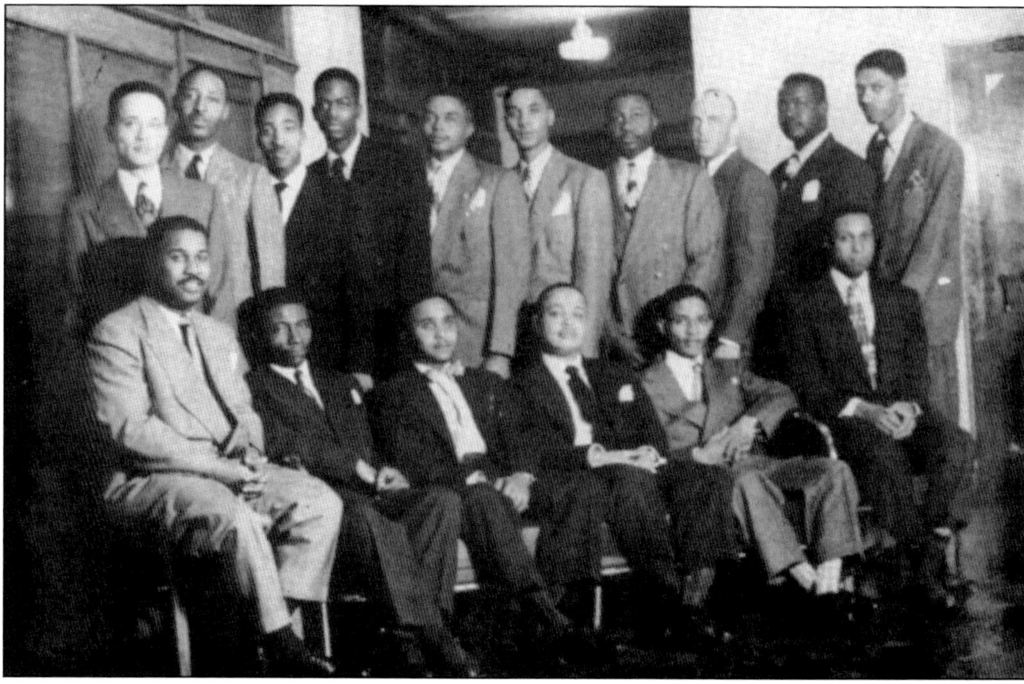

Among the senior students in the 1949 law school class are Benjamin F. Jones, Haywood E. Banks, Roscoe B. Turner, Charles J. Lunderman, Gerald D. Hackett, Henry L. Pearson, Charles E. Coleman, Almer T. Adair, William A. Fordham, Alvin G. Castile, Vernon T. Williams, and Israel M. Augustine.

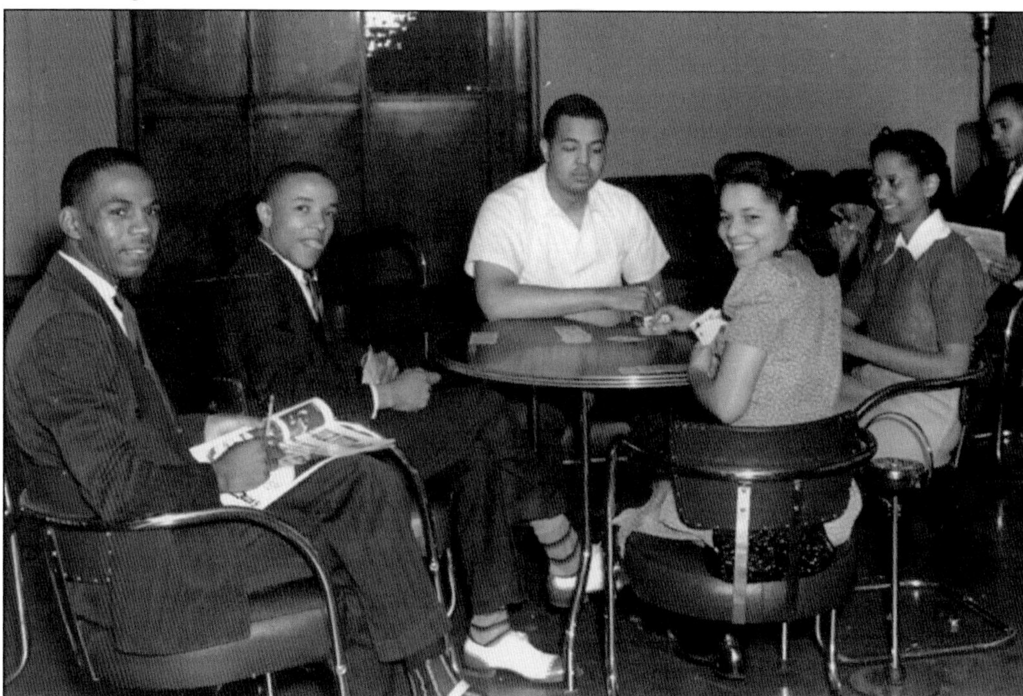

Law school seniors are shown in this 1949 photograph.

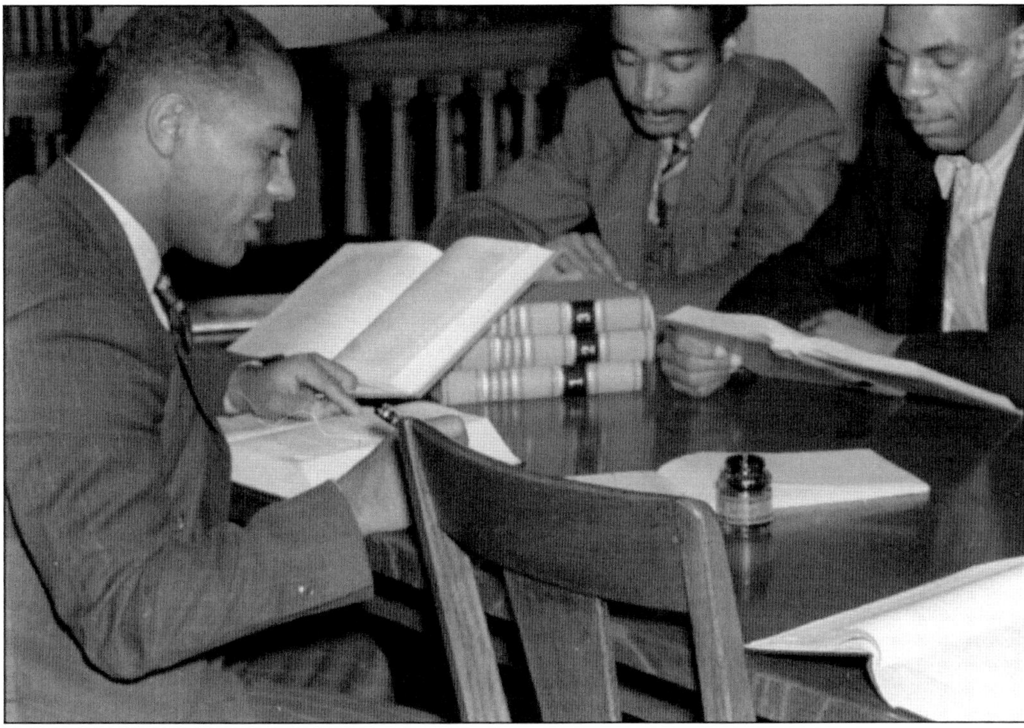

Three students are shown studying in the law library. Even though there was a large volume of books in the library, the NAACP took the position that the segregated law school was not equal to the University of Missouri School of Law program. A suit by the organization to support its claim that the school was not "equal under the law" was thrown out of court because the plaintiff Lloyd L. Gaines could not be found.

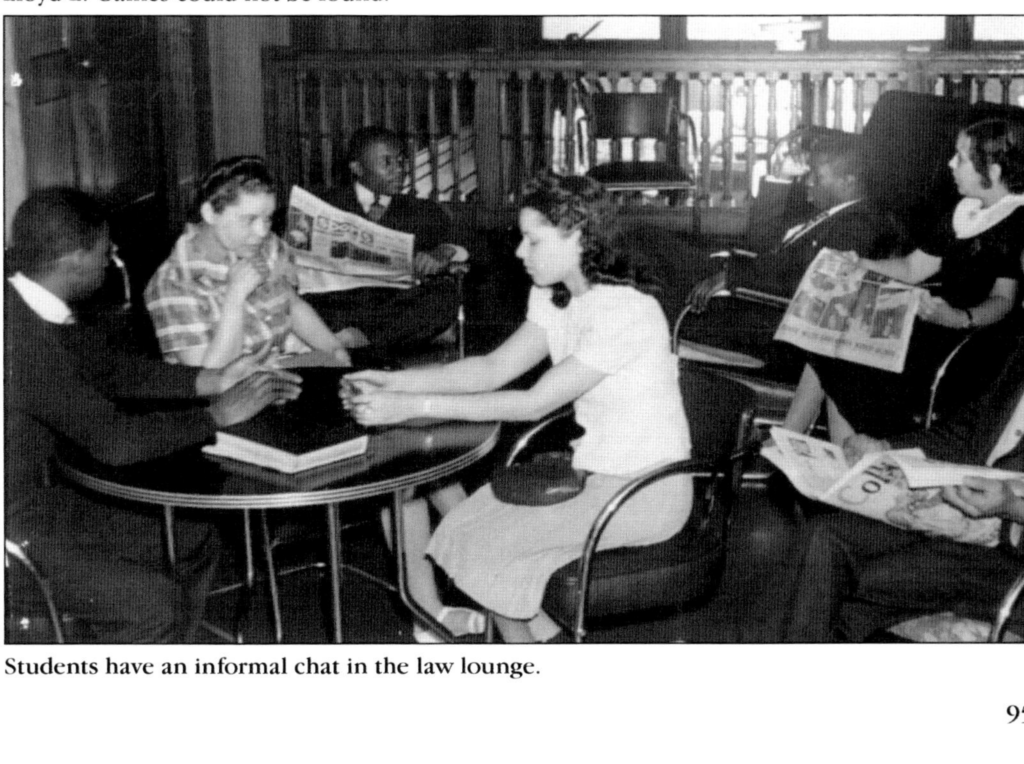

Students have an informal chat in the law lounge.

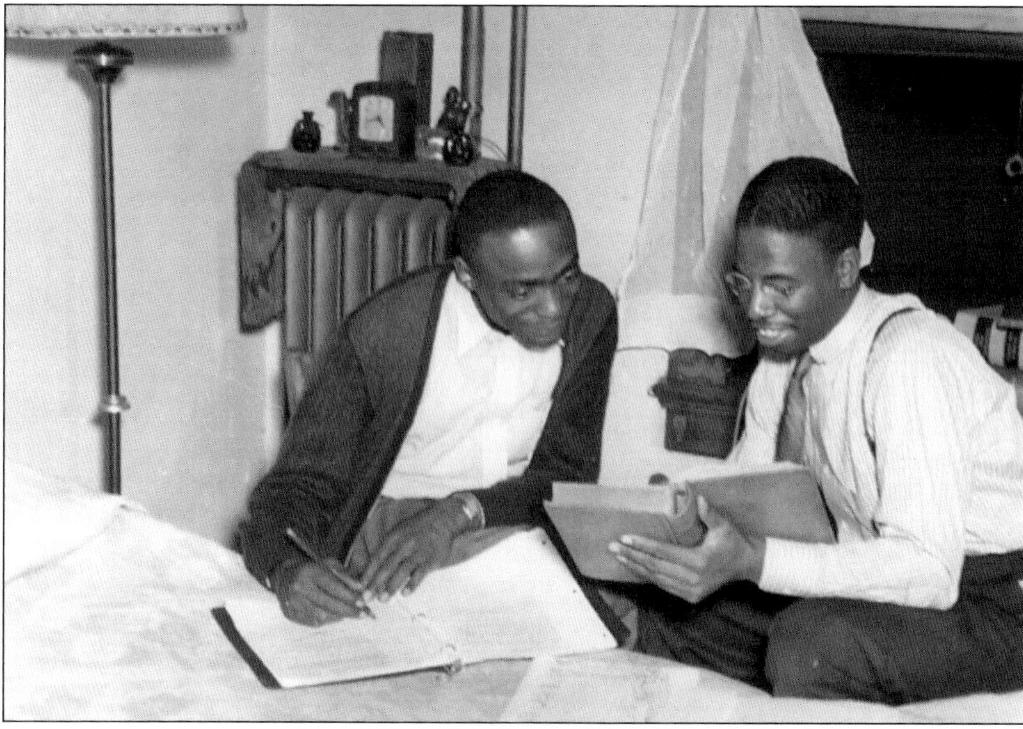

Two law school students study in their living quarters.

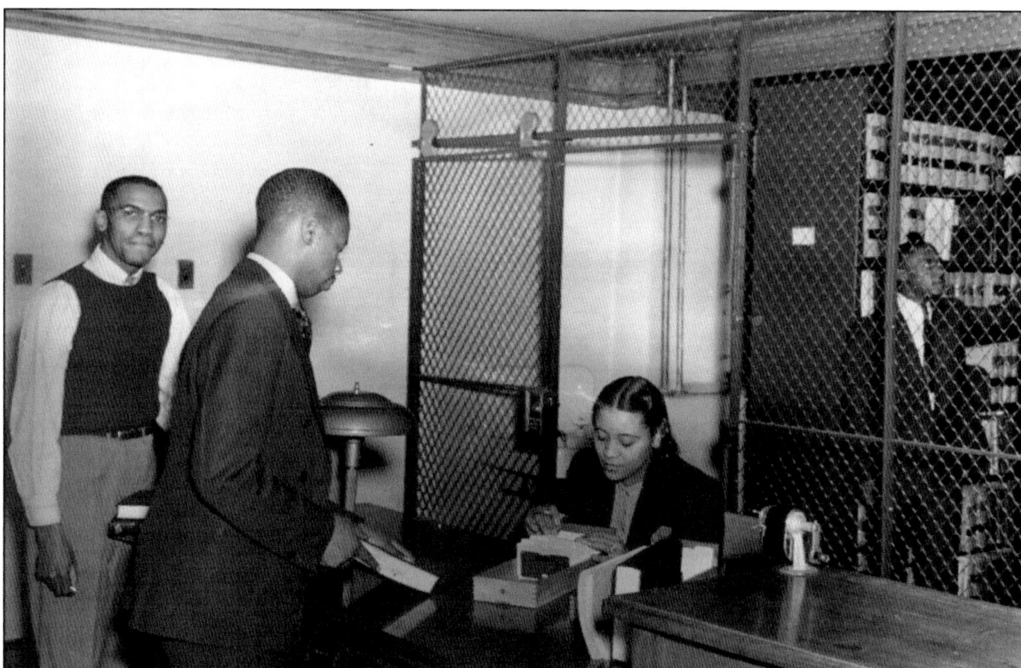

The law school opened with 10,000 volumes, which was sufficient for the school to become accredited by the American Bar Association. These law students in the class of 1940–1941 are waiting to check out books.

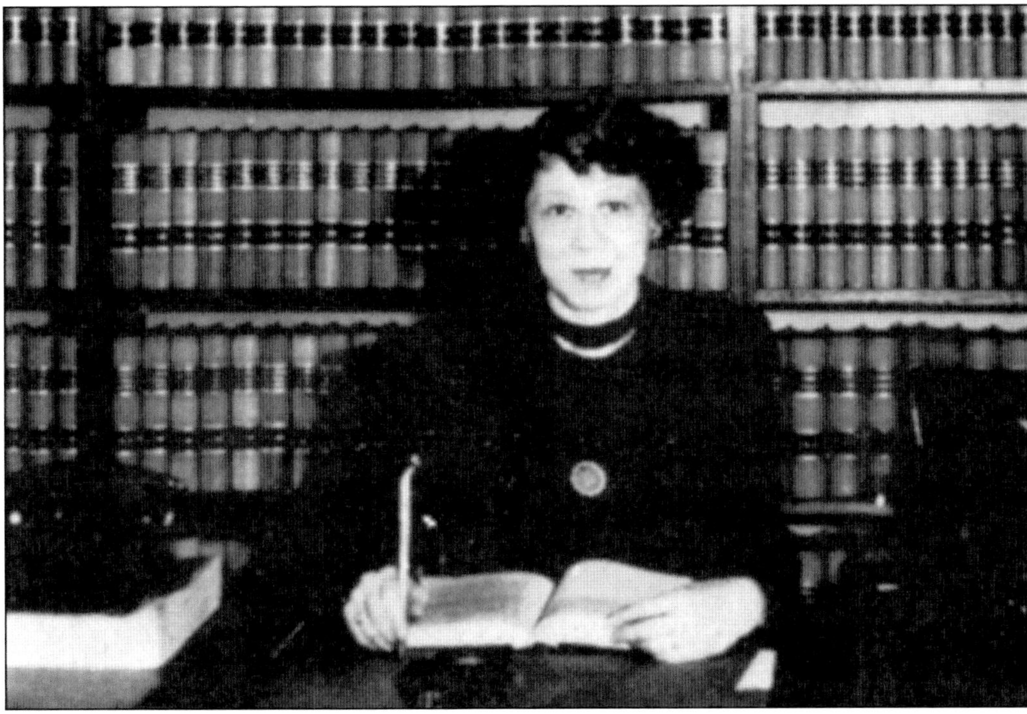

Lula M. Howard was a librarian and assistant professor.

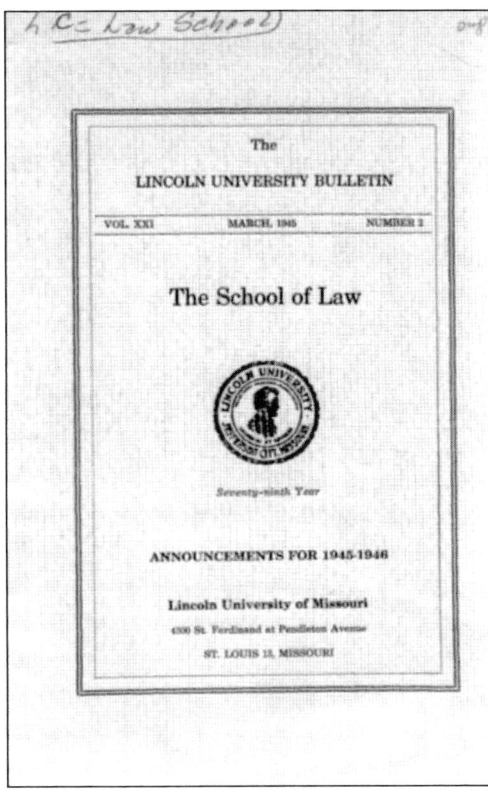

The

LINCOLN UNIVERSITY BULLETIN

VOL. XXI | MARCH, 1945 | NUMBER 2

The School of Law

Seventy-ninth Year

ANNOUNCEMENTS FOR 1945-1946

Lincoln University of Missouri

4300 St. Ferdinand at Pendleton Avenue

ST. LOUIS 13, MISSOURI

This is the cover of the 1945–1946 *Lincoln University Bulletin* for the School of Law.

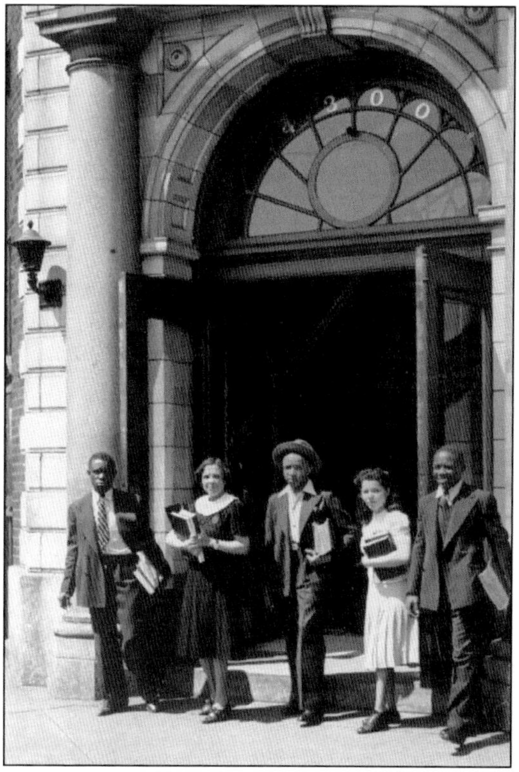

Shown here are five students leaving the law school building. Dorothy Freeman, second from the right, was the first black woman admitted to the Missouri Bar. She accomplished this feat even through she had polio. The person with the hat is Aquinoldo Lemor, who became dean of the law school at historically black Southern University in Louisiana.

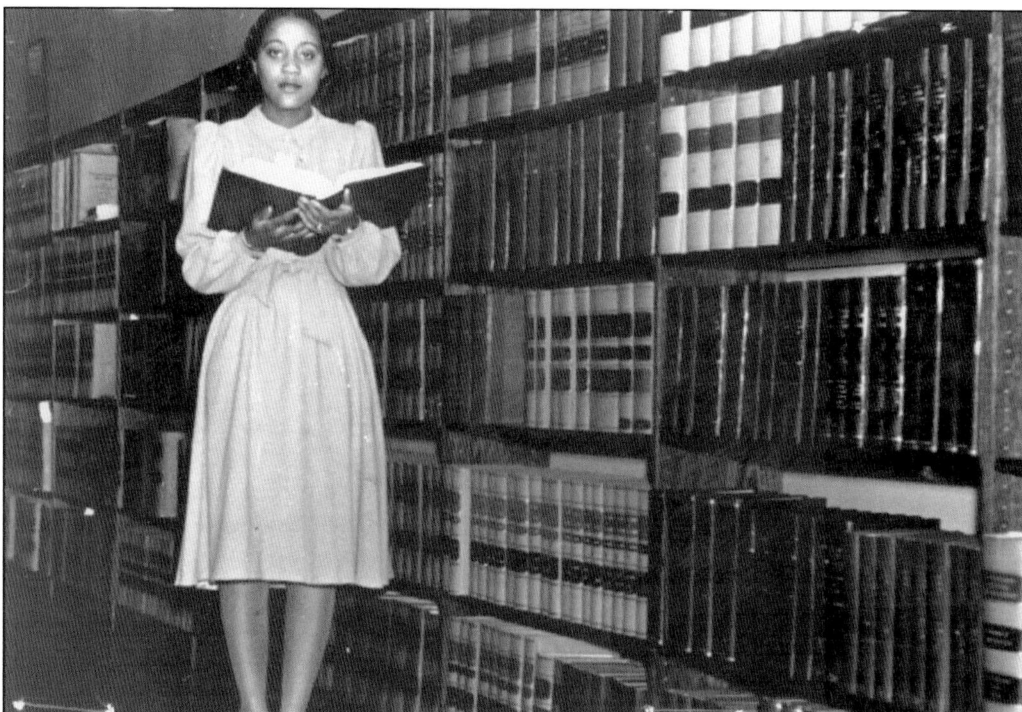

This is a law school student looking at a book in the law library.

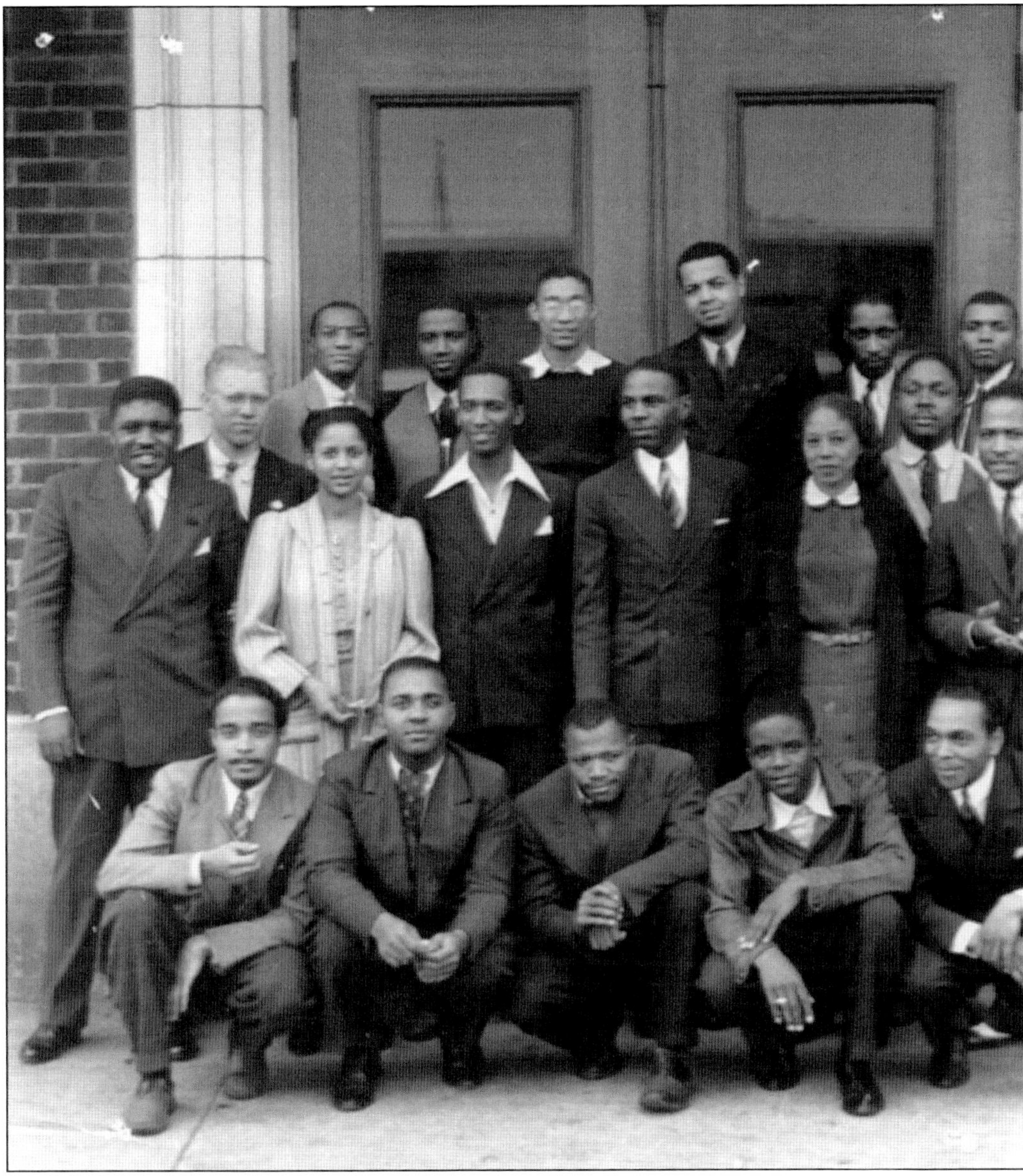

This group of freshman law school students in the class of 1941–1942 has assembled at the front entrance of the school. Many of the Lincoln University law students elected to specialize in civil rights law.

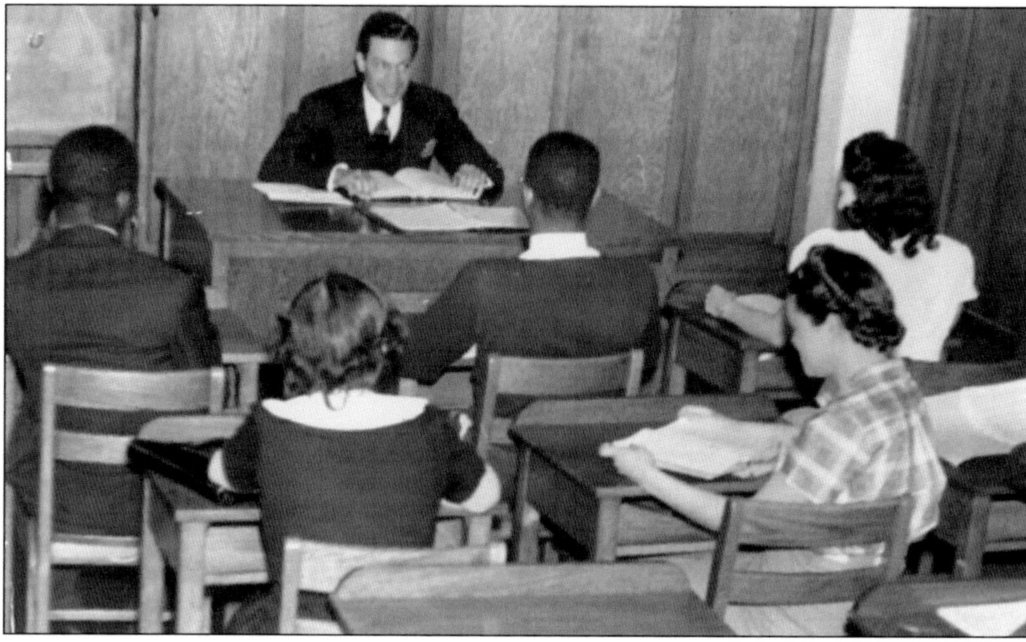

Teaching a law class is attorney Scovel Richardson, associate professor of law. After the school disbanded, Richardson was later appointed by Pres. Dwight D. Eisenhower as a member of the United States Board of Parole and Probation and later received appointment to a judgeship in the United States Customs Court in New York.

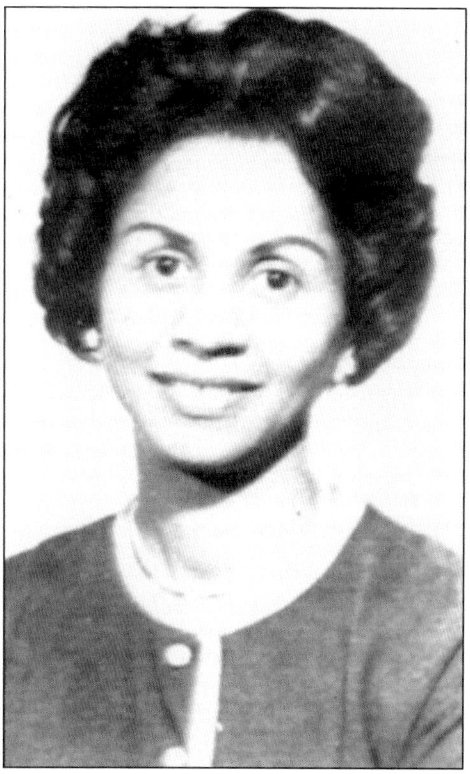

Attorney Margaret Bush Wilson was a member of the second law school class, which had one other woman enrolled at that time. She passed the Missouri Bar and was the second African American woman admitted to practice in Missouri. Wilson's professional experience includes serving as U.S. attorney for the Rural Electrification Administration of the USDA and assistant attorney general of Missouri. In 1975, she became the first black woman to chair the NAACP National Board of Directors, which is a position she held until 1984.

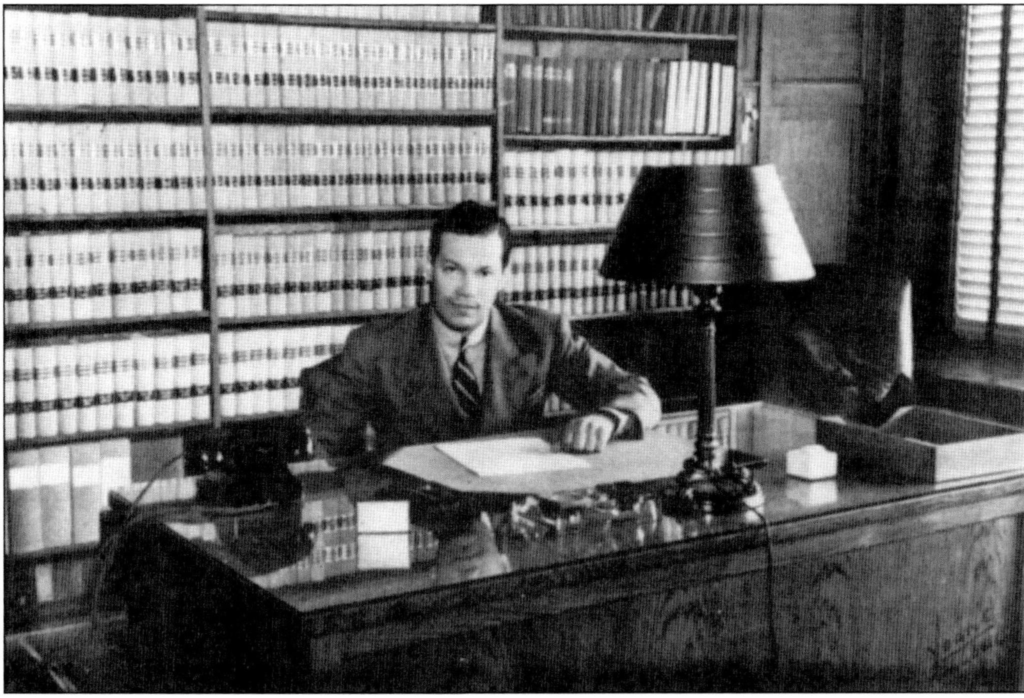

Attorney Scovel Richardson served for a period of time as dean of the Lincoln University School of Law in addition to duties as a faculty member.

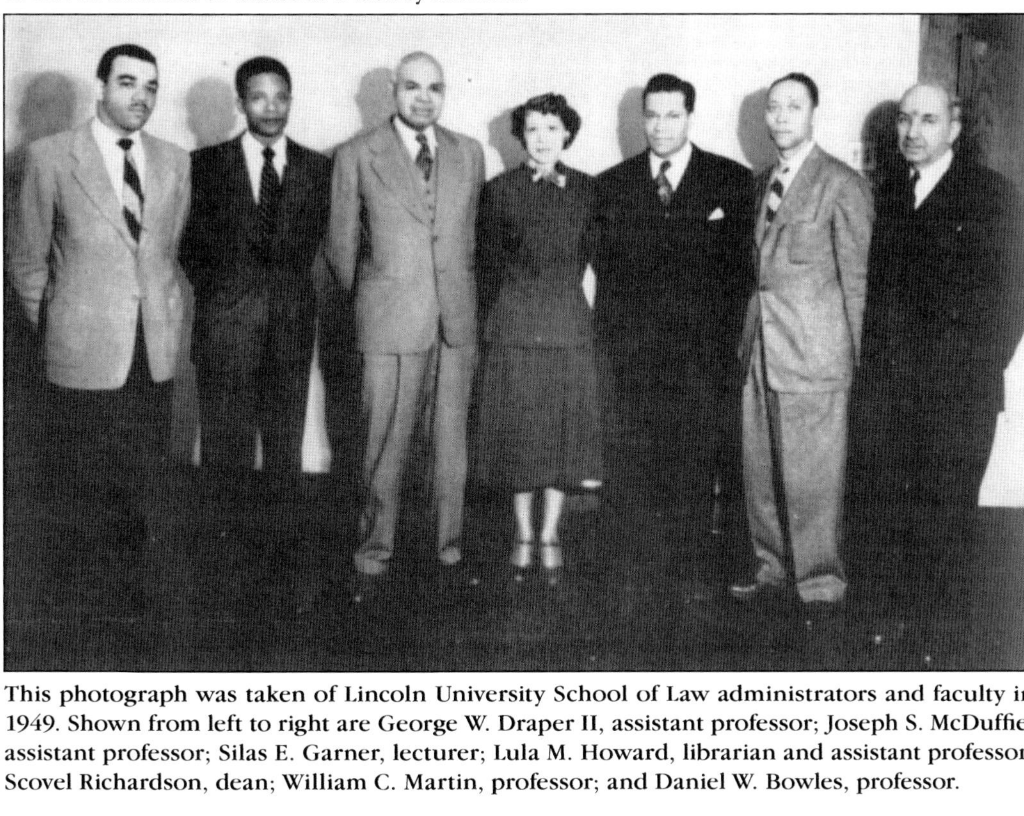

This photograph was taken of Lincoln University School of Law administrators and faculty in 1949. Shown from left to right are George W. Draper II, assistant professor; Joseph S. McDuffie, assistant professor; Silas E. Garner, lecturer; Lula M. Howard, librarian and assistant professor; Scovel Richardson, dean; William C. Martin, professor; and Daniel W. Bowles, professor.

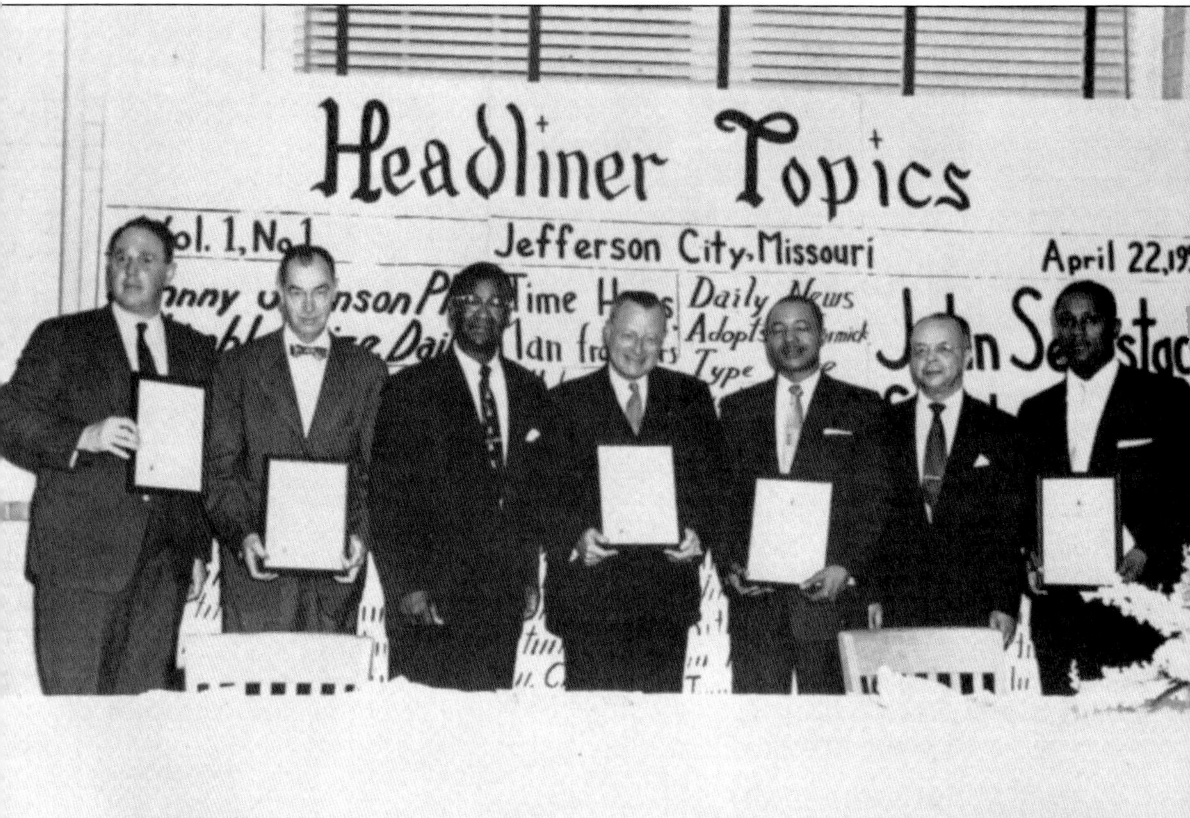


Recipients of awards at the sixth Headliner Week Awards Banquet held in 1954, along with Lincoln University officials, are pictured here. From left to right are Samuel Wells (Midwest manager for *Time* magazine), Dr. James A. Dombrowski (editor, *Southern Patriot*), Dr. Sherman D. Scruggs (president of Lincoln University), John W. Ruettinger (president, City Club of Chicago), banquet toastmaster John H. Sengstacke (publisher, *Chicago Defender*), Dr. Armistead S. Pride (dean, Lincoln University School of Journalism), and John H. Johnson, who received citations of merit for outstanding performance in journalism. The Headliner Awards was a program to recognize significant contributions for better human relations in the print media. Held in April, the event included speakers, workshops, and displays that drew black and white students from as far away as the East Coast. In later years, the program was renamed Unity Awards in Media.

Dr. Armistead S. Pride developed the nationally acclaimed School of Journalism and served as dean of the program. He was a noted journalism scholar who published a considerable number of articles on the black press.

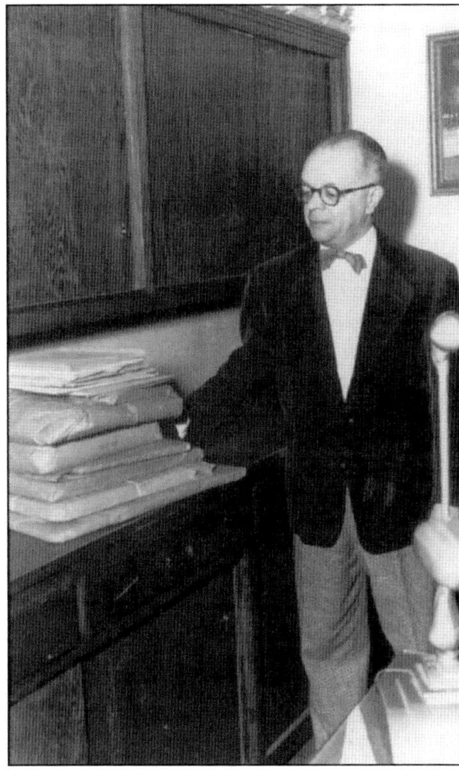

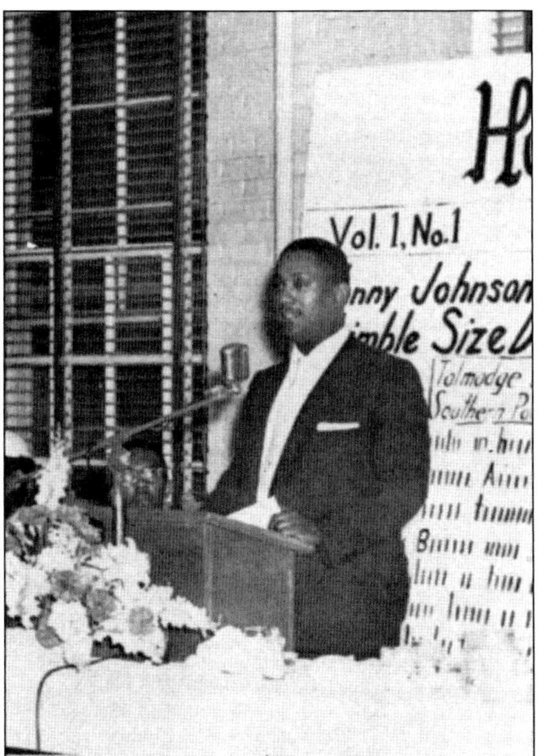


A keynote speaker at a Headliner Awards Program was John H. Johnson, president of Johnson Publishing Company, which publishes *Ebony* and *Jet* magazines.

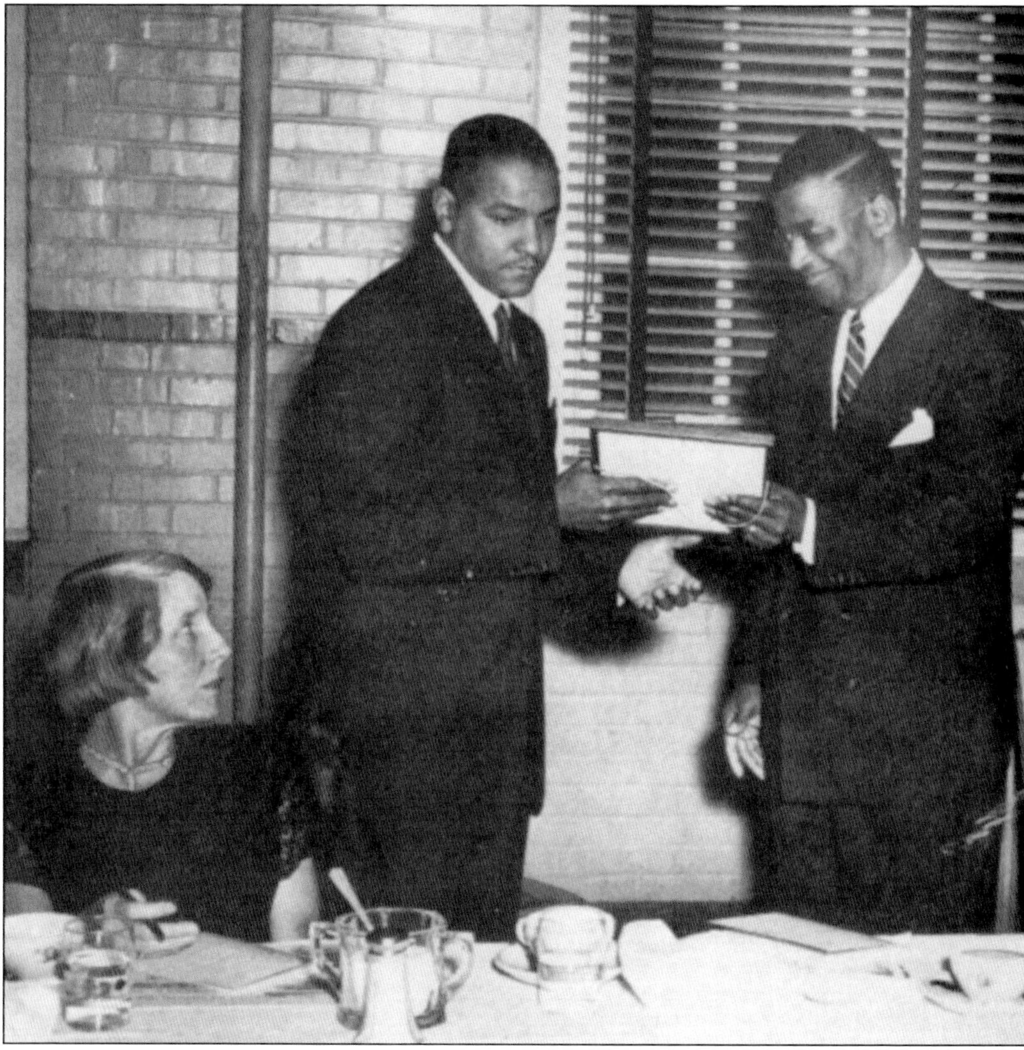

Noted journalist Carl T. Rowan receives a citation from Pres. Sherman D. Scruggs for outstanding contributions in the field of journalism. Looking on is Anne Einselin, associate editor of the *Ladies Home Journal*, who waits her turn to receive the award given that magazine for outstanding contributions in the field of human relations.

*Seven*

# Religion and the Campus

Historically, while Lincoln University is a public-supported institution, religion was a central aspect of campus life. From a nondenominational perspective, during the period proceeding Easter the university regularly held a Religious Emphasis Week observance that included five formal lectures or recitals on religious topics. Moreover, during the administration of Pres. Sherman D. Scruggs, the moral character of the student body was of great importance because the president held a Bible class every Sunday morning in Page Auditorium of Memorial Hall. While not mandatory, the Bible classes were generally well attended. Also, in the 1930s, two very active student organizations were campus chapters of the Young Men's Christian Association (YMCA) and the Young Women's Christian Association (YWCA). As for denominations, the Baptist, Catholic, and Methodist organizations were the most active religious groups between 1920 and 1970. The Methodist Wesley Foundation was the first Protestant religious ministry established at Lincoln University and the first student religious life building erected at the university. In April 1949, during the annual meeting of the North Central Association of Colleges and Secondary Schools, Dr. Earl E. Dawson, then dean of instruction at Lincoln University, and Methodist bishop Matthew W. Clair Jr. discussed the need for a Wesley Foundation to serve the need of Methodist students at Lincoln University. In May 1953, the Central West Conference of the Methodist Church appointed Rev. J. Otis Erwin as campus minister-director of the Wesley Foundation. He remained in that appointment until 1967, serving multiple roles as director of the Wesley Foundation and as a part-time faculty member teaching religion. In 1960, the Methodist Church opened a $30,000 student center just off the east campus for its Wesley Foundation ministry. Also during this period, the Newman Club, the national Catholic student organization active on the campus since 1960, expanded in 1968 into the old Baptist Student Union on Dunklin Street and sponsored forums, movies discussion groups, retreats, and dances. And finally, the Baptist Student Union had an active presence on the campus, and just as the Methodists had erected a student center the Baptists likewise built a campus meeting facility.

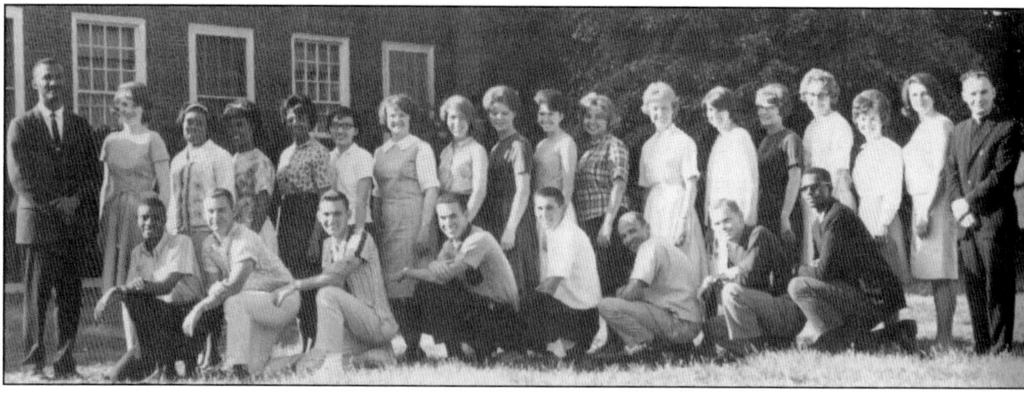

This is a 1965 picture of the Lincoln University Newman Club. Roy M. Collins (extreme left, standing), instructor in mathematics, and the Reverend Thomas Greaney of the Church of the Immaculate Conception flank the members of the campus Newman Club. Collins served as club sponsor, and Greaney was the club chaplain.

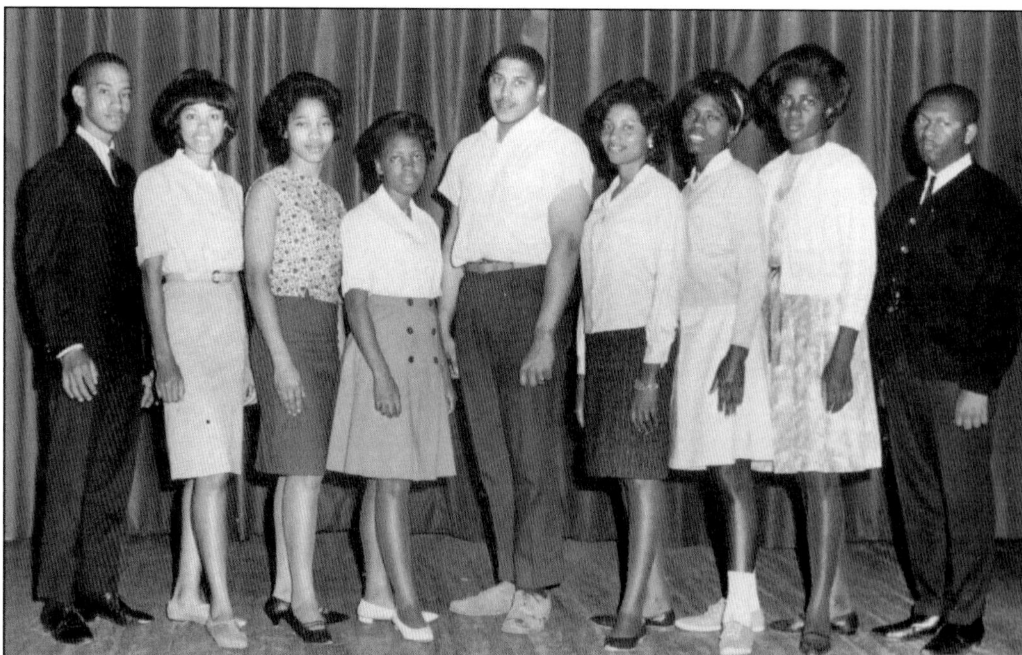

Members of the 1965 Baptist Student Union organization are shown in this picture.

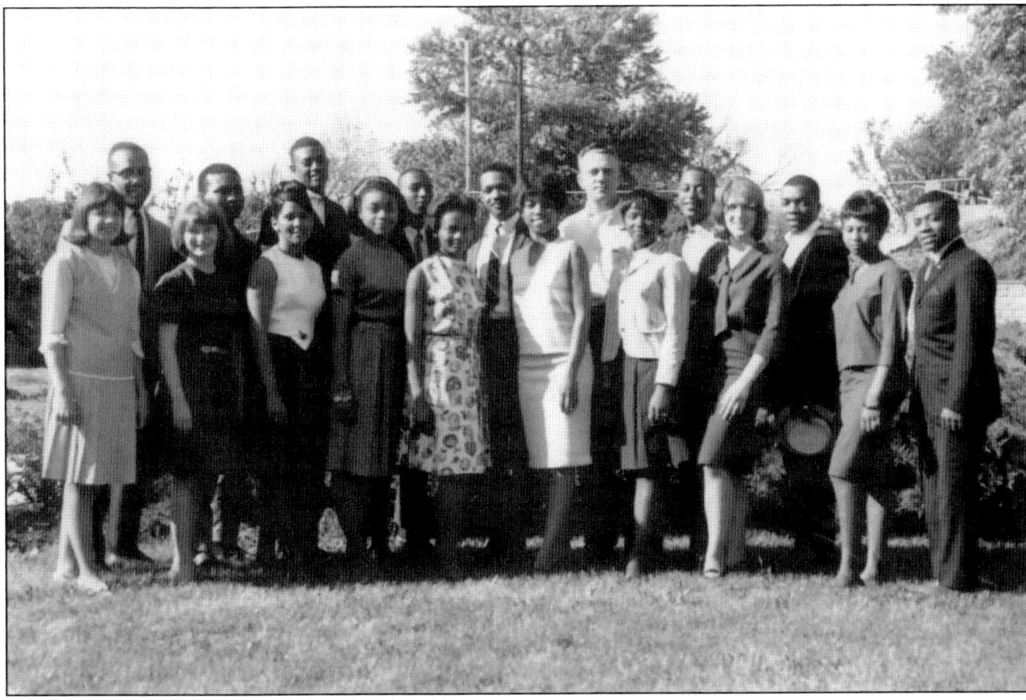

The Newman Club (1963) held religious forums every Monday and a daily rosary every day to aid the students. Besides its daily and weekly activities, the club held a communion breakfast in November.

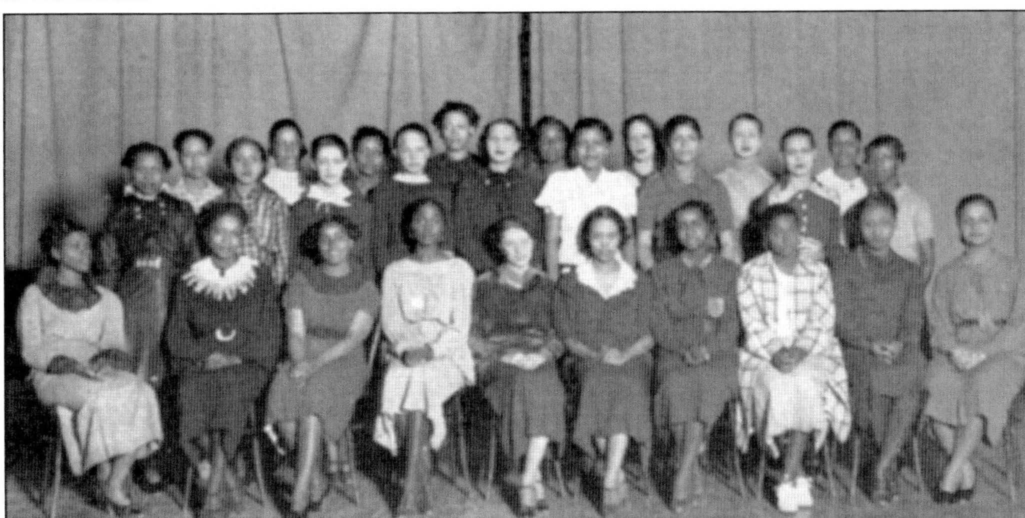

The YWCA offered to the women of Lincoln University an opportunity for practical religious fellowship through discussion groups, opportunities for self-expression, and an opportunity to cultivate her best self through a charm school, helping the person to acquire a broader conception of her classmates. The group in this picture during 1935–1936 sponsored activities including the Freshman Get Together, Halloween Masquerade, hikes, sending delegates to conferences, conducting recognition services, charm schools, and discussions groups. The YWCA also contributed to the Lincoln University Student Loan Fund.

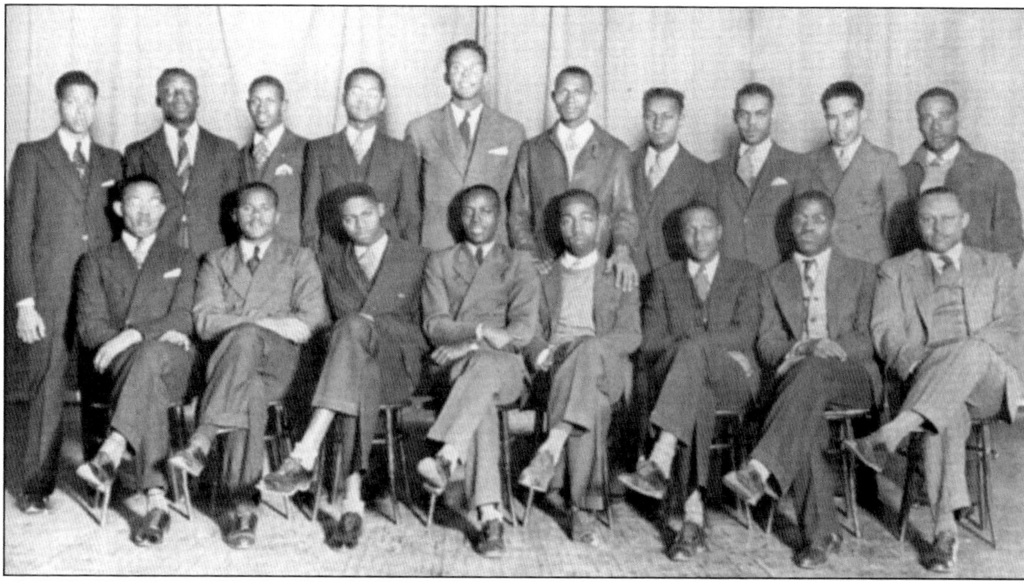

The YMCA existed on the Lincoln University campus as a "fellowship of students, who in seeking the meaning of life, are captivated by Jesus and His understanding of God and man and are committed to comprehending and following its implication in personal and social living." In this photograph, from left to right are (first row) P. Kincaid, F. Clark, A. Lynch, D. Gearin, L. Nicholson, W. Franklin, T. Catlin, and J. McMorries; (second row) K. Moore, L. McField, H. McNeil, H. Moseley, A. Piper, R. Johnson, R. Phillips, A. Chinn, H. Osborne, and H. Belue.

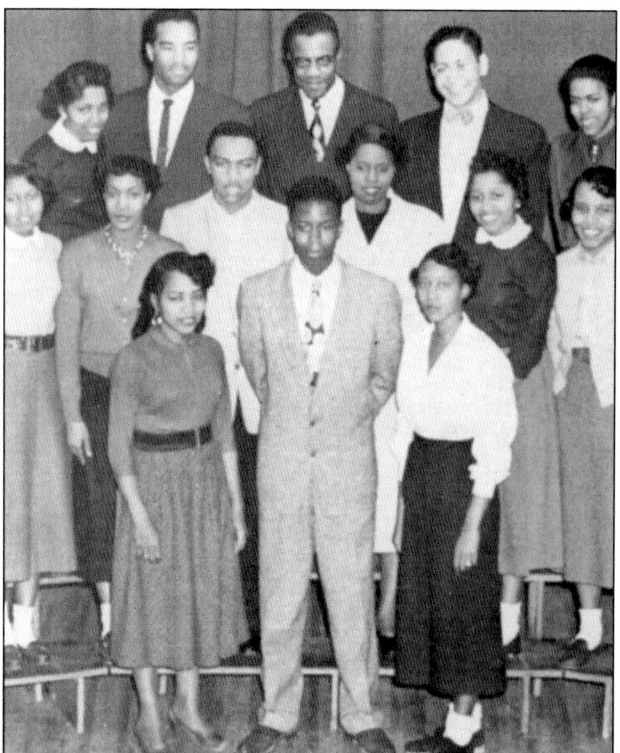

The Bible class was one of the largest campus groups, even through membership was voluntary, attendance at meetings not required, and there was not an elaborate set of criteria for persons desirous of belonging to the organization. The class operated on the simple biblical dictum "whosoever will, let him come." Lincoln University president Dr. Sherman D. Scruggs taught a bible class every first and third Sunday, and each week a campus organization took charge of the Bible class. The university faculty sponsor was Dr. O. Anderson Fuller. Shown in this 1954 photograph, from left to right are (first row) Helen Sandle, Judge King, and Odessa Inner; (second row) Bertha Caldwell, Mary Jackson, Frank Harris, Evelyn Hale, Gwennette Givens, and Lois Moore; (third row) Gwendolyn Givens, Lamar Wilson, Richard Massey (sponsor), James Robnett, and LaVon Woodson.

Rev. J. Otis Erwin served as the minister-director of the Wesley Foundation, which was established at Lincoln University in 1953. Erwin organized the foundation in the fall of 1953, his first year on campus. In addition to his campus ministry duties, Erwin was a part-time instructor in philosophy.

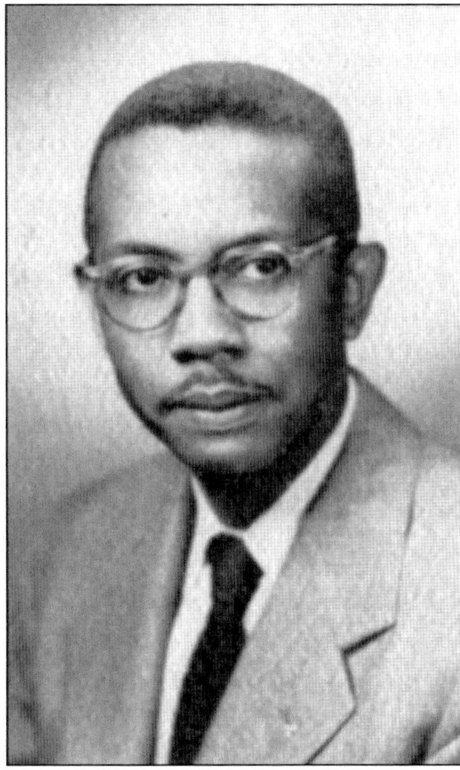

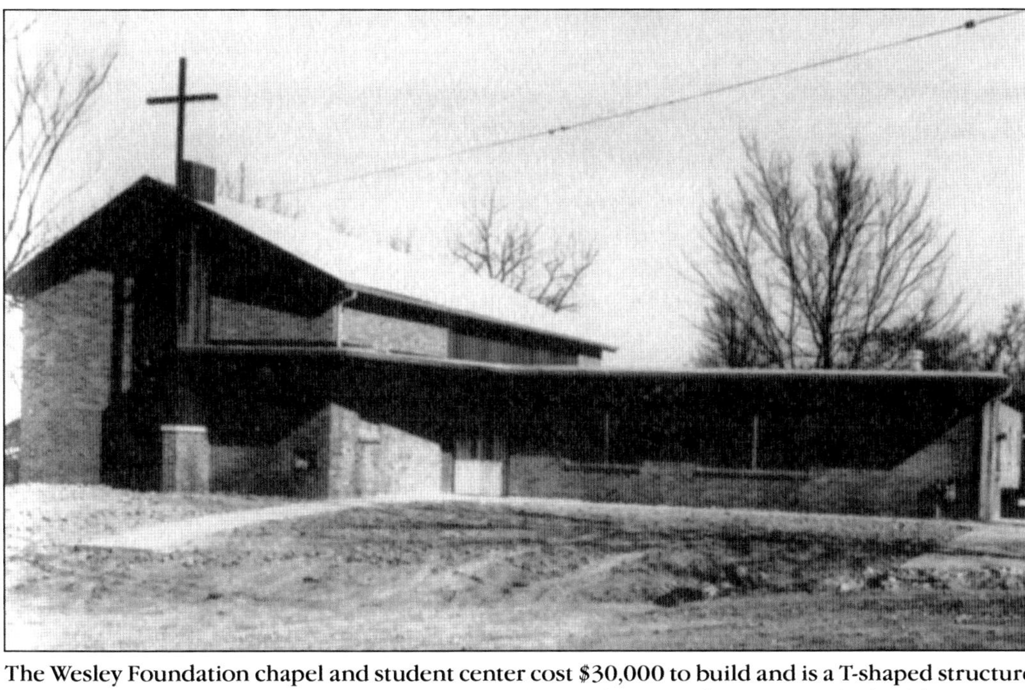

The Wesley Foundation chapel and student center cost $30,000 to build and is a T-shaped structure with a 75-seat chapel and has at the rear a fellowship hall seating 60 persons. The building served as a lounge and social recreation center containing a kitchen, an office, and a student council room above the fellowship hall.

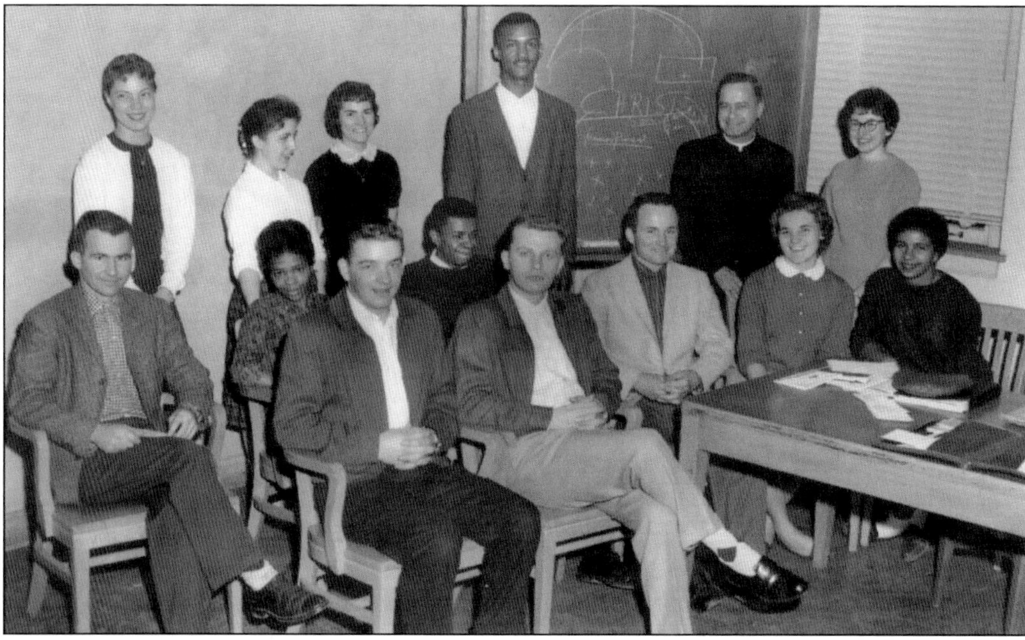

The Newman Club (1960) is shown in this photograph. Members include, from left to right, (first row) Earl Gleeson and Donald Lammers; (second row) Thomas Grassle, Earline Marshall, Kenneth Johnson, John Frassle, Mary Hubo, and Sylvia Soares; (third row) Sandra Bosch, Evelyn Rackers, Verna Tellman, Roy M. Collins, Father Cruikshank, and Betty Plogstead.

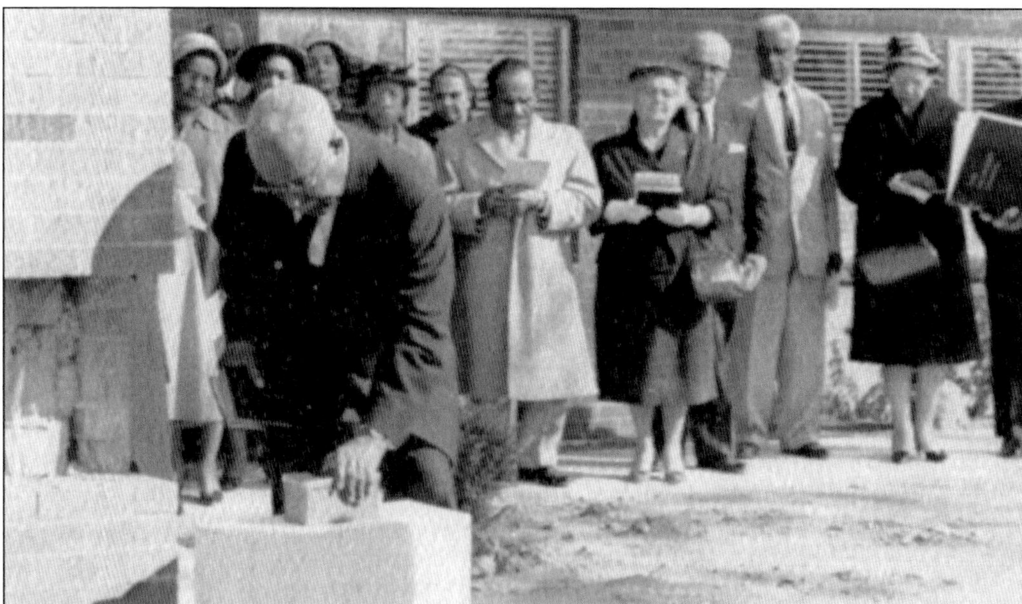

In 1961, the Wesley Foundation Board of Directors, with chairman Bishop Matthew W. Clair Jr., held a cornerstone-laying convocation for the Wesley Foundation and Methodist Chapel, located at 805 Atchison Court. The cross atop the complex was given by Rev. Blain Walker and installed in May 1961.

The Baptist Student Union officials and Pres. Earl E. Dawson are pictured here at a groundbreaking ceremony for their planned campus ministry home.

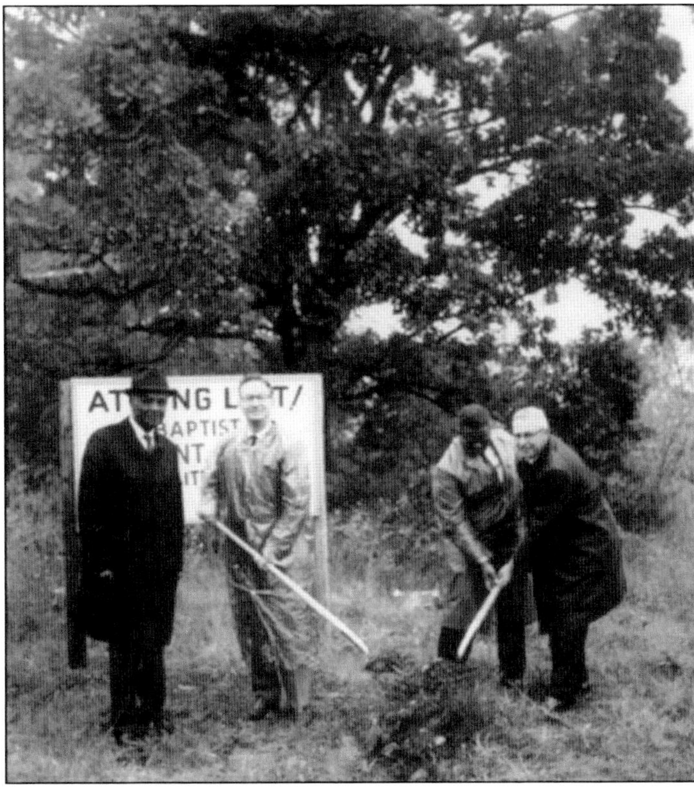

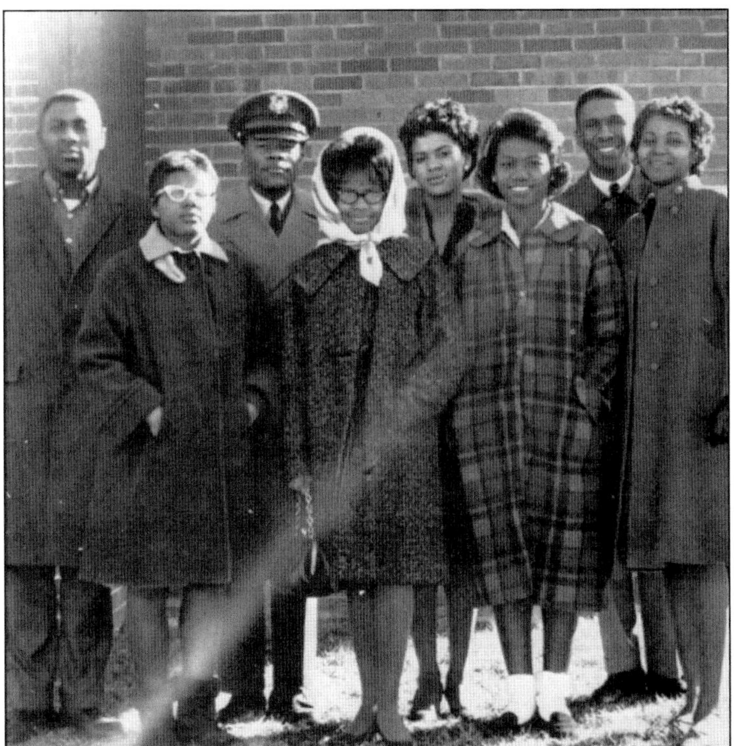

The Wesley Foundation is a Methodist Church organization that exists to meet the spiritual needs of students attending colleges and universities. These needs are met by providing an opportunity for worship through church services, midweek meditations, and private devotions. The Wesley Foundation ministry sponsored a weekly forum on marriage that usually attracted about 50 students.

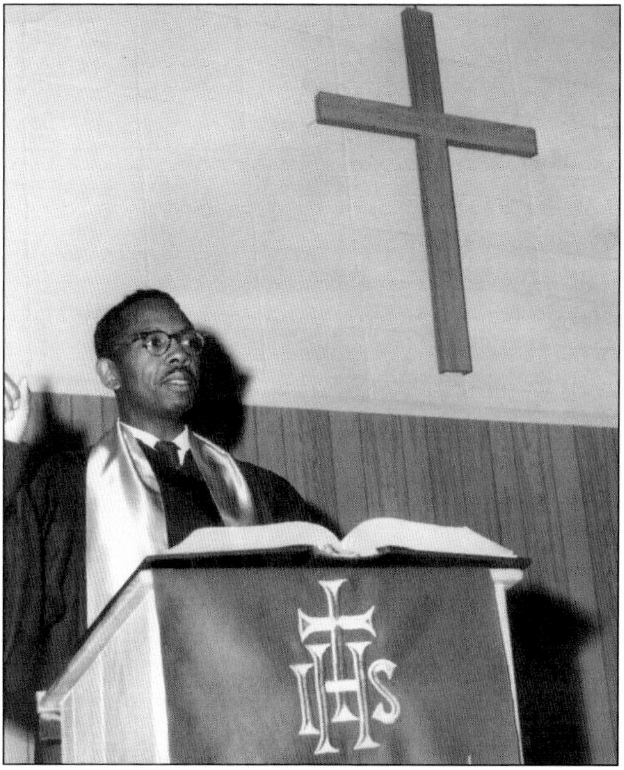

Wesley Foundation minister Rev. J. Otis Erwin is shown at the pulpit delivering a sermon.

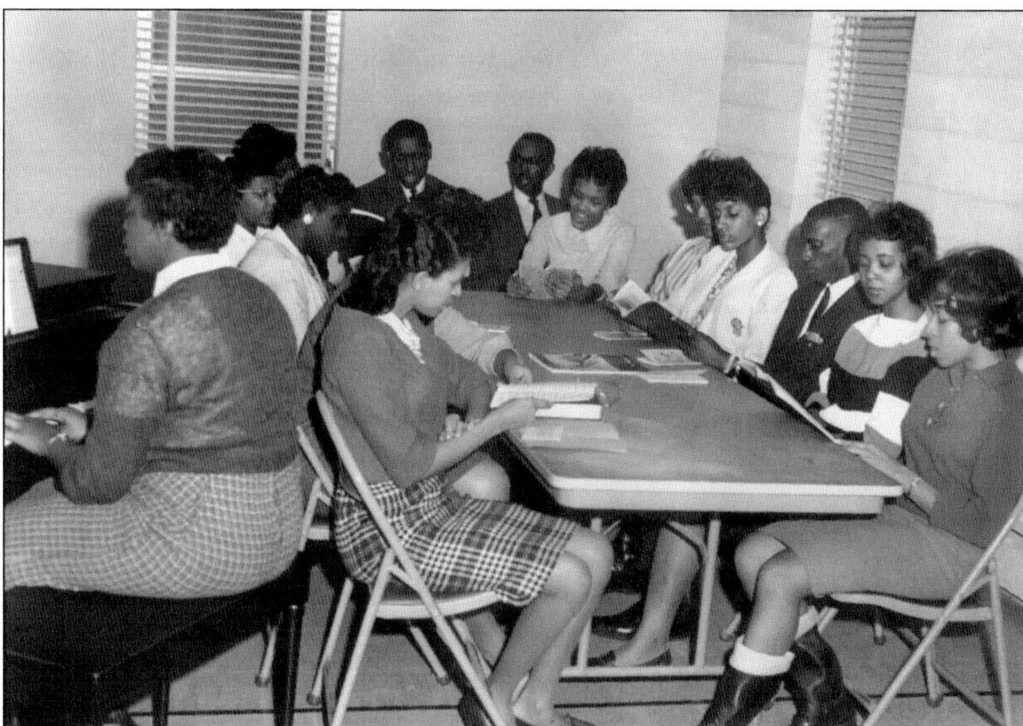

Wesley Foundation members are shown here in Bible study.

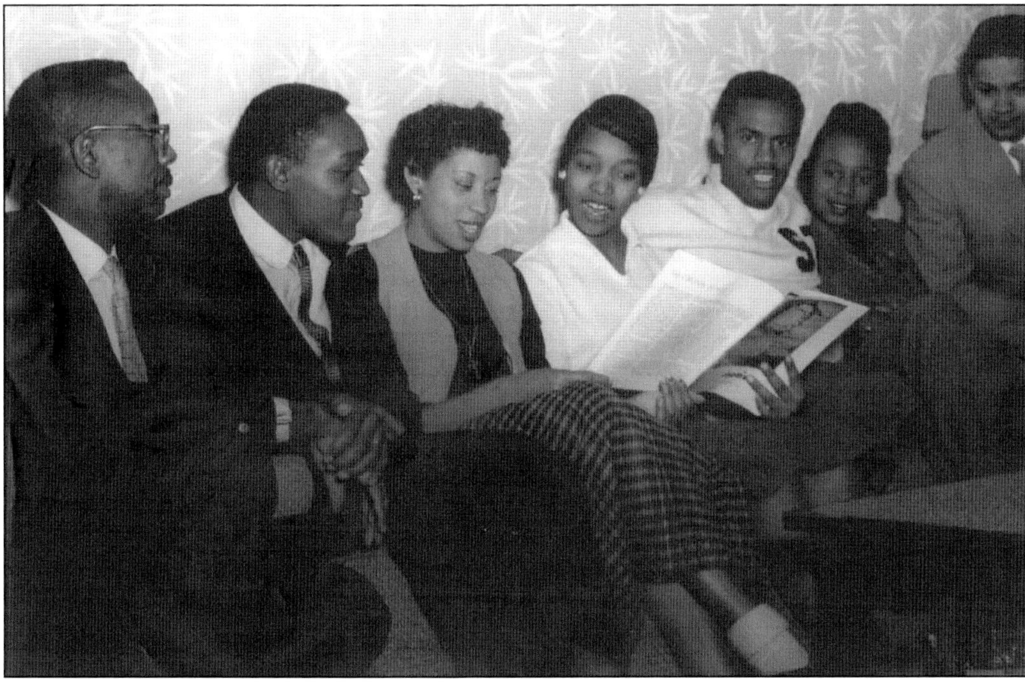

The Wesley Foundation members shown in this 1956 photograph are, from left to right, Rev. J. Otis Erwin (sponsor), James Scott, Rose Wright, Mary Scott, Robert Wright, Delores Graham, and Leland Smith.

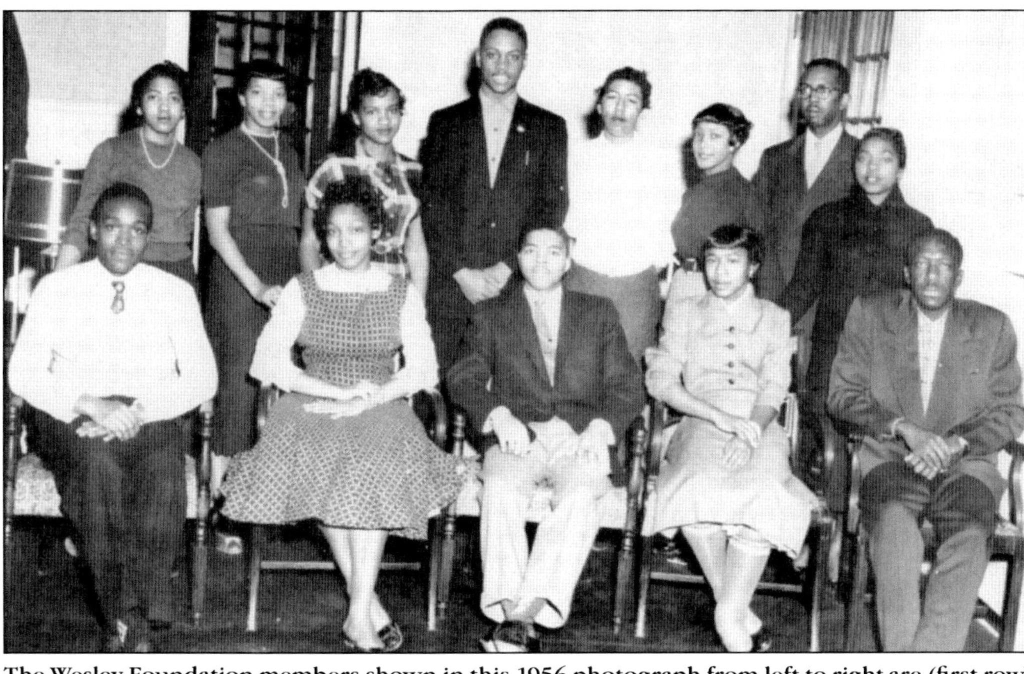

The Wesley Foundation members shown in this 1956 photograph from left to right are (first row) James Scott, Mary Scott, Addison Williams, Ruby Duvall, and John Britton; (second row) Gloria Shanks, Lula Black, Monteel Wilson, Robert Flowers, Beverly Spencer, Thelma Jackson, Rev. J. Otis Erwin (sponsor), and Arnita Graves.

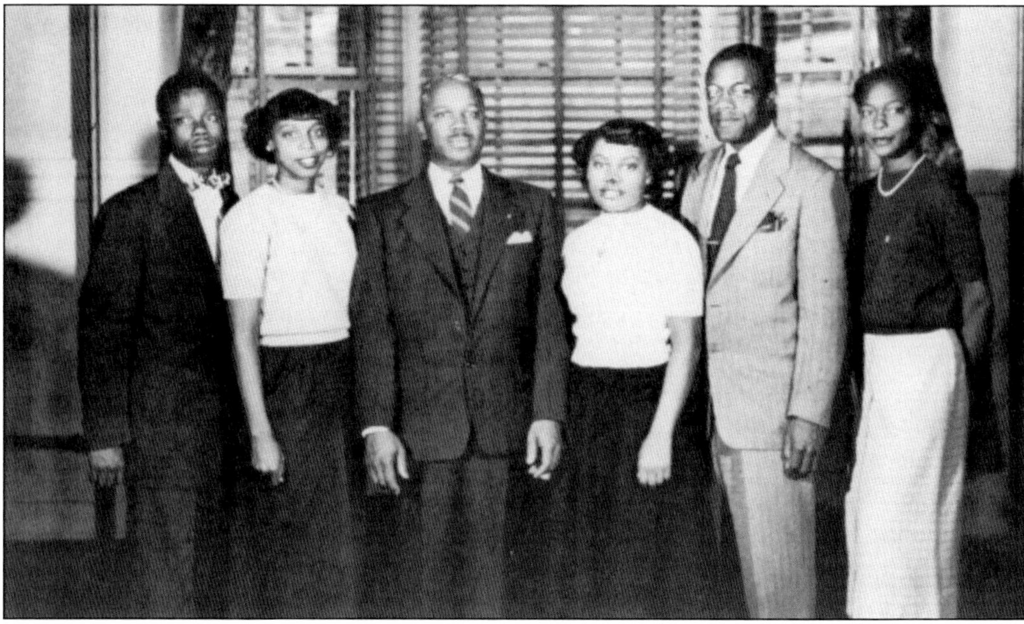

Persons shown in this 1949 Bible class photograph include Richard Massey (president), Lela Shanks (vice president), Dorothy Davis (secretary), Pearlie Ingram (treasurer), Joseph Nash (bookkeeper), and Dr. O. Anderson Fuller (faculty sponsor).

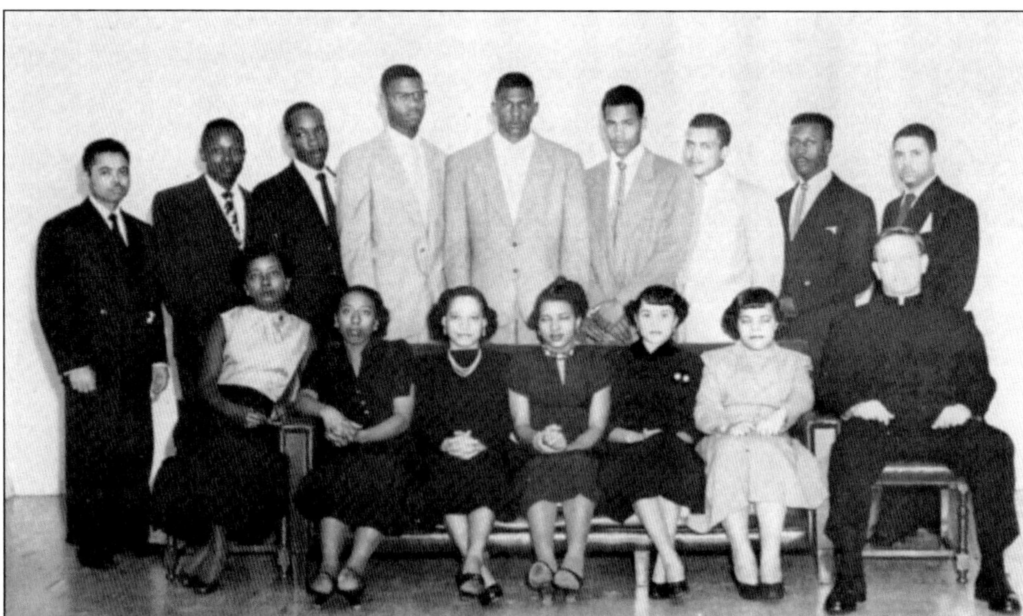

The Newman Center group is shown here in the 1960s.

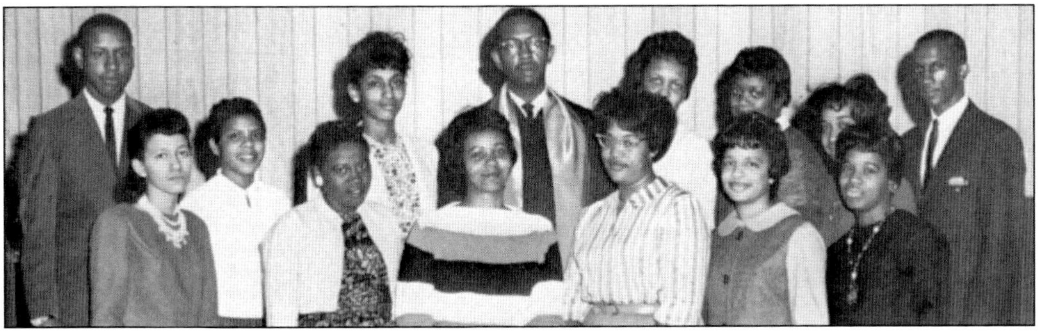

The Wesley Foundation members (1962) shown in this photograph include, from left to right, (first row) Gloria Dismuke, Arlena Casson, Thelma Joyce Blanks, Virginia McNeely, Clara Brown, and Locha Scott; (second row) Archie Price, Margaret Saxton, Jane McIntosh, Rev. J. Otis Erwin, Berrilyn Branch, Nellie Belcher, Jimmye Deffenbaugh, and Bennie E. Rush.

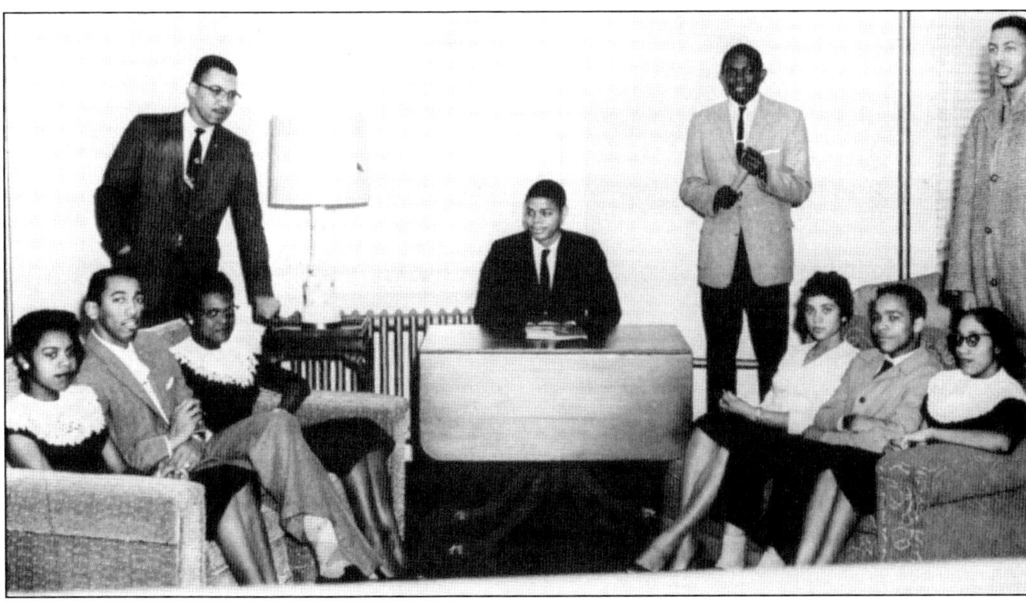

The African Methodist Episcopal (AME) Church had an active Richard Allen Club on the campus in 1958. Members shown in this photograph include, from left to right, (first row) Iola Cheatum, Ray Cox, Bonnie Lain, George L. Williams, Esther Hill, Charles Royston, and Carolyn Diggs; (second row) A. P. Marshall (sponsor), John Hill, and Samuel Hill.

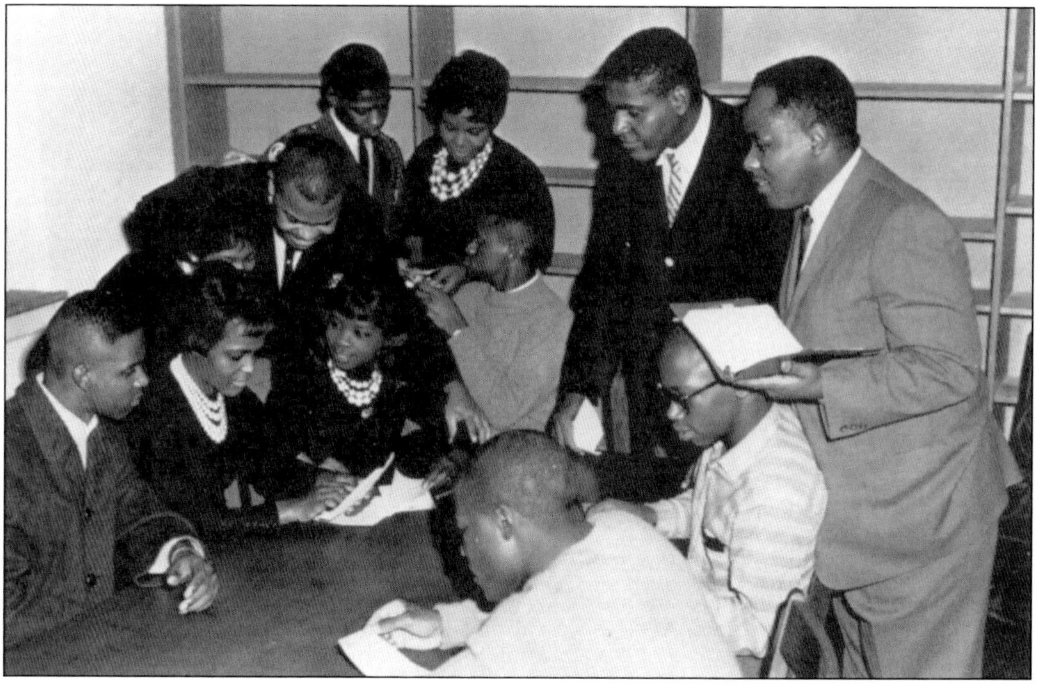

The Baptist Student Union at Lincoln University was organized under the leadership of S. E. Grindstead, national director, with Richard D. Massey as sponsor. In this photograph Rev. B. Daniel Clater conducts a study session for the Baptist Student Union.

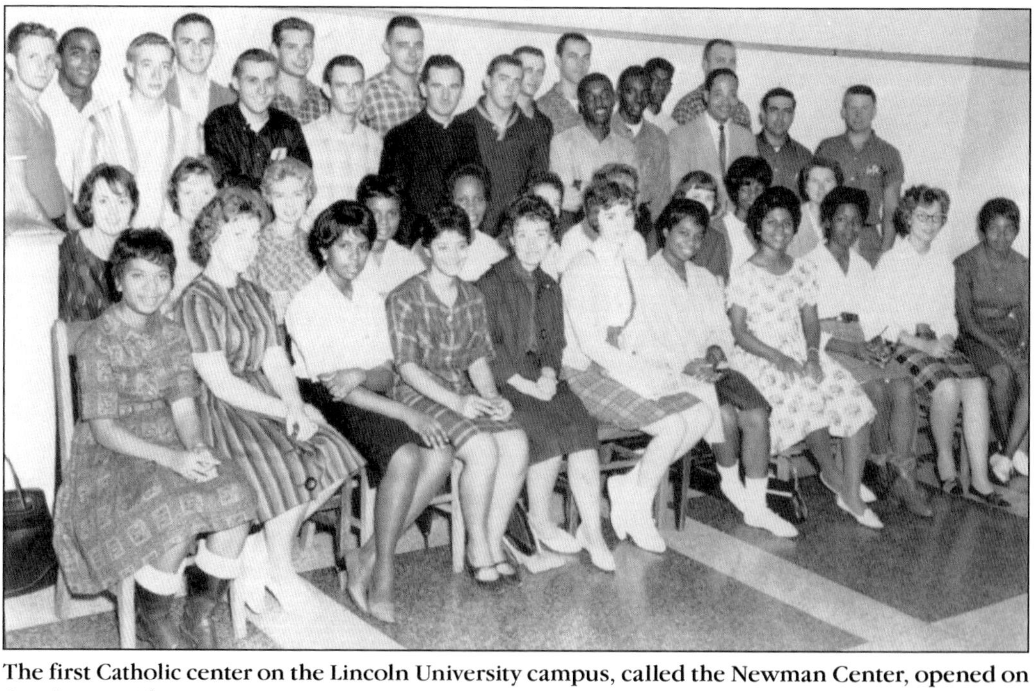

The first Catholic center on the Lincoln University campus, called the Newman Center, opened on October 1, 1968, on Fairmount Avenue across from the new Baptist Student Union. The center was a place where Catholic students could meet and informally study and receive spiritual counseling and guidance. The club met for a weekly Sunday mass and a series of religious lectures.

# *Eight*

# An Athletic Tradition

Until the 1950s, sports had a secondary role at Lincoln University because emphasis centered on academics. In 1950, with a greatly enhanced scholarship program, the university began to actively recruit athletes. This measure was in keeping with a nationwide tendency of colleges and universities to place emphasis upon athletics. In 1951, the Lincoln University athletic program developed a tradition, which lasted almost two decades. In 1952 and 1953, the Lincoln University football teams were undefeated with 21 straight victories and 2 tie games. During the 1953 season, the team scored 267 points while its opponents only accumulated 74 points. Equally significant was the Blue Tiger basketball team. The 1950 team was number one in the Midwest Conference, and the 1953 and 1954 teams came close to winning their conference championships. Also in 1954, under coach Althea Gibson, who later achieved fame as a Wimbledon player, the tennis team was successful in winning tennis championships.

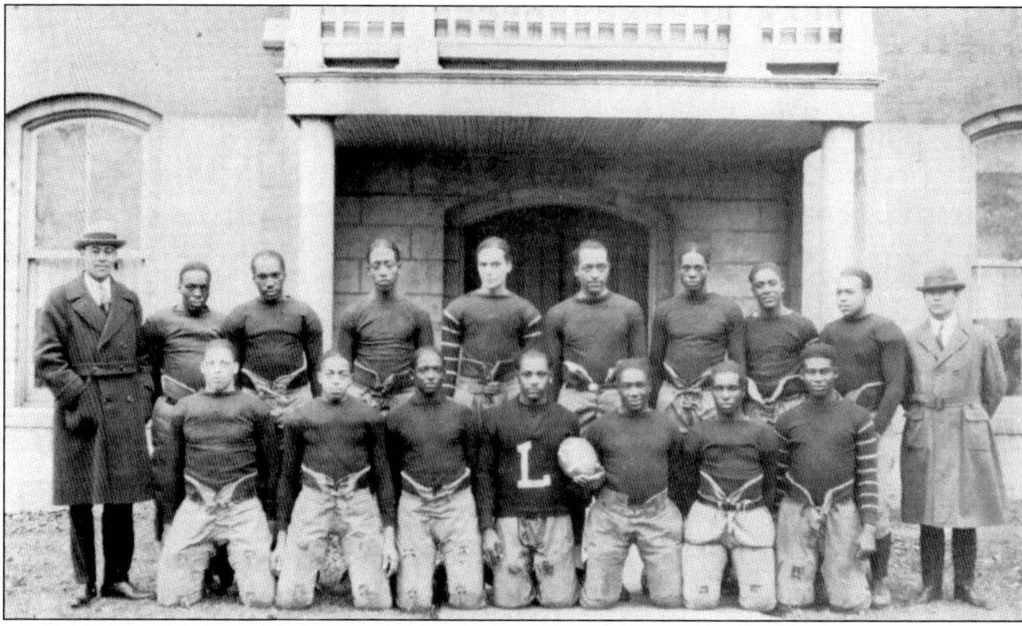

This is the 1925 Lincoln University varsity football team.

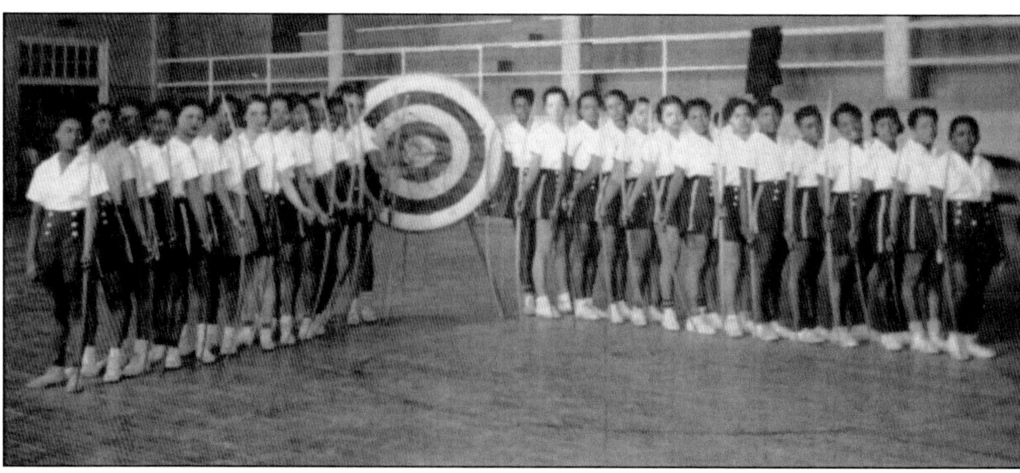

In 1938, Lincoln University had a women's archery team.

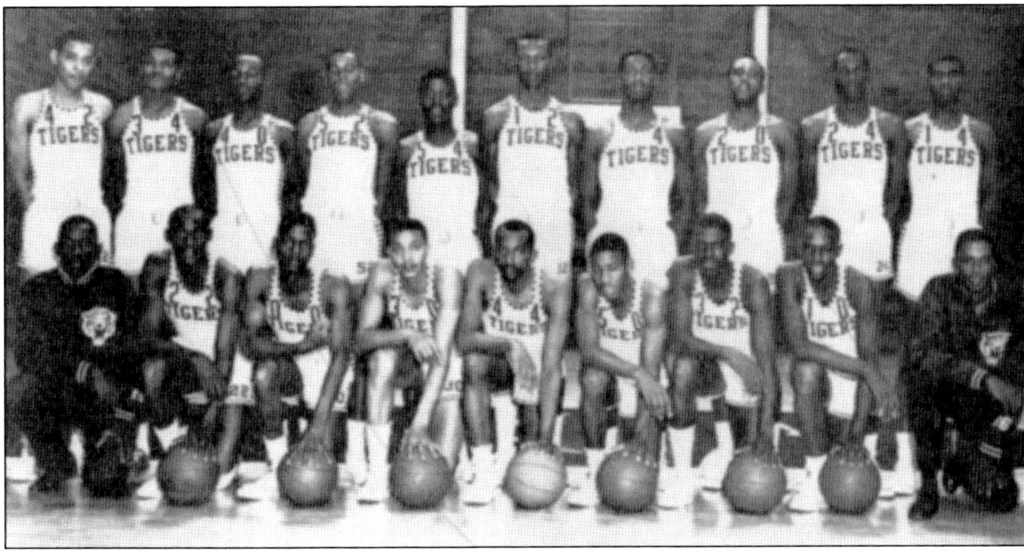

The Lincoln University 1960–1961 varsity basketball team includes coach James Frank; Harry Hairston, guard; Johnny Watkins, guard; Tyronne George, guard; Marshall Abstain, guard; Earl Burgett, forward; Loran Thompson, guard; Cecil Thomas, trainer; Nelson Yates, forward; Bill Perkins, forward; Philip Jones, guard; Norman Stikes, forward; Henry Jones, guard; Charles William, center; Emmit Hooseman, center; Chester Moran, forward; William Thomas, center; and William Johnson, center. Frank left Lincoln University and returned in 1973 and served for a decade as university president.

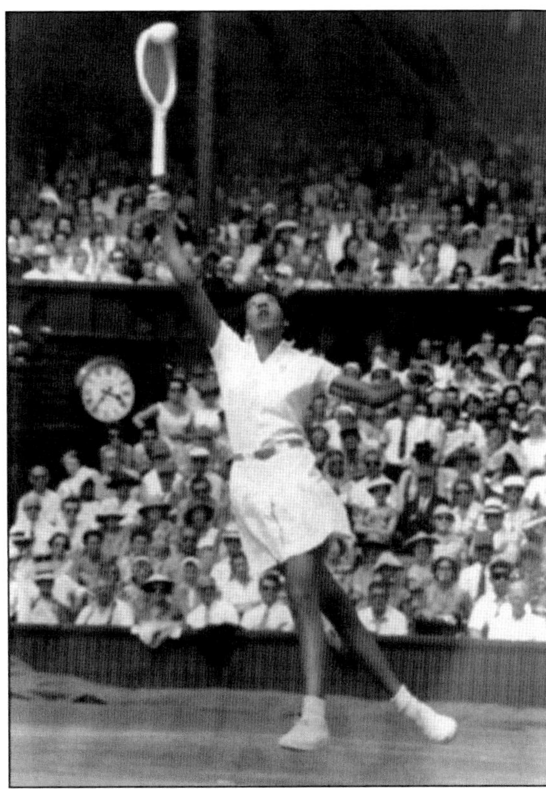

Lincoln University has the distinction of having tennis great Althea Gibson join the university faculty in 1953 as a physical education instructor. This was after she had gained tennis world attention in 1950 as the first African American woman to be a competitor on the world tennis tour. Gibson only taught at Lincoln University two years (1953–1955), and it was after leaving the university that her tennis career blossomed during a period in which she won 11 major titles in the late 1950s. She is sometimes referred to as "the Jackie Robinson of tennis" for breaking the color barrier in her sport.

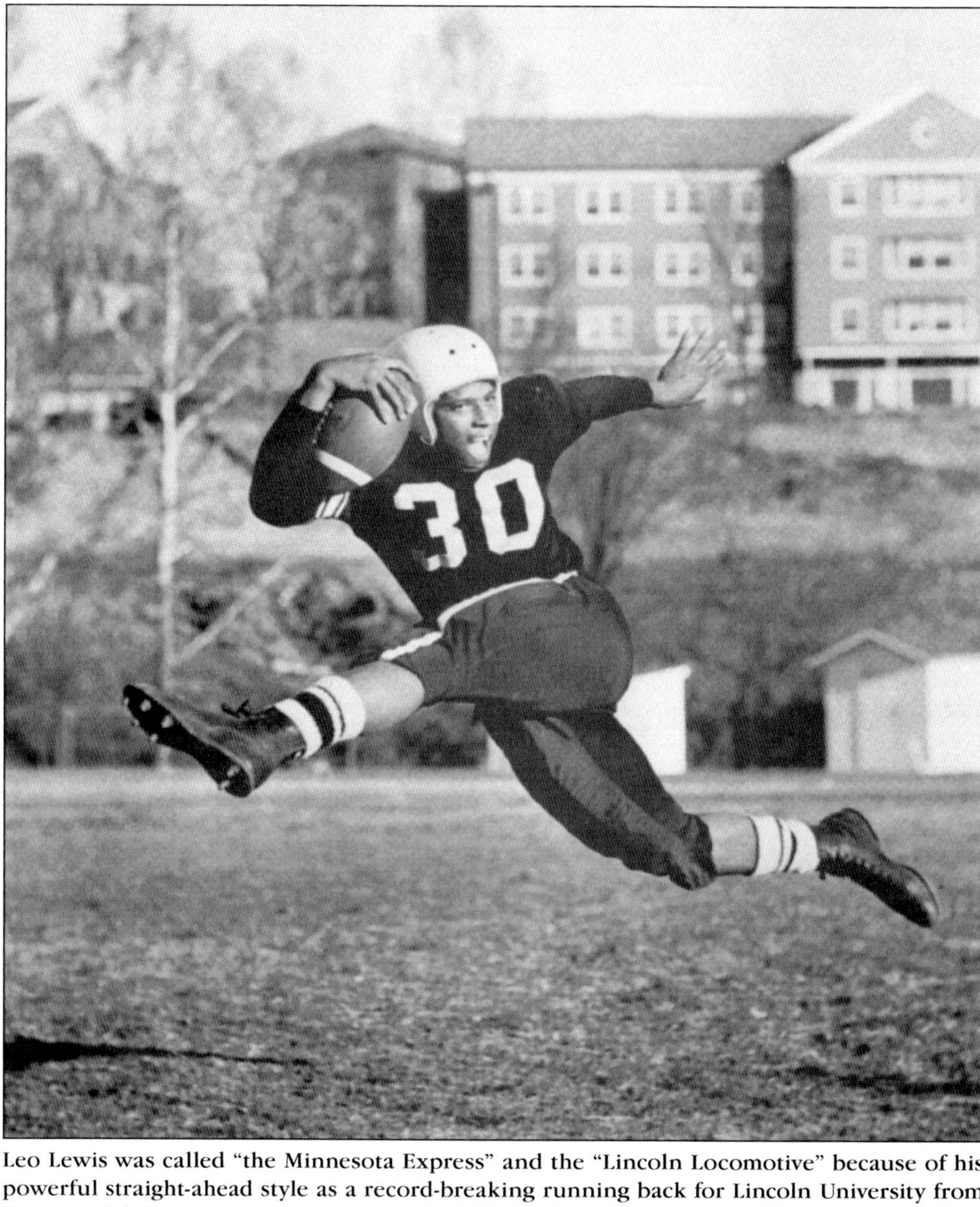

Leo Lewis was called "the Minnesota Express" and the "Lincoln Locomotive" because of his powerful straight-ahead style as a record-breaking running back for Lincoln University from 1951 to 1954. During his sophomore year in 1953, Lewis was named as an All-American, ranking fourth in the nation among smaller colleges with a total of 1,239 rushing yards, the highest average rushes per game with 137.7 yards, and 18 touchdowns scored during the season. Overall Lewis set school records for touchdowns in a season (22), touchdowns in a career (64), rushing yards in a season (1,239), and career rushing yards (4,457). After graduating, the Baltimore Colts drafted Lewis into the National Football League, but the highlight of his career was spent in the Canadian Football League. Lewis played 11 consecutive seasons with the Winnipeg Blue Bombers from 1955 to 1966. During his career, he was honored as a six-time all-star, was inducted into the Canadian Football League Hall of Fame, and is still listed as one of the greatest players in the history of the league.

This page from a program highlights Lincoln University's football success.

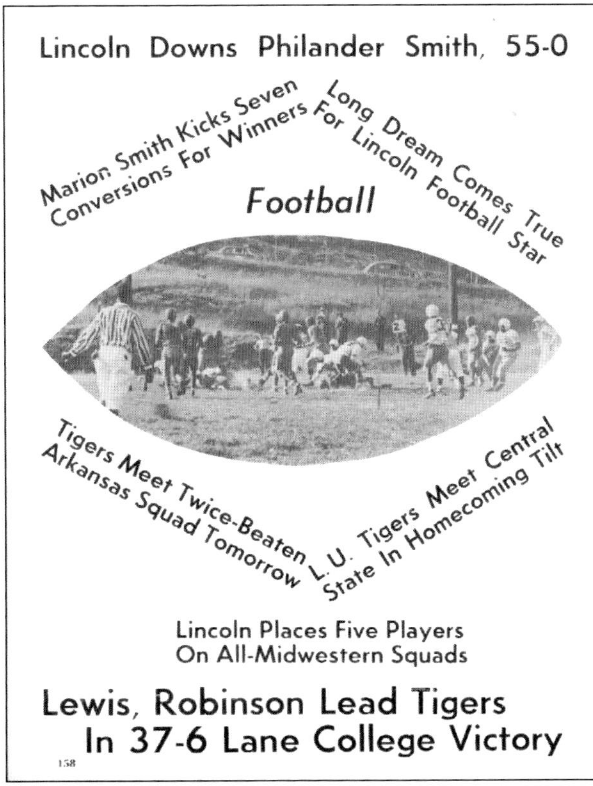

Lincoln Downs Philander Smith, 55-0

Marion Smith Kicks Seven Conversions For Winners

Long Dream Comes True For Lincoln Football Star

*Football*

Tigers Meet Twice-Beaten Arkansas Squad Tomorrow

L. U. Tigers Meet Central State In Homecoming Tilt

Lincoln Places Five Players On All-Midwestern Squads

**Lewis, Robinson Lead Tigers In 37-6 Lane College Victory**

158

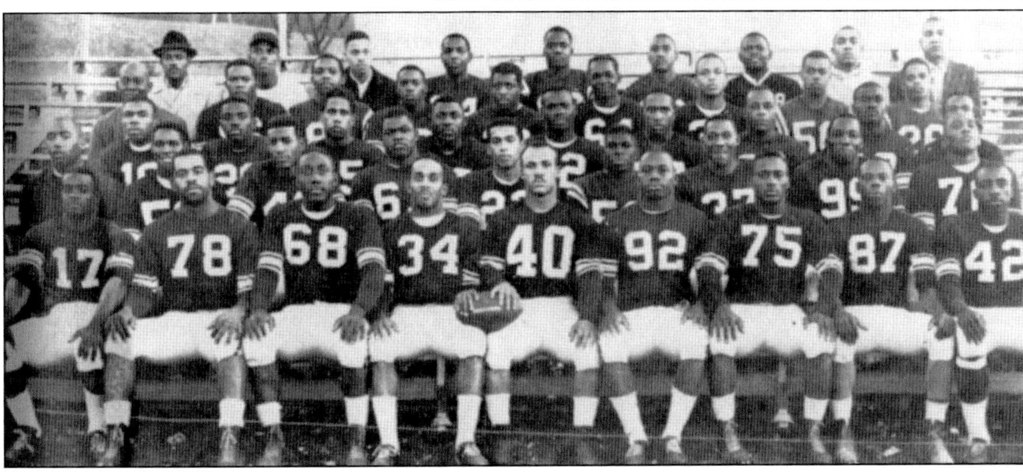

The 1960 Lincoln University football team includes the following, from left to right: (first row) Larry Lott, Frank Glover, Lionel Hopper, Louis Heffner, B. Mabury, James Young, Joe Outlaw, Morris Plummer, and Raymond Hopper; (second row) Lamont English, Moses Lacy, Henry Jackson, Richard Williams, Stanley Scott, Bernard Allen, Samuel Duncan, Robert Walker, and Ronald Copes; (third row) Willie Shamblee, Bobby Michell, Ted Groves, Thomas Whitten, Raymond Nevals, Willie Barnes, Jack Giles, Earl Wheatfall, and Albert Miller; (fourth row) Rudley Robinson, Willie Vaughn, Robert Johnson, Emmitt Hoosman, David Hale, Oliver Stubbs, William King, Kenneth Reed, and Preston Bernard; (fifth row) coach Donald Hudson, Herman Adams, Laurence Harrington, William Anderson, Cleveland Daniel, Jack Marbury, J. D. Brown, Charles Porter, and coach Dwight Reed.

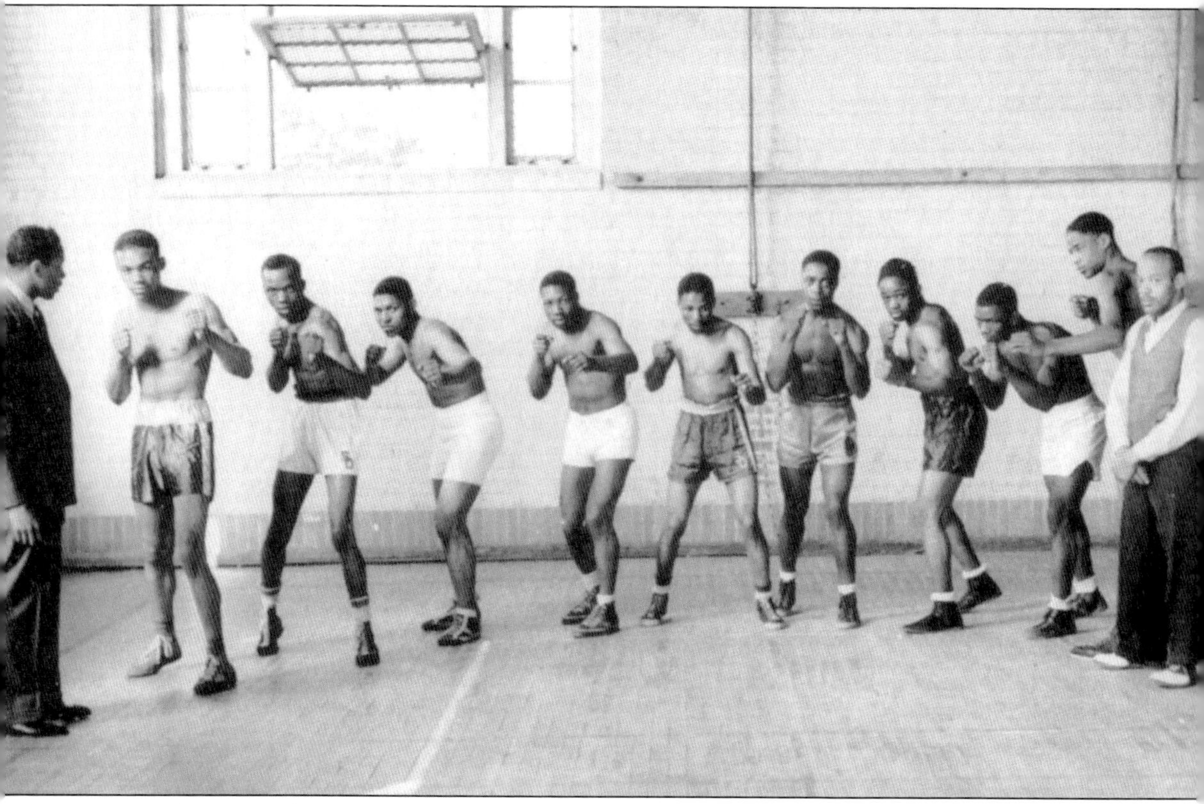

While boxing had been a part of the intramural athletic program at Lincoln University for a number of years in 1942, it was just three years old as a part of the university's intercollegiate athletic program. In this short period, representatives from the university had fought their way to the finals in the Missouri State Golden Glove. In 1941, the team was a runner-up in the Midwestern Intercollegiate Boxing Tournament, whereas in 1942 the team won the championship.

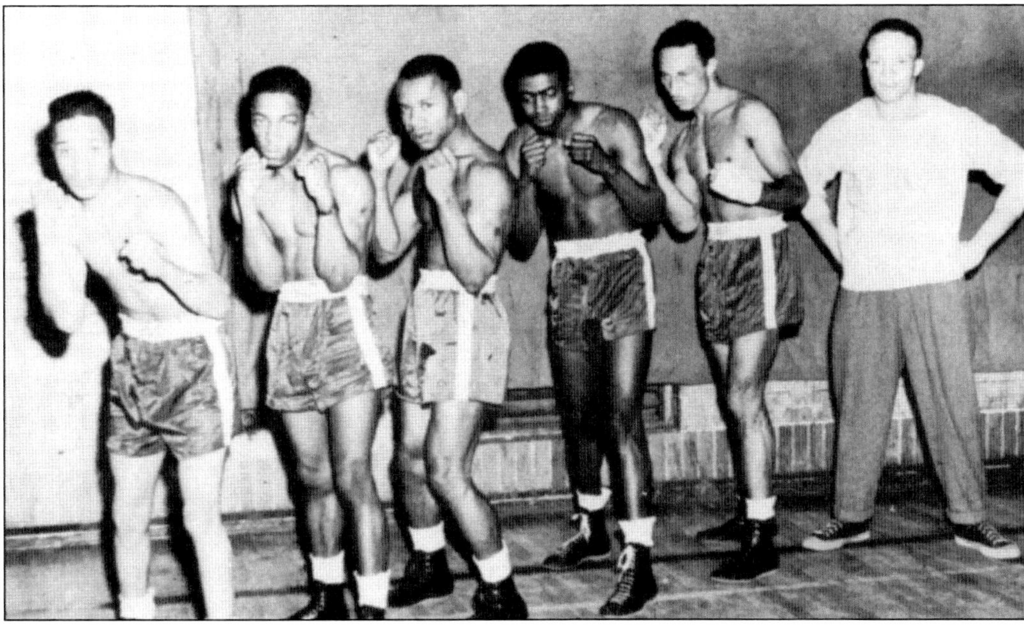

Boxing fast became one of the top sports in Lincoln University's intercollegiate athletic program in 1949. Members of the boxing team entered the Moberly Golden Gloves tournament, and two fighters emerged as champions in their respective classes. The 1948–1949 Blue Tiger boxing team placed second behind Tennessee State University in the Midwestern Intercollegiate Boxing Tournament. Pictured from left to right are Shirdell Hicks (126-pound class), Claude Barge (135-pound class), Paul Saunders (160-pound class), Frank Evans (155-pound class), Frank Price (165-pound class), and Reginald Kimbrough (trainer).

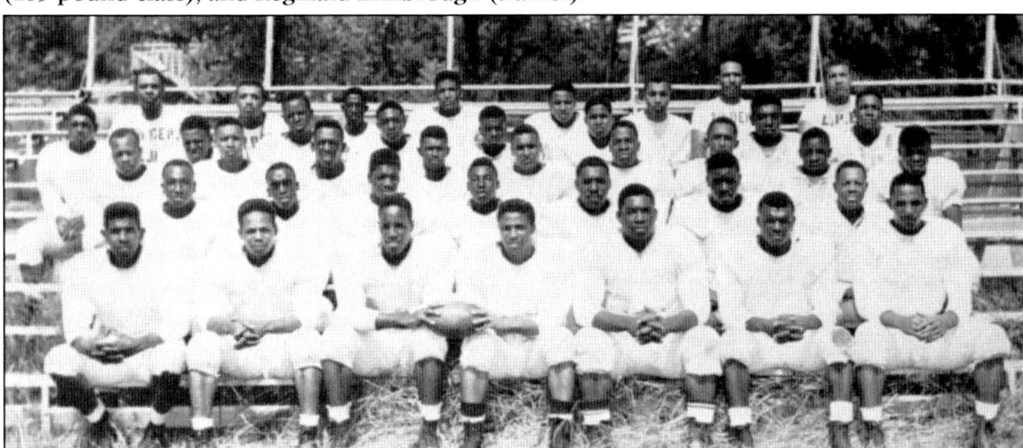

The 1953 Lincoln University Blue Tiger football varsity team includes Robert Wyatt, Joseph Hardaway, Gerald Brown (cocaptain), Leo Lewis (cocaptain), Lamon Ogletree, Marion Smith, Daniel Booker, James Ford, Richard Billinslea, James Dorsey, Lawrence Young, Nathaniel McKnuckles, Robert Wren, Hosie Tenner, Bobbye Egans, Thomas McNair, Hollis Price, Maurice Johnson, Charlie Martin, Robert McGee, Ollie Holmes, Hoover Tolbert, Howard Grimmitt, C. Wayne. Dale Douglass, Otis Lee, Harvard Spenser, Leonard Hardwick, Ozzie Belvin, Theodore Morrison, William McMoore (coach), Ben McCoy (coach), Johnnie Booker (manager), Eugene Hooks, William Meshack, Harold Mabrey (manager and statistician), Earl Beeks (coach), and Dwight T. Reed (head coach).

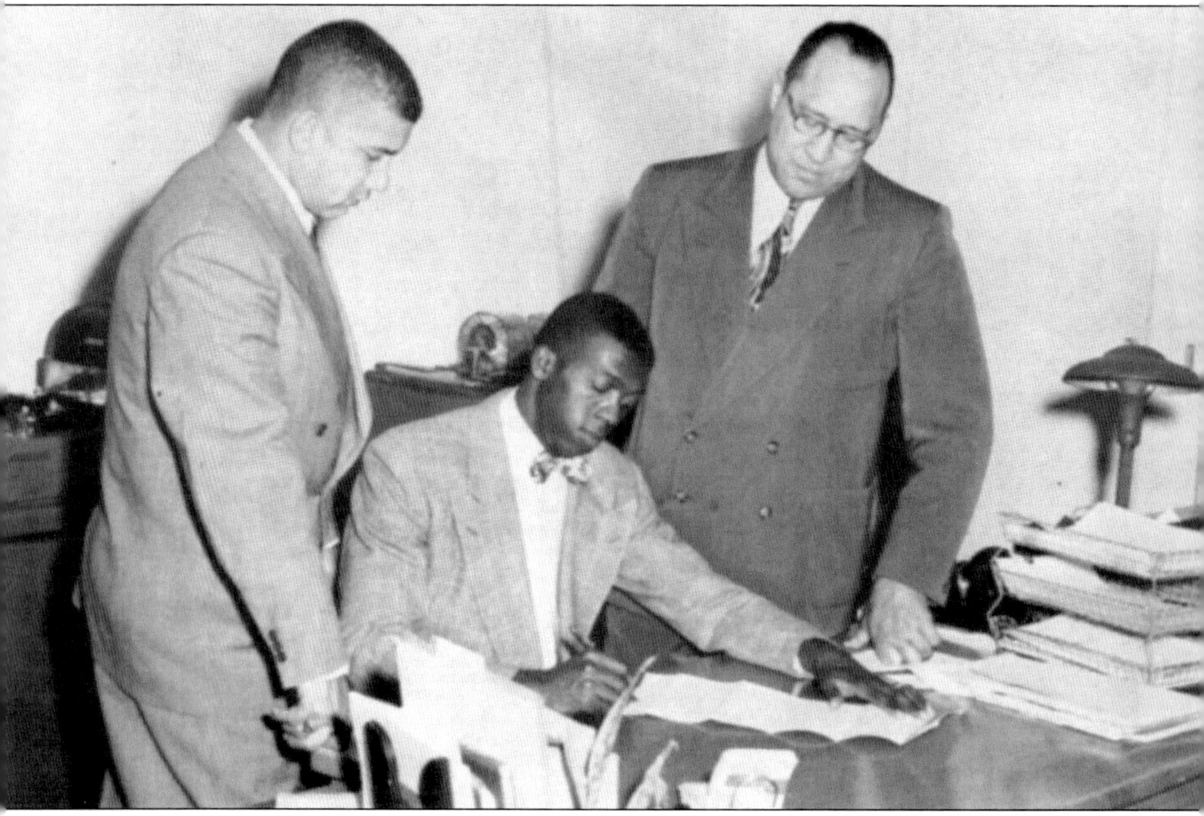

Shown signing a contract to pay football in 1952 with the Pittsburgh Steelers professional football club is Bill "Robbie" Robinson. His initial association with the Steelers came through a chance meeting on a Pittsburgh, Pennsylvania, street corner between Robinson and Steeler president Art Rooney. Each summer, Robinson returned home to Pittsburgh and worked out with his beloved Steelers. Robinson, an art major, was cocaptain of the 1951–1952 football team.

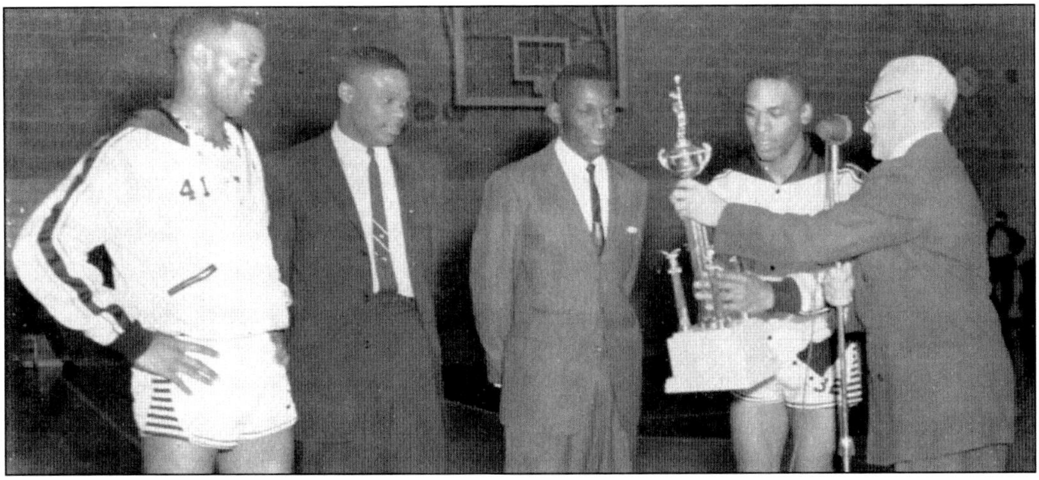

In 1960, the Lincoln University basketball team won the Midwest Athletic Association (MWAA) title giving the Blue Tigers a choice of attending the NAIA contest in Kansas City or the NCAA tournament held in Wheaton, Illinois. The Tigers chose the NCAA college division play-off in Wheaton and won the first round against Augustana, Illinois. Then they beat the Milwaukee branch of the University of Wisconsin. In the finals, the Lincoln University Blue Tigers lost to Wheaton, settling for second place. Cocaptain Carlton Rowe accepts the MWAA tournament trophy from George Davis, association president, as cocaptain Reginald Davis, student coach George Pruitt, and coach James Frank watched with satisfaction. In addition to accepting the trophy, Rowe was selected as a member of the all-conference team, and Chester Moran, the Blue Tigers' six-foot, three-inch forward and the second-highest scorer on the 1958–1959 team, was also selected for the all-star squad.

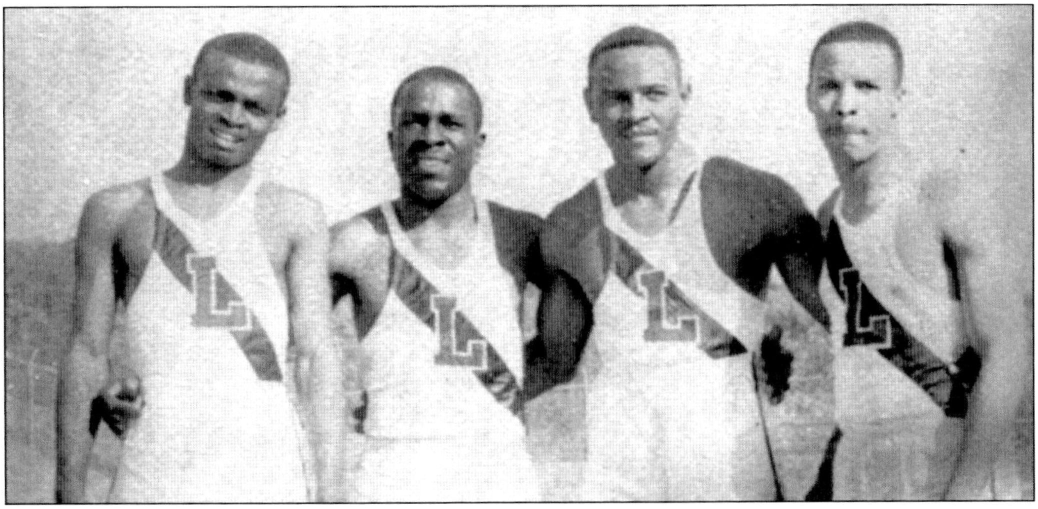

In 1961, the Lincoln University track team participated in 13 meets in Kansas, Missouri, Oklahoma, Illinois, and Iowa winning 2 of them including the second annual NCAA Small College Midwest Regional at the end of the 1961 season. In this picture is Lincoln University's 440-yard relay team consisting of, from left to right, Albert Wheatfall, Donald Williams, Melvin Boyce, and Edward Lane.

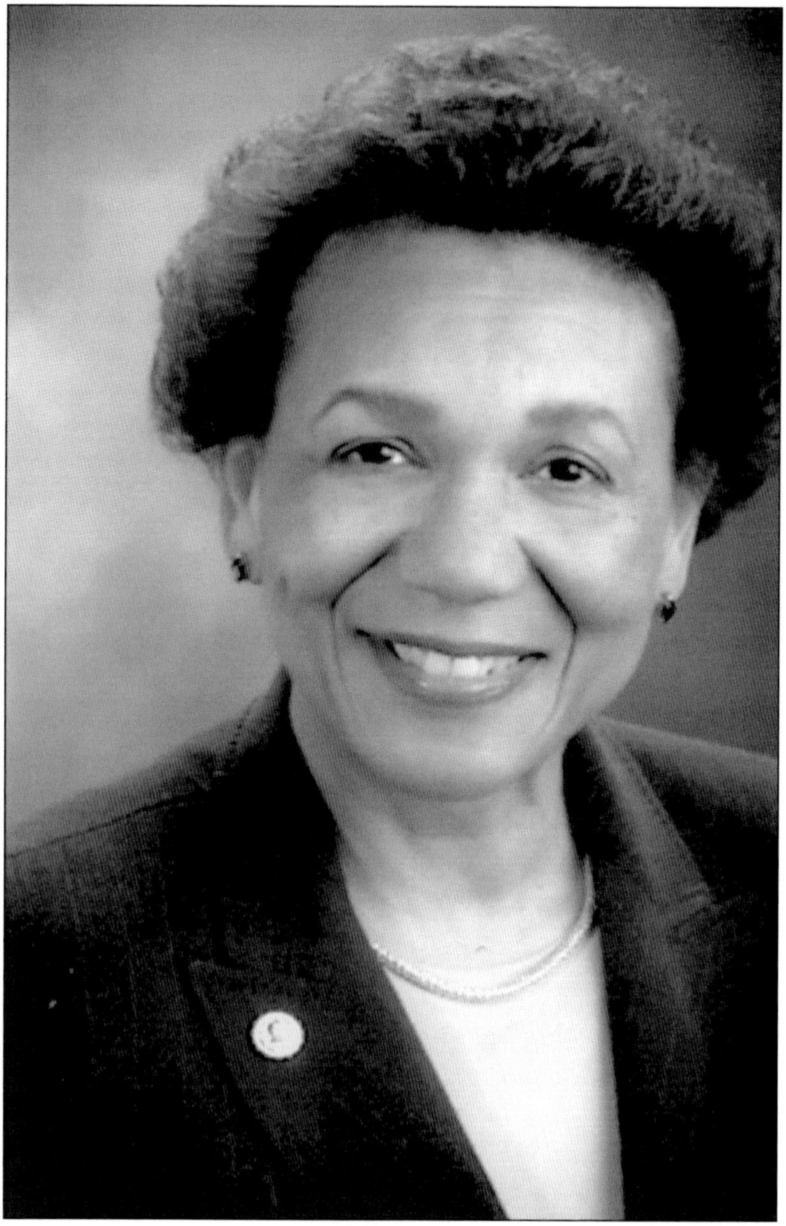

The current president of Lincoln University is Dr. Carolyn R. Mahoney. She is the first female and the 18th president of the university. Mahoney assumed this position on February 1, 2005. She received her undergraduate degree summa cum laude in mathematics from Siena College and her master of science and doctorate degrees (both in mathematics) from Ohio State University. Prior to coming to Lincoln University, Mahoney was one of the 12 founding faculty at California State University San Marcos, where she served as professor of mathematics and interim vice president for academic affairs. Also, she has been a program director at the National Science Foundation in Arlington, Virginia, and provost and vice chancellor for academic affairs at Elizabeth City State University. Mahoney is recognized for her advocacy for students and her service contributions to the education community. She has helped established award-winning outreach and undergraduate retention programs in Ohio and California.

# BIBLIOGRAPHY

Frank, Zelma Lloyd. *A History of the Homes for Lincoln University Presidents.* Jefferson City, MO: Lincoln University Graphic Arts Department, 1981.

Holland, Antonio F. *Nathan B. Young and the Struggle over Black Higher Education.* Columbia, MO: University of Missouri Press, 2006.

———. *The Soldiers' Dream Continued: A Pictorial History of Lincoln University of Missouri.* Jefferson City, MO: Lincoln University Printing Services, 1991.

Kremer, Gary R. *Exploring Historic Jefferson City.* Jefferson City, MO: Jefferson City, 2003.

———. *Heartland History.* Vol. 1. St. Louis, MO: G. Bradley Publishing, 2000.

Lincoln University. *Alumni Line Magazine* 16, no. 1 (Winter/Spring 2006).

Marshall, Albert P. "Soldiers' Dream: Centennial History of Lincoln University 1866–1966." Unpublished manuscript. Inman E. Page Library, Lincoln University. 1966.

Miller, Jayae. *Historic Lincoln Campus Walking Tour.* Jefferson City, MO: Lincoln University Printing Services, 2000.

Savage, William Sherman. *The History of Lincoln University.* Jefferson City, MO: New Day Press, 1939.

———. "The Workers of Lincoln University; Part 1 Boards of Control." Unpublished manuscript. Inman E. Page Library, Lincoln University. February 1951.

*Turn Your Dreams into Reality.* Lincoln University recruitment brochure.

Woodson, Deb. "Dr. O. A. Fuller's Musical Career Has Been Characterized by Noted Achievements." *Jefferson City News Tribune,* February 13, 1983.

Wright, John A. *The Ville Saint Louis.* Charleston, SC: Arcadia Publishing, 2001.

Zagier, Alan Scher. "Disappearance Not Investigated." *Columbia Daily Tribune,* September 21, 2006.

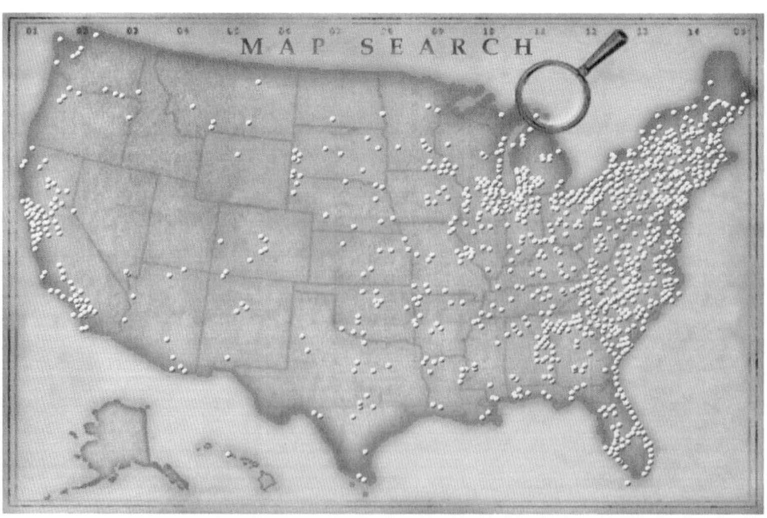
MAP SEARCH